Miracles and the Unexplainable

Chicken Soup for the Soul: Miracles and the Unexplainable
101 Stories of Hope, Answered Prayers and Divine Intervention
Amy Newmark

Published by Chicken Soup for the Soul, LLC www.chickensoup.com

The publisher gratefully acknowledges the many publishers and individuals who granted Chicken Soup for the Soul permission to reprint the cited material.

Front cover photo courtesy of iStockphoto.com/Ig0rZh (©Ig0rZh)
Back cover and interior photo of woman courtesy of iStockphoto.com/AlexSava (©AlexSava)
Photo of Amy Newmark courtesy of Susan Morrow at SwickPix

Cover and Interior by Daniel Zaccari

Publisher's Cataloging-In-Publication Data
(Prepared by The Donohue Group, Inc.)

Names: Newmark, Amy, editor.
Title: Chicken soup for the soul : miracles and the unexplainable, 101 stories of hope, answered prayers and divine intervention / Amy Newmark.
Description: Cos Cob, CT : Chicken Soup for the Soul, LLC, 2022.
Identifiers: LCCN: 2022940324 | ISBN 978-1-61159-094-4 (print) | 978-1-61159-332-7 (ebook)
Subjects: LCSH: Miracles--Anecdotes. | Miracles--Literary collections. | Prayer--Anecdotes. | Prayer--Literary collections. | Providence and government of God--Literary collections. | Providence and government of God--Anecdotes. | Faith--Anecdotes. | Faith--Literary collections. | Self help. | BISAC SELF-HELP / Motivational & Inspirational | SELF-HELP / Personal Growth / Happiness | SELF-HELP / Spiritual
Classification: LCC BL487 .C45 2022 | DDC 202.117/02--dc23

Library of Congress Control Number: 2022940324

PRINTED IN THE UNITED STATES OF AMERICA
on acid∞free paper

27 26 25 24 23 22 01 02 03 04 05 06 07 08 09 10 11

Miracles and the Unexplainable

101 Stories of Hope, Answered Prayers and Divine Intervention

Amy Newmark

Chicken Soup for the Soul, LLC
Cos Cob, CT

Changing lives one story at a time®

www.chickensoup.com

Table of Contents

3

~Coincidences & Synchronicities~

4

~Divine Intervention~

5

~Answered Prayers~

6

~Everyday Miracles~

7

~Dreams & Premonitions~

8

~Angels Among Us~

9

~Medical Miracles~

10

~Miraculous Connections~

11

~Messages from Heavens~

How Did That Happen?

September 15, 1998

Sometimes, our grandmas and grandpas
are like grand-angels.
~Lexie Saige

Some dates are etched into your memory. Your birthday, your wedding day, the birth of your child, or any other date that changed you are dates that are not only remembered but are usually celebrated. Some dates, though, go down in infamy. Those dates force you to relive what happened whether you like it or not.

September 15, 1998 was the latter kind of date. It was the day my daughter was reborn, in the spiritual sense. It was a day I was reborn, as well.

My husband and I had recently purchased a new car, and our daughter had only been driving for a short time, but we agreed she could use it to go visit her boyfriend. She left with a promise to be careful and to call when she got there. Everything would be fine, I told myself, as I fell into my easy chair to catch up on the evening news.

Half an hour after she left, the phone rang. When I answered, I heard what would send any parent into an emotional frenzy. I heard Jess scream. Then there was a brief silence before she calmly said that she had been in an accident. She was sorry and didn't want us to be angry that she had messed up the car. She asked if we would come to her.

My husband and I jumped into our other car. We headed toward the mountain road she had directed us to, but were surprised to see

EMTs, firetrucks, ambulances, and police cars pass us. I worried there had been an accident on this route that could delay us from reaching our daughter. Then we saw all the lights. And our new car facing us on the wrong side of the road.

I couldn't get out of my seatbelt fast enough. My child was in that crumpled car. I ran toward Jess, only to be stopped by a police officer holding a clipboard.

I felt sick to my stomach. I could see her in the car, mostly hidden behind the exploded airbag, but I couldn't see much else. The officer assured me she was being taken care of and that a helicopter was on its way to take her to the hospital. I could barely focus on his words but I clearly heard him say the Jaws of Life. They had to extract her from the car before the rescue flight.

After I gave him some personal information, he told me to walk over to the car and remain calm while I talked to her. She had been in shock, and there were two EMTs in the back seat, bracing her neck and calming her down.

It had rained and the road was slippery. She had hit a van coming from the opposite direction head on. The other driver wasn't hurt, but Jess had hit his van so hard that the front end of her car was pushed in, the dashboard pinning her to her seat. She had blood around her mouth, and they had to wait to discover the extent of her injuries because they couldn't see past her upper chest area.

I remember going to the side of the road to throw up before I went to see her. I needed to be her mom.

I approached the driver's window and smiled. My whole body was shaking. There she sat, with a brace on her neck. She could move her eyes enough to meet mine. All I could think about was the first time our eyes had met when they placed her in my arms after she was born.

I told her in the calmest voice I could muster that she was going to be okay. That she needed to stay strong until they could get her out. She looked back at me calmly. And just like I will always remember the date, I will remember her words.

"I know I'll be okay, Mom. Grandpa was here. He helped me call you."

I stopped breathing for a second. What? I needed to be honest with her. They had told me to just keep talking until help arrived. "Honey," I replied, "Grandpa died last year."

"I know," she said. "He was here in the white golf hat and jacket we buried him in. He told me I was going to be okay."

I didn't respond. I only fought back the tears and smiled as I nodded. Then I was asked to stand back so they could cut my child out of the mangled metal. I thought about the first time she'd been cut out to save her life — when she was born by C-section.

We stood by for an hour and a half, watching, praying, pleading that she would be okay. The officer came back with more questions, but this time our answers were not what he expected. He asked how we learned there had been an accident. I told him about the call we had gotten from Jess. I mentioned the scream that didn't make sense, shared her explanation of what had happened and then added her request to come get her.

"That can't be," he said, shaking his head. "She couldn't have made the call. She's been trapped all this time. Look at her; you can't see her arms at all."

I stuck to my story. It was the truth. "Come with me," he directed.

He led us around to the other side of the car. As he pointed to the floor behind the front passenger seat, he showed us the cell phone on the floor, covered with the white airbag dust. It had clearly not been touched after it flew there during the collision. "You see? She couldn't have called you on that."

Then, without a doubt, her words replayed in my mind. "Grandpa was here." He had been. Oh my God, he had been.

After pulling her out of the wreckage, they flew her to the hospital where we drove, sobbing, and so grateful, so blessed to know she would be fine.

September 15, 1998. The day two miracles happened. The day Jess was spared, and the day that my dad was there to make sure she was okay.

— Kim Garback Diaz —

The Gray Hat

The most beautiful thing we can experience
is the mysterious.
~Albert Einstein

My husband and I were both serving on active duty in the Air Force and were stationed in Wyoming. One cold spring morning we got the phone call no one wants to get; my husband's mother, Mary, had been diagnosed with lung cancer. He took a week of emergency leave to spend time with her.

Among the handful of keepsakes Andy brought back from his childhood home in Tennessee was a hand-knitted gray hat.

He couldn't know that in less than six months, his mother would be gone. And that this hat would end up providing warmth and comfort in every way possible.

You always hear the jokes about the dreaded mother-in-law, but mine was one of those rare, wonderful souls you might meet only a few times in your life. She had the most fantastic, sparkling personality.

The flight back for Mary's funeral was one of the longest, most heartbreaking moments of our lives. I remember feeling a soul-crushing grief, so heavy it was hard to breathe. The kind of grief that clings to you for months, and at times, still pops up with a vengeance years later.

A few months after Mary passed, we took a weekend trip to Denver. As we drove home, Andy realized he'd forgotten his treasured gray hat at the hotel. We pulled over at the next exit and searched our luggage just in case, but the hat wasn't there. We called the hotel but they didn't find it either. Andy's beloved gray hat was gone.

At that moment, the grief came tearing back. My husband was crushed.

Later that evening, after we had emptied the suitcases and searched the car again, we started the laundry. I brought a basket of clothes upstairs, set it on the bed, and went to take a shower. My husband was downstairs napping on the couch.

Then the strangest thing happened in the shower. I thought I was going crazy, but I swore I could smell my mother-in-law's perfume, a delicate and very faint scent. The vanity lights over the mirror brightened, almost as if experiencing a power surge, and seemed to glow through the shower curtain. I poked my head out and saw nothing but had an overwhelming feeling of love and peace.

I got out of the shower; a bit unsure if I should mention what I thought I'd experienced to my husband. Until I went to the laundry basket.

On top of the clothes, in the basket I had just brought upstairs myself... was that gray hat!

I quickly yelled for Andy to come upstairs and pointed to the basket. I was too mesmerized to touch it, but he picked it up and turned it over in his hands. His eyes filled with tears.

It was, without a doubt, the hand-knitted hat that we had accidentally left behind in our hotel room. Andy pressed the hat to his face, breathing in the scent of his childhood home, and the memories forever captured in that home-spun yarn.

Since that day, this hat has traveled the world with us. We've moved across the United States from California to Maryland, and even to Germany with it. It has gone to France, Belgium, Scotland, and England. And it always makes it home with us.

We have no logical explanation for how the hat found its way back to our home that day from Denver and appeared in our laundry basket. I cannot come up with an explanation that doesn't defy the laws of physics or the realm of the possible. It is something that should be impossible.

But it wasn't.

That hat constantly reminds us that miracles do happen. Messages from beyond can come in the least expected of ways and take any form.

Even a gray hat.

— Kristi Adams —

She Came by Prayer

Dogs are miracles with paws.
~Susan Kennedy

Toby, our two-year-old Beagle mix, sat awkwardly on our back deck. He refused to come to me. We had just finished playing ball and frisbee on a warm May evening.

Hoping he'd only overheated, I left him outside so that he wouldn't get sick in the house. After giving him water and affection, I proceeded to make dinner and put our four-year-old son, Jadon, to bed.

Later, when I brought Toby back inside, he walked unsteadily past me.

"What's wrong, buddy?" I led him to his crate, and he vomited inside it. My stomach twisted. "Oh no. Come here boy."

He obediently came out of the crate. Then he wobbled violently and fell over at my feet.

"Jay!" I screamed to my husband. "Get your stuff! Something's wrong with Toby! You need to take him to the vet!"

I dropped to the floor as his body started jerking.

"Toby, no!" Tears streaked my cheeks. "Toby!" I rubbed his soft, tan and black fur trying to get a response from him.

His eyes rolled back into his head. Then he coughed twice and lay unmoving with his eyes and mouth opened.

"Toby," I sobbed and shook him. "Toby!"

Nothing.

James appeared next to me. He carefully lifted our dog and carried him to the car.

That would be the last time I saw Toby.

***

The vet expressed her sympathy and explained that we would never know exactly what happened. She hypothesized that he had an undiagnosed heart defect. I accepted her explanation, but it didn't ease the pain.

He was our son's best friend and only playmate. How do you explain to a young child that he will never see his best friend again?

After this tragic experience, we agreed not to get another dog right away. We already had a new little addition to our family—Jadon's four-week-old baby brother, Timothy. Adjusting to a new pet at the same time would be too stressful.

But Toby's absence created a big hole we couldn't ignore. With the new baby, I had less time for Jadon. And he no longer had a friend to help him cope with the big change in our family.

I started checking local pet rescues online. When I confessed this to James, he admitted to doing the same. So, we agreed to find a dog that wouldn't require high maintenance. She would need to be submissive, relaxed, and gentle with kids.

I also believed in miracles and trusted that if I prayed while we searched, God would answer.

About two weeks after Toby's death, I was snuggling with Jadon at bedtime. We had visited some animal shelters without success. I promised him that God would help us find a new dog one day soon.

What happened next defied logic.

"Mom, we need to go see Bailey," Jadon said matter-of-factly.

"Bailey?" We hadn't met a dog with that name at any of the shelters. "Who's Bailey?

"She's the black, white, purple and blue one at the place where doggie's get haircuts." His blue eyes implored me.

"What?"

Confidently, he repeated the information.

Black, white, purple, and blue? "Well, maybe we can go to the pet store this weekend. Good night, buddy."

I left the room very confused. When did he see a black and white dog named Bailey? And purple and blue?

We'd visited PetSmart a few times in the past where he'd seen dogs being groomed. But we hadn't been recently. However, they did hold regular adoptions on the weekends.

The next day, I searched the Internet for any black and white dogs named Bailey who were up for adoption. I didn't find one, but there was a black and white Border Collie named Lucy who would be at PetSmart that weekend.

On Saturday morning, I took my two young boys to the store. As we entered, I noticed another gentleman walking Lucy. I hesitantly approached one of the adoption workers.

"May I help you?" She smiled brightly.

"Yes, we wanted to meet a Border Collie you had advertised. Lucy?"

My shoulders dropped as she explained Lucy had just been adopted. Then she looked at my crew and thought for a second. "But I think I can still help." She turned and called to another worker, "Can you show them Bailey?"

A chill ran from the top of my head to my ankles. "Wait. You have a dog named Bailey? I didn't see any dogs named Bailey online."

"Yes, her foster family decided at the last minute they wouldn't be able to keep her, so she didn't make the listing. But she's super sweet and good with kids!" She eyed Baby Timothy.

"What color is she?" I gripped my cart for stability.

She pointed. "She's the black and white one over there in that crate."

I raced to the large crate that held the big black and white puppy named Bailey. Oblivious to the barking chaos around her, she was snoozing. A handwritten sign with large letters read "good house manners and great with kids."

Then her puppy belly caught my eye. Because it was so pink, her black spots underneath appeared purplish-brown. And a neat little row of blue stitches from her spaying procedure stretched across her lower abdomen.

Black. White. Purple. And blue.

My hands shook as I dialed my husband. "Are you off work yet?"

"Yes, heading home now. What's wrong?"

"You won't believe it." I sucked in a breath. "We found Bailey!"

Whether by dream, vision, or divine knowledge, God clearly communicated with our little boy about our new family dog. So, at this point, I didn't care if they thought I was a lunatic. With my husband on the way, and our divine gift in front of me, I immediately told the worker we'd take her.

At first she was shocked that we didn't even get her out of the crate. But when I told her our story, she knew we were to be Bailey's new family.

It's been more than six years now, and Bailey Rose, a seventy-pound pointer-hound mix, continues to delight our family. Relaxed, loving and gentle, she's unlike any dog we've ever known. Even as a puppy, she was unusually quiet, easy to house-train and never difficult in any way.

And anyone who meets Bailey also recognizes she's extraordinary. Of course, when they ask, I always smile and say, "She's definitely our miracle dog. Do you have time to hear a story?"

—H. R. Hook—

The Man at the Top of the Stairs

A God wise enough to create me and the world I live in
is wise enough to watch out for me.
~Philip Yancey

It was around ten o'clock when I carefully lifted the phonograph needle off "Sweet Baby James," ending Mr. Taylor's personal concert for the evening. The housemates with whom I shared this old Victorian had apparently settled in for the night.

I sat in the dark, cross-legged on the floor, struggling to sort out a life that was slipping away from me. A collection of leftover prescription bottles filled with remedies for aching teeth, strained ligaments, and sleepless nights lined up in front of me on the carpet. I was certain that collectively they could provide the remedy for what ailed me.

I couldn't think of a single thing I could do to bring hope back into my life. It felt as if there was an expanding hole in the sky that I was being drawn toward, one which I was gradually losing the urge to resist. The reason why I was feeling such hopelessness escaped me. Maybe it was a chemical imbalance, or peer pressure or the stress of my college workload.

There was another possibility that I hadn't considered at that time. I had been raised in a religious household, and now, in college, I was being introduced to all sorts of new possibilities, including the existential philosophy of Camus and Sartre. The idea that there might not be a God was both foreign and oddly fascinating to me. I began to question what proof I really had for God's existence in my life. The truth was, He had never shown me any miracles or hard evidence. What if Camus and his buddies were right… that there was no gardener tending this Earth, that this life was, in fact, a convenient mistake, and that when we die, we die… Adios.

And so, one night at bedtime during my sophomore year I notified God that I would no longer be praying to Him, hoping that if He was, in fact, real and listening, that He'd understand. In no time at all, not praying felt like the easiest thing in the world to do. Normal even. And so what happened? Nothing… At first.

But then, gradually, life began to get messy… very messy. The next nine months became the worst time of my life. Three major car accidents, broken bones, broken relationships, in addition to a life without a moral compass, all resulted in a great deal of hurt to myself and to others. Maybe it was the cumulative effect of all that adversity that caused my tailspin into depression, or maybe it was simply that I had informed God that I didn't want him in my life anymore and he graciously obliged, leaving me with a void which I was ill-equipped to deal with.

So, there I sat in my bedroom, tears welling up in my eyes, as I contemplated Hamlet's to be or not to be question. And the overwhelming thought that filled my head was that not only would my parents be devastated, but also that my mom, in particular, would blame herself, convinced she had failed me. But I knew they weren't to blame. Now the tears were unstoppable.

With nowhere else to turn, I instinctively cried out, "God… Help me! Please help me!" And with my next breath, I whispered, "If you're real, please show me a sign."

The very moment after those words left my mouth, I heard a series of loud rattling knocks at our wooden front screen door downstairs. I stopped sobbing long enough to listen. I couldn't help but consider, was this my sign? I heard the heavy front door open. Someone was entering our foyer.

One of my housemates shouted up the stairs that there was

someone there to see me. As footsteps began climbing the stairs, I quickly scooped up the prescription bottles and stashed them under my pillows. I dried my eyes with my sweater, walked over to the door, and flipped on the overhead light. The visitor had reached the top of the stairs. I tried to compose myself, grabbed the glass doorknob and pulled open my door.

On the other side of the threshold stood a very average looking man, maybe around forty years old, wearing an overcoat and carrying a briefcase. "Are you Don Locke?" he asked very directly.

"Yes," I said, wondering what this could possibly be about. Without introduction or an obligatory handshake, he asked with little inflection in his voice, "Would you be interested in life insurance?"

I recall feeling like the question was both comical and tragic under the circumstances. And I very clearly, to this day, remember the tone of my voice reflecting both emotions, as I answered, "No."

And then this man simply said, "Okay. Good night." And he turned and went back down the stairs.

Stunned by the absurdity of the entire scene, I sat down on my bed and tried to sort it out. Life insurance? So bizarre. Absolutely surreal. I looked around the room. All signs that a person had been contemplating ending his life only five minutes earlier were gone. I had to decide: Was this episode the most amazing coincidence ever, or had I just experienced the divine intervention which I had so passionately prayed for?

For the next two weeks, the hole in my sky gradually closed, until my depression had completely released its grip on me. It has never returned. Needless to say, my desire to pray returned.

I've told this story to many people over the years, and a few have believed it to simply be an incredible coincidence. But about ten years after the encounter, my wife and I met with a real-life insurance salesman at our house. And I learned they don't cold-call twenty-year-old college students late at night. They introduce themselves with a firm, friendly handshake as they offer you their business card. And they never take your first no for an answer, because they work on commission.

Initially I was reluctant to share this story with many people, understanding it might bring pain to those who wondered why God's angels failed to rescue their own loved ones when darkness closed in on them. But I've come to realize how important it is to be reminded that though God may appear distant or unavailable at times, He's always standing by.

—Don Locke—

A Celestial Operator

The relationship between parents and children, but especially between mothers and daughters, is tremendously powerful, scarcely to be comprehended in any rational way.
~Joyce Carol Oates

It was a warm midsummer afternoon and the thunder was coming closer as I sat at a picnic table across from my sister.

A few years earlier, as our mother was dying, she had opened her eyes and smiled at us, saying, "Every year when the flowers are blooming, I want you to get together and have a picnic. I will be there."

So, there we were with our children on what would have been our mother's birthday. We were sending our mother birthday greetings in heaven by attaching notes to helium-filled balloons. My sister and the children wrote "Happy Birthday" on their notes with colorful markers as I sat and watched. Then my sister attached each note to a balloon. The children held them tight until the time came to release them as we sang "Happy Birthday" to Grama.

The balloons were as bright and as colorful as the wildflowers that were blooming throughout the park that day. We watched them until they disappeared.

Then my sister exclaimed, "You didn't send one!" I then realized that in the excitement I had not made a note to send to my mother.

I sat down at the picnic table and chose a bright green marker and an olive-green balloon. My mother's favorite color was green.

On a piece of paper I scrolled, "Happy Birthday Mom! I hope you are having a really nice day in Heaven today. I miss you so much. If you get this note, can you please send me a sign that you got it?"

We gathered to watch my balloon ascend. It progressed upwards at a steady pace, and then, just as we were losing sight of it, the clouds opened. A perfect circle opened up and we saw the green balloon against the blue sky. Then it rose further and the clouds closed around it.

My sister and I stood looking at each other in awe.

A few days later, I was putting up a curtain rod in my bedroom after a painting project. My older son was standing on a stepladder at one end of the large window holding the curtain rod, and I was standing on a stepladder at the other end of the window. It was late in the evening. Nearly midnight.

As I stood on the stepladder holding the curtain rod, my telephone rang. I was startled because it was so late at night, and I was also startled because the ring tone sounded odd. It was higher pitched than usual, and the ring lasted longer, too.

I started to make my way down the ladder to answer the telephone, but it stopped after just one ring. I thought it was probably a wrong number.

A few moments later the phone rang again—that eerie long high-pitched ring, this time followed by a second long high-pitched ring. I hurriedly made my way down from the ladder and around the piled-up furniture to the phone that was sitting on the floor. When I answered the phone, I heard static and it sounded like the static was echoing from far away.

I kept saying "Hello?" and it sounded as though the static was answering me. I thought to myself that something must be wrong with the telephone lines. I hung up. Then I picked up the phone from the floor, and I froze. I was looking at the phone and its cord and I realized it was not plugged in to the phone jack on the wall.

"How is the painting going?" my sister asked me when she called me the next day.

"Great" I replied with a yawn. I had stayed up late to finish the bedroom. We talked at length about the colors I had chosen for my newly painted bedroom.

At the end of our chatting I said, "Oh I almost forgot to tell you!"

"Tell me what?" my sister asked with curiosity.

I replied, "Mom called."

— Barbara Gladue —

Texting Angels

Never lose hope. Just when you think it's over...
God sends you a miracle.
~Author Unknown

The fourth of July holidays. Hot dogs and hamburgers sizzling on the grill. Warm evenings with lightning bugs dancing in the breeze. Patriotic music blaring on your neighbor's radio. Carnivals. Cotton candy. And those fireworks tents that speckle the roadways and parking lots everywhere you go.

So, a few years back my husband and I decided to assist at one of those local fireworks tents near our home. It was much more physical work than we anticipated, but we both are people persons, and we loved the interaction with the public.

Other than the backbreaking setup it was basically like working retail. You rang up the merchandise and the customer paid for it by cash or credit. The incentive to being diligent in your work was that if you didn't charge enough, it came out of your paycheck. You can probably see where this is heading right now.

By the eighth day in we were tired, and worse yet the cash register was also wearing out. We constantly had to restart it and check tallies. During one such fit we realized that a woman had just departed with more than one hundred dollars in fireworks that had not been officially charged. She thought she had paid, and she had even signed the credit card slip, but the sale amount had not printed on the receipt.

I was panic-stricken. But then we realized that she might have provided her e-mail address to get coupons for the following year. I sent one e-mail after another to her, hoping I wouldn't end up in her spam folder.

As the day drew to a close, I confronted the possibility of losing that $100. But then, just as we began lowering the sides of the tent, she pulled up. We ran her credit card again, and this time it worked.

I was so relieved I could cry. She, on the other hand, was slightly irritated. It was no wonder, I thought, I had sent quite a few panicked e-mails.

Surprisingly though, that wasn't the source of her irritation. She was angry that I had somehow hacked her phone number and had texted her about the problem. I assured her that was impossible. I didn't have her phone number. She showed me her phone and sure enough there was a text to her from my phone explaining the problem.

I didn't want to debate it, so I smiled and apologized, and she was off. However, to make things even stranger… I didn't have my phone. I was using my husband's phone.

I didn't have her phone number. I didn't use my phone. But she got a text from my phone.

I guess God had answered my prayer that day when I'd asked Him to help. But who knew that God's angels knew how to text?

— Pastor Wanda Christy-Shaner —

Just What We Needed

Not everything we experience can be explained by logic or science.
~Linda Westphal

New York City. The Saturday after the horror of 9/11. I had just gotten to the first of my three clown jobs for that day when I discovered that I had left my bag of twisting balloons at home. Twisting balloons are the ones you use to make balloon animals.

I was just getting ready to tell the birthday mom that these kids were going to have a balloon-less birthday party when I noticed some balloons that had been left in the bottom of my suitcase. With that, I checked the outside compartment of my suitcase, and noticed some more leftover balloons! Okay, I thought, this would be enough for this party, but what about the next two parties? Would I have enough time to make it home to get my bag of balloons and make it on time for my next two parties? It's not like you can find this special type of balloon easily in a store.

After the first party, I was walking briskly to the subway in full clown attire since I had to get home quickly to grab some more balloons. But there was a barrier by one of the fire stations. Going around this would mean walking a few blocks out of my way, definitely making me late. I tried to cut through but I was stopped by one of the firemen.

With panic in my voice, I told him I needed to get to the subway ASAP or I was going to be late for both my jobs. He thought about it and then he responded, "I'll make a deal with you, Clown. I'll let you through on one condition — that you go into the station and entertain the kids for a couple of minutes."

I agreed without hesitation. When I walked into the back room of the station, I noticed eight sad children sitting at a long table coloring. After trying to cheer them up as best as I could with shticks and jokes, I felt it still wasn't enough. Just on a whim, I reached into my pockets, which originally were balloon-less. There I found exactly eight balloons. I made balloon animals for all eight kids, putting smiles on those sad faces, and then headed for my next job, I still hadn't figured out what to do about my lack of balloons.

When I got to my next party, I again opened up my suitcase, which I could have sworn I emptied out at my last gig and noticed some more balloons! I even had enough balloons to make up for the popped ones!

On the way to my last party, I was approached by some more kids requesting balloons...Yup! You guessed it!! I reached into my pockets and there they were! It happened again when I got to my last party, as well as being approached by some more kids on the way home. Balloons just seemed to be materializing out of nowhere!

Every one of those balloons was a small miracle for a child. I still don't know how it happened, but I know it was just what we all needed on that very sad weekend.

— Susan P. Zwirn —

I Wasn't Quite Done

Blessed are those that know the path out of their carnal flesh, for they shall attain intuition.
~Michael Bassey Johnson

It was my first college party, and I was a very excited, barely twenty-one-year-old girl with no clue about the danger I was facing. I put on my cutest outfit and went to this gathering full of college and grad students, most of whom were much older and more experienced than I was.

I had recently broken away from the religion I had grown up in. Though I always kept God and Jesus and kindness (and spirituality in general) close to my heart, I must admit I was a little bitter about my strict upbringing. I was eager to go and experience what "party life" was like.

Arriving at the tiny apartment building in downtown Salt Lake City where the party was being held, I assumed I was in good company. Everyone around me seemed extremely successful and motivated. Some were graduating with doctorates, some were biologists, and one man was training to become an airline pilot. It was this handsome young man who seemed to take an interest in me throughout the night.

It never once crossed my mind that I was in danger while at this party, so I was relaxed and having fun. I was more concerned about how I looked and making new friends than anything else. I also kept accepting drinks from the guy who was training to be a pilot.

As the night drew to a late close and everyone attending had begun ordering their Ubers and Lyfts home (all of us being sufficiently buzzed or drunk from drinking) I began to make my own plans to Uber home. It had been a wonderful time and I'd made new friends and felt on top of the world.

Suddenly, my admirer said there was no need for me to get an Uber. Instead, he offered me a ride back to his place, where he assured me I could safely crash on his couch and he'd take me out to breakfast the next morning.

I definitely should have been wary, but this guy was a motivated college student and was training to fly airplanes! He was cute and sociable and seemingly friendly. Naïve twenty-one-year-old me sensed absolutely no danger as I thanked him and crawled into his car, planning to crash on his couch for the night.

You can probably guess what happened next, so I will leave this part of the story somewhat vague. I fell asleep and when I woke up I was being brutally attacked. He hurt me in a way I will not describe, and the searing pain put my body into flight mode. I screamed and tried to escape the place, but he kept picking me up and throwing me back onto the bed I had woken up in.

I believe the only reason he eventually left me alone was because I began throwing up so violently. In fact, I was puking so aggressively, my body in complete panic mode, that I actually choked on my vomit in the bathroom and began to suffocate.

I can tell you that suffocating to death is much more peaceful than you can imagine—at least it was for me. When I stopped breathing for long enough, I consciously experienced myself leaving my body. I saw my physical body still lying on the bathroom floor, up against the toilet.

I was hovering in the top corner of the tiny bathroom and I remember looking at my body and becoming very sad. The first thing I experienced was a deep love for myself. I remember looking at my body and sadly saying, "Wow. I'm so beautiful."

I don't believe I said this in a vain way, but more out of respect for all that my life had become at that point and all that I had made of myself as a person.

My conscious attention then turned to the fact that I had left my body and that I was surely going to die. "I can't believe this is how it ends. I die at the hand of this jerk," I remember thinking to myself somberly. I was mostly at peace, but there was quite a bit of sadness and even a slight bitterness that my life would be taken this way.

What comes as a surprise to me and probably will to you, is that when I left my body, it was as if I had always been in this ethereal state, like the super conscious or higher self is a part of you that is always present and watching. The transfer from my physical body and into my "soul" was as natural as blinking.

Looking at my body and mourning, I then looked to my right and saw these breathtaking streams of color—aqua, ice blue, teal. Those waving colors meant something to me—that I should go back to my body. I heard a loud clap and I was back in my body, gasping for air.

I was completely conscious of what had just transpired. For whatever reason, my attacker had decided to leave me alone. I washed up and called my mom for a rescue. I would never report what happened to me that night. I was afraid no one would believe either story: the horror, or the miracle.

—Jessica Joe—

Come and Meet My Son

Believe in miracles. I have seen so many of them come when every other indication would say that hope was lost. Hope is never lost.
~Jeffrey R. Holland

It was Mother's Day 2017. My daughter and I were sitting in the living room watching the early morning news when we heard my son call out. "Mom," he said, "Mom." And then there was a bumping sound as he fell against his bedroom doorframe.

We were beside him in seconds and while I got him seated Sarah called 911. That was at 7:15 A.M. By 8:30 A.M. he was in the neurology department at St. Luke's and it was apparent that he had suffered a stroke. I was terrified and broken hearted.

By 9:00 A.M., we three — my daughter, my other son, John, who had come immediately from his home in Liberty, and I, stood beside Brian's bed as the neurologist explained to him what they thought was happening and what they intended to do. My daughter and I watched as he listened attentively, made steady eye contact, and asked questions appropriate to the situation. It was a few minutes before the realization that something significant had happened came to us. This was my fifty-one-year-old son, who was high functioning but severely autistic with multiple ancillary disabilities. He had never acted like this before.

My daughter turned to me and we searched each other's faces while we both wondered: "Who is this? Is this our Brian who was lost?"

I gestured toward the door, and we fled into the hall.

"He called me 'Mom,' Sarah. He called me 'Mom.'"

Even as a very small child he had called me "Mother." The other children called me "Mom" but from him it was always "Mother." From the time he could talk his vocabulary was totally out of sync with that of a child. My friends said he spoke like an old man. He had never, and I mean never, called me "Mom."

"And he's talking to the doctor… and looking right at him," Sarah responded. My son had been unable to make eye contact since the age of five. We stared at each other, overcome with the wonder of it… but the question hung there. "Will it last?" she asked me.

"Well, if it doesn't, for how long will he…?" I couldn't finish the question.

A month later we came to believe the change was a lasting one and it has been. Although Brian still needs care and support, my son is home.

He had been far away in that land of autism, which has its own laws. It is a land that requires constant vigilance against any and all human contact, both physical and emotional. It demands from its residents an extreme effort to process the cacophony of sound and senses in the world, leaving no room for everyday things like affection or joy. It is a land of sorrow, both for the residents and for those who miss what could have been.

Brian had left us slowly when he was a child, but he came home in an instant thanks to the stroke. For how long no one knows, nor do they know why he is here with us again.

Now we must learn new rules. Accept new happiness. Give up old habits. We are surprised to hear his voice in conversation. We're unprepared for his soft questioning of something he sees on television. Unused to his smile or chuckle, his steady gaze. Totally overcome with his pleasure in experiencing tastes and smells and the loveliness of the world in spring.

I yearn to run up and down the street… knock on all doors… tell all who will listen, "Come and meet my son. He has returned. Come and meet my son, Brian."

—Laura Lewis—

Heaven-Sent

The Birthday Gift

The prayer that begins with trustfulness and passes on into waiting will always end in thankfulness, triumph, and praise.
~Alexander Maclaren

"It'll be $1900, and that includes parts and labor." the mechanic told me over the phone. It was the last week of October in 2001 and the transmission had gone out on my car. Money was tight, but if I maxed out the only credit card I had, along with using everything in my checking and savings accounts, I would have just enough to pay for the repair.

"Okay, go ahead and fix it," I replied with a sigh. I needed transportation to get to work and to get my kids to school, so it had to be done. After hanging up with the mechanic, a thought struck me and I uttered it out loud to myself: "What about Shane's birthday gift?"

My son Shane was turning nine on November 1st. For the last six months or so, we had been making weekly stops at the local skateboard shop so that Shane could browse. He dreamed of having a skateboard made just for him and he spent hours with the owner of the shop discussing the pros and cons of the different brands of decks, trucks, wheels, and bearings. After one particularly lengthy visit to the shop, I had apologized to the owner for taking up so much of his time. He said that Shane was always well-mannered and respectful and he genuinely enjoyed talking with him. He told me that we were welcome there anytime.

The skate shop owner was right about Shane; he was a good kid. He'd sometimes struggled in school, but the extra effort he had been putting in this year was already being reflected in his grades. That was one reason I'd promised to get the new skateboard for his birthday. He deserved to be rewarded.

Shane often spent hours trying to piece together a working skateboard from a few old ones that we had bought at garage sales, but eventually there weren't enough usable parts remaining and he was left without a board at all. How could I explain to him that I wouldn't be able to buy a new one? It broke my heart to have to break a promise to my son. I prayed that I could find a way to keep my word.

November 1st arrived way too soon and Shane was up early that day. I made his favorite breakfast and listened as he chattered away about all the tricks he would be able to do with his new skateboard. I hadn't told him yet that the money for his gift had been used to fix my car. I tried to tell him several times, but the words always seemed to get stuck in my throat. I was still holding out hope that I could find a way.

In the car on the way to school Shane went over the plans for his big day. I was to pick up Shane and his friend Derek after school and we would go straight to the skate shop. Shane would get his skateboard, then we would pick up his sister, Scarlett, from her school. We would all go to the skatepark for a couple of hours, then stop for pizza and then finally, go back home for birthday cake. I smiled weakly and nodded in agreement, all while fighting back tears.

On the way to Scarlett's school, I began to rationalize in my head. I thought "I can still manage to afford a pizza and I can bake a cake at home instead of getting one from the bakery. Shane can probably borrow a skateboard from Derek's older brother so we can still go to the skatepark. Maybe he won't be too disappointed?" But I knew that he would be.

I continued holding back the tears until after I'd dropped off my daughter. But as soon as she was out of sight, I let them flow. Life had been difficult for too long and the struggle had finally caught up to me. I felt guilty for not being able to keep my promise to my son and for not explaining it to him sooner. I felt guilty for not being able to provide better for my children and for other things that had happened that were beyond my control. I felt so tired, overwhelmed, and sad.

I was about halfway home when my crying began to subside, and I started to pray. I prayed for one thing and one thing only and that was for help in finding a way to get Shane's birthday gift. I told the Lord that if He would help with that, then I would work hard to make everything else better for my family.

I finished my prayer while pulling up to a stoplight. As I waited for the light to turn green, I casually glanced out my window and something caught my eye on the other side of the street. "Is that money?" I said aloud. The morning sun was in my eyes, and I squinted to get a better look. "Yep, that sure looks like money!" I quickly looked around and there was not a single car on the road in either direction, so I hopped out, ran across the street and picked up the cash. It was a one-hundred-dollar bill! My heart was flip-flopping in my chest! I saw that there were four more bills nearby, so I quickly gathered them up and ran back to the car.

The light was still red, so I took the time to count the cash that was tightly clutched in my hand. It was one hundred and eight dollars! The cost of a custom skateboard was one hundred dollars plus sales tax for a total of one hundred and eight dollars! My prayer had been answered for the exact amount that I had requested!

As I think back now on that strange event, I am still baffled. At that time of morning there was always bumper-to-bumper traffic on that street, so where were the other cars that day? The cash was across the street, three traffic lanes away and in the shadow of the gutter, so how could I possibly have seen it? What were the odds of me finding the exact amount that I had asked for in my prayer? Some might call it coincidence, others might say that the universe provided, but my heart tells me that it was a miraculous gift from God.

It was several years later before I finally told Shane the story of how he got his first new skateboard. He gave me a hug and thanked me for always trying to make his birthday special.

I still smile when I think of my son's ninth birthday. Shane passed away in 2012 and those precious memories are all that I have left of him now. I'll always be grateful for that answered prayer and the birthday miracle that it provided for my son.

— Tammy Childers —

More than a Coincidence

Do you think the universe fights for souls to be together?
Some things are too strange and strong to be coincidences.
~Emery Allen

Unable to sleep one night, I began to craft the perfect man for me in my head. The few dates I had had in the past seven years were hopeless, and I was only fifty-four, still young enough to enjoy a relationship with a man. "Okay, Moira [my guardian angel's name], I'm gonna ask one more time: I'd like to meet a nice man, not too fat, not too thin, not too rich, not too poor, older than me, good sense of humor, easygoing, educated, halfway decent looking, knows how to dress..." The mental litany of what I wanted in my dream man lulled me to sleep.

The next day at work my supervisor called me into her office. "Here's a new patient for you, Kathleen," she said as she handed me the paperwork. I was working for a hospice in Charlottesville, Virginia, as an R.N. Over the weekend the intake nurse had written a long note on a patient, detailing her cancer, that she had been diagnosed two years prior to hospice's involvement, along with personal information. She and her husband Ed had four children, were long-time boaters and went to the same church I attended. Ed was a retired Air Force pilot who had been overseas many times. Hmm, I thought. Lots of similarities to my life — boater, grew up overseas, regular churchgoer, four children, military people in my family. Other than that cursory thought I didn't dwell on it. I picked up my bag of medical supplies and headed for their home in the city.

Ed met me at the door. He welcomed me into their home, an upscale condo in the historic district. His wife sat in a wingback armchair, an attractive blonde in her early sixties. She looked tired but smiled and said "hello" quietly as I introduced myself. Ed, a slender man with thinning gray hair, slightly older than his wife, stood by while we chatted. His wife and I had a lot in common.

As the week wore on, I visited three more times, and during my visit on Friday, I found my patient sitting up in bed, but dozing off now and then. As I sat down next to her on the side of the bed, she extended her arms toward me but was silent. I scooted closer to her, put my arms out and we hugged. She began to cry softly. I had the feeling she was asking me to take care of Ed. It seemed strange because I barely knew her and she barely knew me, but I felt the message almost as if she had spoken out loud. I said goodbye to her and then to Ed, taking the message with me in my heart. She died the following day.

The standard follow-up after a person's death involved two more home visits. Ed and I chatted about his wife and her importance to him and their family. I maintained my usual professional manner, suggesting he join the hospice support group, which he did.

In the month following the death of his wife, I found myself thinking about Ed more and more. I was definitely attracted to him. On a Tuesday, one night after work I called him to chat and see how he was feeling.

"Hi, how're you doing?" I asked.

"Oh, I'm okay. I miss my wife, but I'm managing. The support group is helping."

We talked about the wine festivals in the area, and how much we each enjoyed a good red wine. "Would you like to join me for a glass of wine at the Court Square Tavern?" he asked.

Located in the downtown area between his home and mine, the tavern was a popular watering hole for locals. You could also get a hearty meal there. Fortunately, he didn't see my wide smile or hear my rapidly beating heart when he asked. "Sure," I answered. "Not tomorrow though, but Thursday is fine." I didn't want to seem too anxious!

I walked into the tavern after work and there he was, sitting at a table in the bar area reading the local paper. Just one look at him told me I wouldn't have to teach him how to dress. He looked handsome in a navy-blue blazer, a striped shirt, khaki slacks and loafers. After a few glasses of wine and a good meal, we headed for the door, presumably to go our separate ways. Outside, a soft spring drizzle sparkled in the streetlights. As he opened the large blue and white striped umbrella he was carrying, he turned to me and asked, "How about walking down to the mall?"

Charlottesville has a lovely open-air mall complete with twinkling lights in the trees, good restaurants and cute boutiques. I agreed. Sharing his umbrella, with my arm entwined in his, we headed toward the lights of the mall in the rain. It was so romantic.

As we came to know each other better I told him about my prayer. We laughed about it and marveled at it. He told me when his wife's doctor informed them that her cancer had moved into her liver and she had a limited amount of time left, she made Ed promise he would try to find a suitable woman and get married again. I guess I was it. I never told Ed about the unspoken message I had received from her the day before she died.

One year later, we were married in the banquet room of a lovely hotel in Charlottesville. The hospice chaplain performed the ceremony, and all our family and friends witnessed the happy occasion. For the next nine years we traveled extensively, lived on a boat for a while, and just enjoyed each other's company. There was no doubt about it: Ed was the man I had prayed for and dreamed about.

Sadly, nine years after we got married, Ed was diagnosed with an incurable cancer. He died peacefully in our home four days before his seventy-fifth birthday. I still feel his presence every now and then and I know he is watching over me. I will be forever grateful for our ten years together, and for the answered message from Moira, my guardian angel.

— Kathleen Cox Richardson —

Show Yourself

The love between a mother and daughter
knows no distance.
~Author Unknown

On March 18, 2020, my ninety-year-old mother lay sedated and non-responsive in a hospital bed in New Hampshire. It was two days after she suffered a debilitating stroke that would shortly lead to her death. The Covid pandemic was just rearing its ugly head and the hospital had an absolute no-visitor policy. The closest I could get was on speakerphone from my home in Vermont.

I stood on my deck on that drizzly, gray March day as a nurse held a phone for my mother. I clutched my phone tightly as if I were holding my mom. Through wrenching sobs, I cried out, "You can do this, Mom. It's going to be beautiful. So incredibly beautiful. You will be free from your body, free from suffering." Weeping, I paused. Finally, catching my breath, I said, "I love you so much and you love me so much and this love will not die with your body. It's just the next season of the two of us. Go, Mama. You go and I will look for you." Two hours later my mother left her body.

The fear of the pandemic combined with my enormous grief and it was overwhelming. I took refuge in the forest behind my home, sometimes dragging a sleeping bag with me and lying beneath the trees and sky to feel the pull of gravity under my body. I needed to be held. I wanted to feel protected. And I wanted a sign. God how I wanted a sign.

As spring shifted into summer, my twenty-year-old son Max and I lay on inflatable rafts on the little pond in our woods. "I miss her so much," I said.

"I know," he said. "I do, too."

Floating quietly, I noticed the birds calling each other, the frogs' occasional splash, and something else. What was it? Something walking? "Max!" I whispered, "Over there!"

Astonished, we watched a big black bear tromping around close to us. My mom had been afraid of bears and of nature in general, but she was seriously terrified by bears. She was also the biggest worrier I ever knew. It was sad how much she worried, but on this day, as we witnessed that big black bear walking around so close by, I looked to the sky and heard my mom say, "Don't worry."

Don't worry!

A bear. My mom. Don't worry.

Here she was, on the other side of everything, giving me this advice. Could it be that simple—just stop worrying? I realized that if my mom was working that hard to send that message, I should take it seriously.

The next month, our family spent a week at our cabin on the Maine coast. By then the wisdom from the bear was drifting away and all that remained was a deep emptiness and an insatiable desire to receive a message from my mom. One morning, as Max and I paddled our kayaks around the cove, I wanted a sign so badly I cried out into the cloudless sky, "I want to see you, Mom! Show yourself!"

There were many times in the past few months when I asked for a sign, and all I received was a fluttery feeling in my heart, a reminder that her love did not leave when her body died. But I wanted more. I wanted visual proof that we were still connected, so looking up to the sky I demanded, "Be an eagle!" And by golly there she was. A bald eagle flew above us, circled around, and flew away out of our sight.

"Did that really happen?" I asked. Max nodded. The sweet satisfaction of my wish fulfilled only lasted a moment. *It's not that unusual to see an eagle out here,* I thought. *It's probably just a coincidence.* I wanted more confirmation that she was with me, so I called out, "Okay, Mom, that was cool. Now be an eagle and catch a fish and bring the fish to a nest with baby eagles and feed the fish to them."

When this happened exactly, when the eagle came back, dove into the water, carried a big fish to an enormous nest high in a giant pine tree, when the eagle tore off chunks of fish and fed them into the wide-open mouths of her two eaglets, well, all I could do was sob. And trust. And believe. And rejoice.

"Did that really happen?" I asked Max again, this time in a whisper. Again, he could only nod, both of us wide-eyed. We slowly drifted back to the cabin, our paddles lightly lapping the water. I realized that my insatiable need for a sign from my mother had finally waned. I was still grieving intensely, but now I knew I was not alone. My mother's love was ever-present.

In the two years that have passed since my mother's physical death, I have realized three things: 1) Grief is a very fierce form of love and it will come and go as it pleases; I need only hang on tight and let it pull me under when it chooses to do so. 2) Miracles absolutely do happen. And 3) Life is a lot more fun without worrying!

— Lava Mueller —

Butterflies, A Sign of Hope

Butterflies are nature's angels. They remind us
what a gift it is to be alive.
~Robyn Nola

"Look! That tree is alive," our nine-year-old son, Caleb, called out. It was as if the tree were breathing butterflies; it was spellbinding. My daughter and mother-in-law tried to photograph it, but it was impossible to capture the grandeur of it.

The monarchs were migrating to Mexico and a storm had blown them off course. It was the only time in the twenty-five years we lived there that we witnessed their journey south.

We didn't know it then, but all too soon monarch butterflies would be adding more wonder to our lives. Everyone knows that butterflies are beautiful, graceful and wonderful to behold, but they became even more than that for my family.

A few years later my dad had a heart aneurysm and was life-flighted to a hospital near Kansas City. He endured thirteen hours of surgery, but the surgeon had to stop because they kept losing dad and bringing him back. They finally decided that he couldn't endure any more, so they closed him up to wait for another chance to finish the surgery. The surgeon said he needed rest and healing before they could complete it.

Dad lingered for a few days, and we never left his side. Tubes and machines helped him fight for his life, but after two weeks, he was too tired to go on.

My mother-in-law noticed a monarch butterfly resting on her screen door that day. She began to grieve because she felt it was a sign that my dad had passed. We had not spoken with her, but in her heart she knew. She watched the butterfly for hours before she received my call that my dad was gone.

She and my father-in-law arrived at the hospital as soon as they could get there. She hugged me and said, "There are butterflies on your shirt! Monarchs!" I didn't usually wear anything like that, but that day I wore a T-shirt with beautiful monarchs on it. Then she told me about the visitor on her screen door that day, and how she intuitively knew that it was a sign that my dad had passed.

After that, every time I took a walk in our woods, which was almost daily, a monarch butterfly would cross my path. "Why do you think this is happening?" I asked my mother-in-law. She said, "The Lord is showing you that your dad is still with you, not that I think he has turned into a butterfly, but it is a sign that his presence is near." He was with me, I felt him, kept hearing his voice in my mind, and knew he was close by. And yet, I longed for the way it used to be. I wanted to hug him, see him, talk to him.

Our daughter's wedding was in August that year. It is when we gather for such events that my heart aches and longs for my dad the most. My dad did not get to meet Drake, my daughter's fiancé, before he died, but we know they would have adored each other.

I didn't know it at the time of the wedding, but Drake's grandmother had also passed away, and she had loved butterflies. She had them displayed all over her house in various forms. Drake's mom was going through a very similar period of grieving over the loss of her mom.

The wedding was held in a park in North Carolina. We knew it would either be hot or raining, so we had supplied our guests with umbrellas to shield them from the elements, whichever way it went.

I walked down the aisle that day in the most beautiful dress I've ever owned and took my place in the front row, feeling like a queen. The sun was scorching hot even at 11:00 that morning, so I put up my umbrella to shield me. The beautiful ceremony ended and I was escorted back up the aisle to the buffet. My husband's aunt met me there with great excitement. "You couldn't see it!" she said, "There was a monarch butterfly resting on your umbrella through the whole ceremony."

He was there! He was with us that day. My daughter was his pride and joy and he wouldn't miss her wedding. Tears streamed down my face as I whispered, "Thanks, Dad! I love you!"

The next morning at breakfast we learned that a monarch butterfly rested on Drake's mom's knee and hovered about her through the whole ceremony, too. She felt it was a sign that her mom was present. We hardly knew what to think! It was a beautiful sign from heaven that our loved ones who had passed were there with us in spirit, celebrating, making a beautiful wedding even more extraordinary.

Over time my encounter with butterflies has seemed to wane, but each time I see one I am reminded of how they inspired hope and gave comfort to our extended family.

—Cheri Bunch—

Dad's Journey Home

Someday a loving hand will be laid upon your shoulder and this brief message will be given: "Come Home."
~Billy Graham

Dad had been experiencing intense chest pain from what the doctors called a "three-day stress heart attack." He finally gave in and let my mom take him to the emergency room. He was immediately admitted to the cardiac care unit.

Mom stayed with him until he was considered to be stable. As she turned to leave, Dad said goodbye, but it wasn't like "see you soon." It was more like a final goodbye. She turned to look back just as alarms started going off. She heard the call of "code blue" and knew that it was for Dad. That was the beginning of his first after-death experience.

Dad was blessed to have a wonderful nurse who was also a devoted Christian. She was in the room when Dad coded and asked if he would mind sharing his experience with her. Dad said, "I remember leaving my body and I went up to the corner of the room near the ceiling. I could see several people working on me. I'm not sure how long I was out of my body, but I remember suddenly coming back down from the ceiling and reentering my body."

The nurse asked his permission to bring in several members of the code team, including some who had not been in attendance, to see if he could identify who was in the room at the time of his near-death. To their amazement, he accurately identified each one.

Upon further tests, it was determined that Dad would need immediate surgery to insert a pig valve and repair the major damage to his heart. He went into surgery, and halfway through the procedure a nurse came out to the waiting room and asked Mom questions pertaining to Dad's spiritual beliefs. Something had occurred in that operating room.

An hour later we were summoned to the hallway leading to the CCU recovery unit. We saw Dad coming toward us on the gurney, but something about him was very different. He was actually glowing! Then, to our amazement, Dad sat straight up and said, "I can't wait to tell you where I've been!" The nurse who was with him during surgery told us they had lost him for more than four minutes. Post-op, she was able to visit him in CCU and document the details of his journey. Two nurses were also in the room while Dad was sharing his story and were so moved that they accepted the Lord at Dad's bedside.

We went to visit Dad soon after he returned home and were sitting by his bedside when he asked if he could share his near-death experience with us. We listened intently as he told us about his journey to heaven.

"I remember being in the operating room and was aware that the doctors had started the procedure. It wasn't long before I realized that life was slowly leaving my body. It began at my feet and had reached the point of my waist when I cried out, 'Lord, I'm dying! Please help me!' I heard a voice tell me, 'Reach up and take My hand.' I did as I was told, and I could feel my soul leave my body, exiting through my head. All at once I was transported through a long dark tunnel with an extremely bright light in the distance. I wasn't afraid, as there were two angels, one on either side of me, who had been sent to guide me to my heavenly home. As I got nearer to the end of the tunnel, I began to hear the most beautiful music! It was something like I had never heard on earth. It sounded as if it could be coming from the angels moving their wings."

We were awestruck as he continued: "I exited the tunnel and saw what I thought was the greenest, most beautiful golf course that I had ever seen in my life! The flowers were beautiful and the colors were vibrant. There was a river running through the valley, and on the other side was the heavenly city." Dad had seen the Valley of the Shadow of Death!

He went on to say, "The streets were really gold, just like the Bible says, and the gates were made of huge pearls. Friends and relatives came to greet me, and we spoke, but not with our mouths. It was more like mind transference where we knew each other's thoughts. I was greeted by the Lord and He told me that if I crossed over the valley to the gates of the city, I could never leave. I was experiencing such peace and I never wanted to leave, but the Lord said, 'It's not your time. You have to go back.' I had no choice in the matter and was quickly and painfully transported back into my earthly body, entering through my head, just as I had left."

Dad fell into a deep depression after this experience. He kept questioning why God didn't want him in Heaven. But I said, "Dad, do you remember those two nurses who accepted the Lord after they heard your testimony? You were sent back for them, and for so many others who will be moved by your testimony."

At a subsequent checkup, Dad was told that the pig valve in his heart had developed a small tear. Left untreated, the valve would give way unexpectedly, and Dad would be gone in a matter of seconds. The doctors urged him to have the valve replaced, to which his answer was an adamant "no." "You robbed me of heaven once, and you're not going to do it again!" he said. He was told to curb his activities in order to avoid stressing his heart, but he continued to play golf and walk every day. I think that Dad was longing to go "home" again.

That year on Christmas Day Dad had his favorite dinner and spoke with each of his children and several of his grandchildren. Around 9:00 P.M. Christmas night, my brother drove my parents back home. He usually dropped them off with a quick goodbye, but that evening, he felt compelled to go inside and visit for a few minutes. My mom was showing him the Christmas cards that friends and relatives had sent when my dad stood up suddenly and cried out, "I think that I'm having a heart attack!" My brother ran to catch Dad as he was going down, but it was apparent that Dad was already gone.

At Dad's memorial service, Mom said, "Look at your dad's face!

He looks so peaceful, as if he's smiling."

I said, "He's seen the Lord. I'd be smiling too!"

— Sharon E. Albritton —

"L" Is for Louis

There's no other love like the love for a brother. There's no other love like the love from a brother.
~Author Unknown

The anniversary of my brother's death was approaching. It didn't matter that it had been several years since his passing. It still hurt.

I had become my younger brother Louis's guardian upon the death of my mother seventeen years earlier and I took my responsibility very seriously. Through those years, I attended his school functions and meetings, accompanied him to medical visits, chaperoned playdates and everything else a true mother would have done. As he grew older and moved into his own home, I still saw him at least every other week and he phoned me each morning and evening without fail.

Louis was not a complainer, so when he told me during one of these morning conversations that his throat was bothering him, I became concerned. The fact that he repeatedly said his throat felt irritated and he was having trouble swallowing sent me right back into "mommy mode" and I urged him to see his doctor. When he phoned later that evening, he told me that though his primary care physician had not been available, he had gone to an urgent care center. The diagnosis: a simple case of strep throat. He was given a prescription and told to follow up in two weeks.

I breathed a sigh of relief; it was only strep. Yet, my relief was short lived. When I visited with my brother two weeks later, I could plainly see his throat was significantly bulging on one side. He admitted, also, that he was not feeling much better. What happened next was a whirlwind. I accompanied him to every doctor imaginable. Not one was willing to make a diagnosis or take further responsibility for his treatment. Louis was feeling worse every day. I couldn't understand any of it.

Ultimately, I took Louis to a local hospital emergency room when he finally admitted he was too weak to lift his toothbrush. After a full battery of tests, the diagnosis was made—advanced lymphoma. He was gone by the end of the week.

My grief was indescribable. For weeks, I cried in my sleep, upon waking, and then throughout the day. I kept the urn filled with his ashes on my dresser and hugged it each time I passed. I don't know what it's like to lose a child and pray I never do. But I do know what it's like to lose my brother, best friend and someone who was like my child in many ways. It was crippling.

Months later, I still continued to seek solace, but none ever came. At my husband Bill's suggestion, I moved the urn that held Louis's ashes to a less prominent spot in my home—a bookshelf in a spare bedroom. There, he said, it would not be such a constant reminder of my loss. Only, to me, with the urn out of sight, it felt like my brother was moving even farther away.

After dinner that night, I took a walk as my tears once again flowed. How was any of this possible? I wondered over and over again. I had taken my brother to the best doctors. We had remained on top of the situation. What about medical advances? Had there been no way to help him?

I looked up at the stars, imagining that Louis was as far away and as inaccessible as those tiny sparkles of light. Then I brought my gaze downward. Through my tears, my eyes caught a glimmer at the edge of the curb. I bent down for a closer look. And there, I found something I still consider amazing to this day. I picked the glittering item up. In my hand, I held a silver chain on which a silver heart and a silver "L" charm hung. Now, I could understand finding a lost heart necklace. But finding a heart and an "L" together on the same chain? It was as though Louis had sent his love and gratitude down to me from heaven.

I can't say that from that point I felt instantly better and that my grief was miraculously healed. Yet, I can say I took this as a beautiful sign that my brother was, in some way, still near me, seeing me and hearing me and, wherever he was, he was strong enough to send this message. And that revelation set me on my own road to recovery in the days, weeks and months that followed.

—Monica A. Andermann—

The Jackpot

Timing in life is everything.
~Leonard Maltin

I had let a credit card back into my life. But now I was going to free myself from debt. I'd watched my online financial guru, Dave Ramsey, on dozens of YouTube videos about eliminating debt forever. I got out my scissors. It was time! Snip, snip, snip. The credit card was sliced to smithereens.

I had moved to Albuquerque for affordable housing. I only took what fit in my sedan and donated the rest. I was staying in a free guest room at the apartment complex while I waited for the tenants to move out of my intended rental. It was supposed to be ready in a few days. But I ended up staying in their guest room rent-free for over a month.

I had just enough cash for my rent and deposit, so it was quite possible that I would end up sleeping on the floor once I got inside my new carpeted apartment. I didn't care as long as I had my own space.

But then, while taking my trash out one morning, I spied a discarded queen mattress and box spring leaned up against a brick wall. I looked them over. Would I look like a low life dragging them across the parking lot? But then I thought of Dave Ramsey, my hero. He said, "Live like no one else for now, so that later you can live and give like no one else." He said not to worry about the broke Jones's, just live within your means, or more bluntly, "Act your wage! Eat rice and beans if you have to but PAY OFF THAT DEBT!"

I knew he was right. It was time to get serious about money and debt. I was motivated. I dragged that heavy mattress across the parking lot, repeating to myself, "Live like no one else." This bed was free. I'd paid $1700 for my last queen bed, and I ended up giving it away to my friend Vicki because it didn't sell on Craigslist.

This secondhand bed would do just fine.

I went back for the box spring, not caring who saw me now. My goal was to be debt-free, and this would help me reach my goal.

Now they were leaning against my guest room wall. "Yay! I have a bed!" I would buy a thick mattress pad covering and I'd be all set. I had a whole apartment to furnish and this was a great start. I was happy I'd humbled myself enough to haul the bed to my room.

Later that afternoon, I took out my trash again. This time I saw a small white bookcase on top of the Dumpster. I carried it over my shoulder to the guest room. I was now the proud owner of a bed and a bookcase. I was being supplied. It felt good to have these useful things for free.

While sponging down my new treasure from the trash, I heard a knock at my door. It was a young man who I'd seen loading a U-Haul truck in the parking lot. "I saw you take the bookcase," he said. "We're moving today, and our truck is full. Do you want some other stuff? We don't have any room for it."

I said yes to everything they didn't want. If I couldn't use it, I would sell it or give it away. In any case, it would be repurposed instead of going into the Dumpster.

I got seven patio chairs, a deck lounger, a folding table I could use for a desk, a nightstand, end tables, stools, a wicker laundry basket, a trash can, even a director's chair that said VIP on the back.

I felt overwhelmed by this abundance. I'd given away everything I had in San Diego to my church, and now it was all coming back to me like a boomerang… plus more!

I lived another two weeks in the crowded guest room surrounded by all my free furniture.

After I got it all into my new apartment, I saw three ottomans on the side of the road for pick-up. I took a beige leather one I liked and put it in my car. As I lugged it up to the building, I noticed a pretty blond woman standing by the locked building door.

"I forgot my key," she said, waiting.

"I'll let you in."

"I'll hold the door open for you."

"That will be great. Thanks. I'm Carolyn."

"I'm Carolyn, too, but I go by 'Susie.'"

"Hi Susie. I found this ottoman for free." I laughed, "I like free."

"Everybody likes free stuff," she said.

I carried the ottoman inside my apartment and then I heard a knock at my door. I opened the door.

It was Susie. "Do you need lamps? Do you like elephants?"

"I love elephants," I said, "Yes, I was sitting here in the dark. I'd love elephant lamps."

Susie brought them in. I loved them. What a month I'd had! I'd slept in a rent-free guest room for several weeks, received all the furniture I needed for my new place, and now had a new friend next door. I had really hit the jackpot.

— Carolyn Jaynes —

The Tradition

Deeply, I know this, that love triumphs over death.
My father continues to be loved, and therefore
he remains by my side.
~Jennifer Williamson

When I was very young my family had a tradition. On Fridays we would eagerly wait for my father to come home from work because Friday was payday. Dad always gave us our allowance on Fridays. My mom got a twenty-dollar bill, and my sister and I each got five dollars. It was the 1960s and that was a lot of money to give a child back then for doing their weekly chores.

This tradition continued for many years. As time went on though, things changed. I was married in the late seventies and then had my daughter in 1981. I had moved to downstate New York for several years but would travel upstate whenever I had the chance to see my parents. We went up for holidays, birthdays, or any other reason just so that my parents and daughter could form a bond.

As my daughter grew up, my father continued the tradition by giving me a twenty-dollar bill and my daughter a five whenever we visited. This went on until my dad passed in 1997. At the cemetery, my daughter threw her last five-dollar bill on top of my dad's casket as it was lowered into the ground.

For years, we talked about my dad and what we called "the tradition."

One Father's Day, with our grown daughter far away, my husband

and I decided to go for a ride up north for a change of scenery. As we drove, we came upon a small-town diner that I had frequented several times as a child with my parents and sister. I remembered that my dad had done some accounting work for the owner, and he had taken me along when he met with them to go over their books.

My eyes welled up when we entered the diner and I spotted the familiar orange Formica tabletops. As we slid into our booth the waitress walked over to us with a big welcoming smile. Before she took our order, I told her about my history of visiting the diner with my dad.

Her face lit up. She said it was her parents' diner. I remembered a little girl running around back then, and this was her, all grown up. Then, much to my surprise, she told me that her mom was not only still alive but was the cook. She was in the kitchen!

I immediately sprang to my feet and ran over to the kitchen window. I peeked in and smiled. She asked if there was something I needed, and I spilled out the story. She was all smiles. She not only remembered my dad, as he had been their accountant and friend, but she remembered me! She remembered a little girl who sat at the counter spinning her seat, drinking her vanilla milkshake, and waiting for her daddy to finish his work meeting. We hugged and promised to see each other again to reminisce.

We left and I felt a bit melancholy. It had been a special day for me so far but I so missed my father on Father's Day.

On our way home, we stopped at a supermarket to pick up ingredients for dinner. At the checkout I was prepared to do my normal thing, which is to not ask for cash back, but then something told me to ask for ten dollars... in two five-dollar bills. My husband took one of them and gave me the other.

I still wasn't sure why I'd asked for cash back, never mind the request for the two separate five-dollar bills. But as I folded the bill to place it in my wallet, I couldn't believe what I was seeing. Written on the bill was my name in blue ink... KIM!

My knees felt weak, and I told my husband I had to go outside while he finished packing the groceries we had bought.

When he came out, he found me leaning on the car clutching the five. It was my Father's Day gift. I was sobbing. So grateful. So blessed.

That memory is something I carry with me every day in my wallet — the "tradition" that will always remind me that my dad is still part of my life.

— Kim Garback Diaz —

The Christmas Coat

Life is a series of thousands of tiny miracles.
~Mike Greenberg

"I don't think we can afford it right now. Maybe it will go on sale after Christmas," said my mom.

"It's okay, I can make my pea coat last one more winter. We can pray for God to provide one at a reasonable cost, too."

I didn't mean to eavesdrop on my parents' conversation, but we lived in a small house.

I was about seven years old and the third of four children. Christmas was coming and we were getting excited about what might be under the tree for us. Hearing my dad talk about making do with his coat, though, made me a little sad.

Dad had worn the blue wool coat for as long as I could remember. He'd been in the Navy years earlier—before he married Mom. I am ashamed to say I remember being embarrassed when he wore that coat. The wool had been patched in spots and I can't remember how many times my mom sewed on the buttons with the anchors on them. He needed a new coat, but I'd never thought about how much it would cost—or how often my parents made sacrifices like this so we children could have the clothes or shoes we needed or, in this case, some presents under the Christmas tree.

Earlier that day, my parents had gone shopping and he'd seen a winter jacket that he really liked. It was a heavyweight green and black plaid wool. He felt it was the coat for him, but then he saw the price. It was far more expensive than their budget would allow. He'd recently started his own business, and it was a daily struggle just to pay the bills and feed and clothe four children. As far as he was concerned, unless God had other plans, the coat would have to wait.

It was only a week or so later when Dad came home with a large box and an incredible story.

On the way home from work he'd seen a box fall from the back of a truck that was several car lengths ahead of him. He tried to catch up to the truck to let the driver know something had fallen off his vehicle, but he lost sight of it in the traffic. He decided to backtrack and see if the box was still there.

He was amazed when he saw the large red box still sitting where it had fallen in the middle of the intersection. He pulled over and went to get it—surprised that it hadn't been run over in the twenty or so minutes since he saw it fall. It was a gift box from a local department store. He took it to his car, opened the box, and could not believe his eyes. Inside was the coat he wanted—and it was his size.

It was tempting to keep it, but he thought about the person who obviously bought this coat as a gift—and the person who was supposed to receive it. He drove to the department store and took it to the men's department. The cashier did not recall selling the coat to anyone that day. There was a cash receipt in the box, so there were no credit card records with the name of the purchaser, and no one had called or come in to report it missing, so she told him to just keep it.

He couldn't in good conscience keep it without trying to find the person who bought it, so Dad took out an ad in the Lost and Found section of the local paper naming the intersection, type of truck he saw the box fall from, day and time, but no one ever called to claim the coat. After about a month, he finally felt like it was meant for him.

I remember Dad wearing that coat for years—long after it was threadbare and out of fashion. For him it was something that he could point to and tell the story of how God provided for his need in a very unusual way. More than half a century later, it is still a reminder for me to always have faith that God will provide for my needs.

—Donna Anderson—

Coincidences & Synchronicities

A Gentleman's Game

The probability of a certain set of circumstances coming together in a meaningful (or tragic) way is so low that it simply cannot be considered mere coincidence.
~V.C. King

"Checkmate, Papa!"

My grandfather surveyed the board, adjusted his bifocals and smiled. "Appears the teacher has been bested, Grandson! Well done!"

It took me three years to beat Papa. He had started teaching me to play chess when I was ten. Blockade, attacking, breakthrough—Papa taught me everything he knew about chess, or the gentleman's game as he called it. Now, as a teenager, I had taken all those strategies and won.

Delicately, Papa removed the remaining pieces from the weathered, foldable chessboard and flipped it over. I was amazed by what I saw. It was covered with dozens of names and dates.

"What is this, Papa?"

My grandfather swept a trembling hand over the board. "These are the men… and some women… who have beaten me at chess. Most are from World War II; fellow soldiers, passing the time with me on the front line. Whenever someone beat me, I let them write their name on the chessboard."

"What about this one, Papa? It says Betty, with a two after it."

"She was a nurse when I was recuperating. Good nurse. Even

better chess player. Beat me twice."

"You got hurt, Grandpa?"

"German infantry mortar round caught me out of my foxhole. And this fella," Papa pointed to a name on the board, "carried me off the field. Saved my life. And then, while convalescing in the hospital, he beat me at chess. Course, I was flat on my back and had to have him move the pieces for me." Grandfather considered this and laughed. "Son-of-a-gun probably cheated."

"There are so many names, Papa."

"Yes, and now there's one more. Here." And Papa handed me a pen.

Over the ensuing years, Papa and I played hundreds of games of chess. Soon, I was old enough for college and our games became fewer. When I graduated with a degree in social work, I returned home, and we played what was to be our last game of chess together.

And like so many times before, Papa won.

Then Papa methodically removed the chess pieces, placed them in a little wooden box, folded up the game board and handed everything to me. "I want you to have this."

"Papa, I can't take this. It's special to you."

"And now, it'll be special to you, Grandson. That's the way it is in life: we pass our love on to the next person."

Sadly, it wasn't long after this that Papa passed away. I was heartbroken, of course, but determined to take the things I had learned from him, and the love he had shown me, and pass them on to others.

I didn't have to wait long for an opportunity.

I was hired to be the social worker for a retirement community that sat on the edge of a park. Each day at lunch, I observed elderly residents milling aimlessly about, sitting alone, heads down.

Game on.

In the middle of the park, there were several concrete tables with chess/checker boards imprinted on them. One day at lunch, I sat down, set up my chess pieces and waited.

Nothing.

I came back the next day and tried again. An elderly man cautiously approached.

"Care for a game?" I cheerfully inquired.

The man smiled weakly and sat down.

"Your move… um, didn't catch your name."

"Paul," he said.

"Your move, Paul."

The man hesitated, as if he wasn't sure how to proceed. I was beginning to wonder if he'd ever played chess before.

Finally, he moved king's pawn two spaces, a standard opening move.

We played in silence, the only sounds the click-click of our chess pieces. I tried not being aggressive in my play, but I could only delay the inevitable.

"Checkmate," I said apologetically.

The old man sighed in a way that only someone very old and tired can do. "It's been a while since I played," he explained. "Will you be here tomorrow?"

"Yes, and every day after that."

When I returned the next day on my lunch break, I was surprised to see Paul already there, playing another elderly gentleman. I set up my pieces on a vacant table but before I could finish, an elderly woman approached and plopped down opposite me.

"Ready to get beaten by an old lady?"

My chess venture was a huge success, with ten to twenty people showing up each day around lunch and that many more spectating. Our play soon extended to the weekends, at which point we decided on a name for our merry group of chess-playing seniors: The Nobody's Pawn Chess Club.

Because we were running short on chessboards, I decided one Saturday to bring Papa's. I knew he would have approved.

Paul approached once I had set up the board. I hadn't played him since the first day we had met but he had shown up every day since.

"How 'bout a rematch?" he asked.

As soon as we began, I could see Paul had refined his chess skills. His moves were tactical and swift. But it was what he said next that surprised me.

"You know, before you came along, I rarely left my room. I had pretty much given up. But now, I've reconnected with old friends, made new ones. This may sound silly, but I think our chess club may have saved my life."

Before I could respond, Paul made his next move and jubilantly cried out, "Checkmate!"

I smiled, shook Paul's hand and he got up to go.

"Hey, wait a second, Paul. My grandfather had a custom. The victor gets to write his name on the bottom of the board."

Paul turned slowly, smiled and winked. "Don't need to. Last name's Ward. Paul Ward. Upper right-hand corner. See ya tomorrow."

I flipped the chessboard over and there it was. Sergeant Paul Ward 6/10/44. Papa's words flooded over me: "and this fella—carried me off the field."

Sergeant Paul Ward had saved my grandfather's life. And now, years later, Papa's love and passion for chess had returned the favor.

—Dave Bachmann—

Just What We Needed

Angels love to create synchronicities because each synchronicity produces an illumination point for a soul to connect the dots on life experiences.
~Molly Friedenfeld

My tears dropped onto the baby I held in my arms. She was wrapped in a pale pink muslin blanket with a burp cloth tucked under her chin. I cradled her close as I fed her a bottle in the back of the church. In front of me, a couple hundred women sat in pews listening to our Wednesday morning Bible study lecture. I shifted myself from side to side, rocking the baby as she half-ate and half-slept.

Six months earlier, a caseworker had pulled into our driveway. She unloaded an infant carrier from the back seat, rang our doorbell, and handed me a baby. The baby's name was Addy—and she brought our all-girl-gang total to five.

Our life was full, but in the words of our four-year-old, "When you become a foster family, your love grows and grows, and there's room for everyone."

Child Protective Services had removed Addy from her biological mother, Liz, at birth. Her biological father, Brad, was in jail. Addy spent her first couple of months in a different foster home, several hours north of us. I don't know much about her time there.

Addy was a delight. The center of attention, the recipient of a hundred kisses a day, cuddled close for most of her waking hours.

Her kitchen bouncy seat was my husband's first stop when coming in from work. Our other girls doted on her, fed her, read her books, pushed her stroller, and spoke to her in that gentle big sister way. We all loved her.

Brad and Liz were unable to make the necessary changes to provide a safe environment for Addy, and termination of their parental rights seemed imminent. As the court date drew near, we began paperwork to request her adoption.

During this transition, a new sadness welled up inside me. I was sad that I knew nothing about the day Addy was born — no memories, no photos, no information. I imagined Addy turning five and then nine and then seventeen, and while my other daughters have baby books bursting with photos and memories of their entry into the world, I would have almost nothing to share with Addy. All I had was a partially filled out card from the hospital that looked like it had been used as a coffee coaster. I desperately wanted to give her more than that. I longed for a photo of Addy snug in the arms of the mother who had carried her for nine months.

So, there I was, in the back of the chapel, cradling this baby. This baby, who had not come from me, but who was becoming mine. This baby, who had two mothers, but would likely only ever know one. This baby, who deserved more than what I felt I had to offer.

The lecture ended with the Romans 11 Doxology. There was a promise in those lyrics — God would meet Addy's needs and mine.

As the song ended, I exited quickly, hoping to find space to untangle my feelings and hide my tear-stained face. But as I ducked into an adjacent room, Becca, a woman I barely knew approached me.

"Hi," she said with a cheeriness I couldn't match. And although my weary heart wanted to be alone, I asked her how she was doing. She told me that she'd recently quit her job at the homeless shelter in town. My curiosity was piqued — Addy's biological mother had spent some time there.

"Did you know Liz Burrows?" I asked.

"Yes," Becca said. "How do you know her?"

And although I didn't make a habit of sharing Addy's story with just anyone, I didn't want to miss the opportunity for a glimpse into this unknown part of her life. "This is Liz's baby," I said. "I'm Addy's foster mom."

Becca stared at me. My heart rate quickened. Was there anything Becca would share that would give me a new piece of Addy's story?

"I have been praying for this baby." said the woman. "I have been praying for her foster family." She was praying for us?

Becca continued, "I drove Liz to the hospital the night she went into labor. I was there when Addy was born."

This woman, who was almost a stranger to me, told me the story of my daughter's birth.

Later that night, I laid Addy in her crib, feeling grateful and overwhelmed by the events of the day. After slipping out of the nursery, I checked my phone for e-mails. There was a message from Becca—and photos. Five beautiful photos of a newborn baby, snug in the arms of the mother who carried her for nine months.

— Kate Rietema —

The Painting

When two people are meant to be together,
they will be together. It's fate.
~Sara Gruen

Abstract paintings adorned the walls of the student union during my freshman year of college. Each was a unique expression by one of the art students. But one painting stood out for me. The vibrant yellow, the movement of the red and orange, the calming violet drew me in. I couldn't explain it. My fellow students knew that was my spot on the couch in view of the painting. It was there that I studied for sociology, statistics, history, and health. No matter the class, that painting exuded comfort.

Abstract art was not my thing. I preferred van Gogh or Monet—starry nights and water lilies. I couldn't explain it, but this painting was special. I tried to buy it, only to be told it wasn't for sale. Then, at the beginning of my sophomore year it was gone, replaced by something that was not memorable.

Five years later I had a job, an apartment, and more than one breakup behind me. I was finished with love. My sister told me to quit being dramatic. She insisted that I go Christmas shopping with her and her friend. I didn't know it was a blind date.

Frank was sweet and funny. However, he was a single dad with two kids under age six. What was my sister thinking? I really liked him, but did I really want to go there? A date or two wouldn't hurt. But if I was going to risk my heart ever again I needed a sign. A big one.

Frank wanted me to meet his children — they were a package deal — and he invited me to his younger son's birthday party. A birthday party for a kid wasn't a date so I agreed to go. I arrived early and met his two little boys who were bouncing here and there, so proud of their Christmas tree. They led me to the den area. As I entered the room, the twinkling lights of the tree faded for me because hanging behind Frank's couch was my painting.

"How did you get this?" I was amazed. "The lady in the art department told me it wasn't for sale."

"That was you?" He gave a little smile of disbelief, shaking his head.

"How did you get it?"

He looked at me and grinned. "It's mine as in I painted it."

I had no words for a moment, so he continued.

"Do you like mythology? It's Andromeda in chains." He pointed to the yellow. "The Kraken is coming to take her, but Perseus is there. He's rushing in to break the chains and save her."

And he did save her. Not Perseus, but Frank saved me.

That was more than thirty years ago, and here I am, still married to Frank — now we have four grown kids. I'm still sitting by the painting even though I had to marry him to get it.

— Lisa McCaskill —

An Inexplicable Encounter

When you live your life with an appreciation of coincidences and their meanings, you connect with the underlying field of infinite possibilities.
~Deepak Chopra

"I can't believe our dream trip is almost over," I lamented to my husband as we waited to board our plane. After forty-four years of saving and waiting, our trip to Hawaii was about to become a beautiful memory. Smiling, we leaned into each other and lapsed into a comfortable silence. Simply having this trip come to fruition after so many years of envisioning it seemed miraculous.

It wasn't just the peaceful beauty of this trip we hoped would be nurturing, but also the timing. We were continuing to come to grips with the death of our son a few years earlier. Life would never be the same but we were learning to adapt. We'd hoped the change of scenery and climate would be a catalyst to opening our hearts a little bit more.

Now, awaiting our return flight home, I was grateful for our dream vacation.

The gate attendant began boarding rows for our red-eye flight and soon my husband and I settled into our aisle seats across from each other. As I buckled in, I offered a smile and a polite hello to the couple in my row. The wife, seated next to me, returned the pleasantry and we both shared that it had been our first time in Hawaii.

What she said next stunned me. "My husband and I were a bit

apprehensive about traveling as our son died a few years ago and it has been hard to go on." My widened eyes locked with hers as I whispered, "Me, too!" Our conversation revealed we each had three boys raised in similar environments and our deceased sons were both the middle child. The boys had the same interests, were the same age at the time of their deaths, and the circumstances of their deaths were fairly identical. Almost every detail was a mirror of the other's experience. It was like I was having a conversation with myself.

She and I talked for most of the six-hour trip as if we were dear, old friends. We freely shared our grief experiences. We talked about how one child's death impacted our other children, our families, and our friendships. And when we felt sated, we embraced and then clasped our hands for the remainder of that plane trip. We had never met before and would never see each other again but we understood each other. I felt like the vise that had seized my heart at my son's death had finally released its grasp.

I have no way to explain the convergence of events which enabled this unexpected healing encounter. On a jumbo jetliner, what were the odds my seat would be next to another mother whose loss mimicked mine, who intimately knew my pain, and who could empathize with me as if we were twins? Typically, my husband and I book seats immediately next to each other, not across the aisle. What caused us to book differently for this trip? If we hadn't, I would have never met that other mother. As it was, I stepped back on the mainland a little stronger. I felt emotionally lighter.

I had erroneously assumed the wonders of my trip had ended when I boarded our return flight. How wrong I was. I had forgotten miracles can happen in the most unexpected of places, at the least probable time, and often because of truly inexplicable circumstances.

— Rose Robertson —

Shannon Saves the Day

And, when you want something, all the universe conspires in helping you to achieve it.
~Paulo Coelho, The Alchemist

He seemed nice enough as he regaled me with stories of the ponies running at Del Mar. He had good hair for a man who was likely above legal drinking age when I was born. "Chris," he said, already taking it upon himself to find a shorter version of my name, "we could have some fun."

And he did look like fun. His gold chain, his slick hair, the roll of cash that he tapped on the table until he was sure I noticed it. The way he touched the tip of his tongue to his finger before parting the bills. I wondered if he knew the Rat Pack.

"I wasn't going to reach out because I'm a little older than the range in your profile."

I nodded politely the way my mother had taught me. I covered my mouth with a napkin so he wouldn't see my sudden smile. But I knew my eyes showed it, so I avoided his eyes too.

As I looked at him, I saw in his eyes a fancier me. One who would wear ridiculous high heels with bright lipstick and big hair. I saw someone who would stop doing things for herself because he would pay someone to do them for me. I saw a blond Christina, possibly with hair extensions, who would laugh at his jokes and stroke his ego.

And I wondered if I could be all those things and what it would cost me. Then I thought of my ten-year-old sons and wondered where they would be when Tony and I were "playing the ponies" for the weekend. Who would pick them up from school and take them to baseball? Tony would probably get me someone for that.

That night, I turned the key in my door certain Tony wouldn't call again. I picked up the lone sock in the middle of the living room. How had it gotten there all by itself? It looked lonely. I sat on the couch with the sock in my hand and wondered how we had both gotten to where we were.

Why did I bother with online dating? Sure, I was lonely but not enough to make this quest for the perfect guy worth the effort. Dating was exhausting.

As I walked over to my jewelry chest to remove the jumbo earrings I saved for dates, I wondered aloud why I bothered. I popped open the top of the case and scanned its contents. Most of what I owned was from my mom and my ex, except for my guardian angel pin, a tear-drop-shaped crystal with gold wire wings and a halo. It was something you'd give a ten-year-old, but it had appeared in my stocking one Christmas and no one admitted to placing it there.

I picked it up and watched it shimmer in the light. The crystal was bright enough that you could barely see how her wings were no longer the bright gold of her halo.

I sighed deeply, feeling sorry for myself, the angel, and the lone sock. This was certainly not the Saturday night I had envisioned. My phone buzzed and I looked down to see a text from Tony.

Chris I was thinkin'—you me Vegass, baby.

Double the s in Vegas. This guy was not for me.

I held my angel close to my mouth like I was whispering a secret in her ear.

"You know what I want, Shannon?"

I had named my angel pin after a girl in my kindergarten class who had died in a car accident. When my mother told me she had died, she told me Shannon was now an angel. Since then, every angel was Shannon.

"I want a man who can fit flawlessly into my life. Someone who is good with kids but isn't one. Shannon, I want someone who knows me, and I know him. I don't want to start from scratch only to get halfway to knowing this person and find out he's a creep. I want him to realize I'm special, not because of how I look, but how I think. Is this too much to ask?"

I looked at her sparkling self as if she would answer. I might've even waited for her to. But eventually I grew tired, put her back in her case, and tossed the lone sock in the hamper.

The next evening my phone rang. An ex-boyfriend of mine, and now friend, was asking me how the date went.

"Meh, he wasn't the right fit." I said.

"What's wrong? Not smart enough?"

"No, I mean, he wasn't smart but wasn't dumb. We're just different."

"Different can be fun."

"It's not. I mean, I just don't think I'm ready."

"You'll never be ready," he pointed out. "You're just not a dater."

"What is that supposed to mean?"

Bart and I were engaged decades earlier, but distance and immaturity had ended things for us. And here he was suggesting that at forty-five I should jump into online dating even if I wasn't a "dater."

"I just don't see the point," I said and prepared my argument as to why I was correct, and he was wrong.

"Agreed," he said.

"Good. Wait. What?"

He wasn't supposed to agree with me. He was the one who was supposed to push me out there beyond my comfort zone. He was supposed to practice tough love and tell me I was being ridiculous. And he was the only one who could because he was the only one who knew I was trying online dating.

"It's just that I was talking to a friend last night and she told me that you should always tell people how you feel. So, I need to tell you I love you. I don't want to be just your friend. I want to be your guy. I want us to see where this goes. I don't want you online going out with strangers, I want you going out with me."

I held my breath, suddenly twenty-three again, butterflies swirling in my stomach.

"Who was this friend?"

"Well, okay not a friend, exactly. She was a lady at the florist."

A knock on my door interrupted Bart's admission. I opened it to find flowers on my doorstep. I plucked the card from the bouquet and read it: *You have always been my one. Love B.* I noticed the florist's name, Shannon's House of Flowers.

One year later we were married, and my angel pin Shannon was attached to the ribbon on my flowers.

—Christina Metcalf—

It Truly Is a Small World

There is always another layer of awareness,
understanding, and delight to be discovered
through synchronistic and serendipitous events.
~*Hannelie Venucia*

My cousin Ellen Toby ripped open her invitation and started to read: *Please join Sharon and Michael Segal as they celebrate the joyous occasion of the Bat Mitzvah of their daughter, Shawn…*

Ellen Toby wanted to be at the joyous occasion; however, we live in Houston, Texas, and she moved halfway around the world to Israel many years ago. It was just too far. However, she wanted to get Shawn something very memorable.

One Friday morning, Ellen Toby was browsing at an outdoor bazaar near Tel Aviv for Shawn's special gift. The bazaar had many merchants trying to sell clothes, trinkets, and jewelry but my cousin could not find that special gift. That was until she saw a merchant with jewelry that looked promising. She looked through the many pieces in the case and then she saw it: the perfect necklace charm. Ellen Toby asked the merchant to show her "that unique charm up close."

When the merchant responded in Hebrew, my cousin replied, "Obviously, you're not a native Israeli as I can tell by your accent. I am not a 'Sabra' [native Israeli] either. Where are you from?"

The woman replied, "I moved from Texas a few years ago."

"Texas!" my cousin said. "My uncle lives in Texas. He lives in Houston and is a rabbi there… Rabbi Jack Segal."

With those words the merchant began to sob.

Ellen Toby could tell that something was wrong, but she did not know what it was: "Ma'am, ma'am… what's the matter?"

The young woman wiped her eyes as she explained: "When I was a little girl, my dad lost his job. My family was kicked out of our apartment for not paying the rent. We didn't know what to do, so we lived in our bus. It was very difficult finding a place to park the bus as most organizations that we asked would not let us live in our bus in their parking lot. That was until we met your uncle.

"He let us live in our bus on the synagogue's property. He let us use the bathrooms inside the synagogue. He let us stay there until my dad found a job and an apartment. He also invited us to eat breakfast with the congregants after the daily morning service, have lunch with the congregants after the Saturday morning service, and dinner with the congregants after the Saturday night service. It might not sound like much to you, but to me and my family it was huge. This is why I am crying. My tears are happy ones because I thought when I moved to Israel I would never see him, or anything that reminded me of him, ever again. That was until just now!"

The merchant hugged my cousin and insisted on giving the special charm to my cousin in gratitude. Ellen Toby wouldn't let her; she insisted on purchasing it. True, the charm was very beautiful; however, its deeper beauty was in the memory of a caring heart.

— Michael Jordan Segal —

Our Miracle House

If you can heed only one piece of advice from the universe,
make it this... Pay attention. Do this and
everything else will fall into place.
~Bryan E. Wright

A couple of years after college, my partner Jon and I were tired of living in one run-down apartment after another. There was the one that was overrun by drain flies and was across the street from an elementary school, which clogged traffic on the only road out of the complex when Jon needed to leave for his evening shift at the local newspaper.

Then there was the apartment with wine stains on the carpet, peeling linoleum in the kitchen, and appliances three decades past their prime. Not to mention the neighbor we called Mystery Meat who peddled steaks from a chest freezer in the back of his pickup truck. He kept it plugged in via an orange extension cord that stretched from his truck in the parking lot to his apartment on the second floor. He was known to throw raucous parties and offer apologies in the form of free steak the next day.

Wanting a quiet place to ourselves, Jon and I started looking at houses for sale around town—surely a fairly simple process given my mother is a real estate agent. We found a listing for a cute bungalow that noted a fresh coat of paint, original hardwood floors, antique crystal doorknobs, and a prime location—across the street from Piggly Wiggly and walking distance from the neighborhood arts district. Perfect!

I bounded onto the wooden porch of the house and through the door. I was already oohing and aahing over the skeleton key locks and the big porcelain tub, dreaming of where we'd put our many books.

But Jon didn't share my excitement. From the moment we stepped onto the porch, I sensed him tense up, like he didn't want to be there. He looked around with a crease in his brow and finally went to a corner of the kitchen and took out his phone.

"Well, this is… interesting," my mother said, opening a slender cabinet in the kitchen and finding a hole in the floor that went down into the dirt basement.

"Okay, so the house has a dungeon! We can live with that, right? Maybe it's like an old root cellar?" I said, tugging Jon's sleeve.

I've always had a love for vintage clothes and antique decor, so I thought the old house had charm. Jon seemed less enthused.

"You don't like it," I ventured.

"It's okay," Jon replied.

"Okay? If we're going to live here you need to feel more than okay about it."

I then caught a glimpse of his phone. He wasn't checking social media or texting friends. He was texting his ex-girlfriend.

I felt my jaw tense with the will not to cry and I turned away so neither Jon nor my mother would see. Not only did Jon not want a house with me, he didn't even want to be with me! I told my mom this wasn't the house for us and got out of there as quickly as possible.

Later, I confronted Jon. I don't remember what I said, only that there was a flood of tears and choking sobs and questions like "How could you?"

"I'm so sorry," Jon said, wrapping his arms around me and letting me drip snot onto his collar. "I don't want to get back with her! I was texting her because that was her house!"

"What?"

"That was the house she moved into after we broke up and I remember dropping some of her stuff off there. I was making sure that was definitely the house, because if she lived there, we ain't buying it."

Out of all the houses in Birmingham, Alabama, Jon and I managed to nearly buy the one that had been rented by his ex.

That was enough to put me off house-hunting for a long while. Later, we moved to Columbus, Ohio and decided to look for a house there—especially since there was no chance of one of the houses being an ex's residence.

Columbus was experiencing a population boom and was one of the fastest-growing cities in the U.S. After we picked the neighborhood we wanted, we met up with a real estate agent who drove us around to a couple of listings. One had a bedroom that wouldn't have held our queen-sized bed and had walls painted a toxic green like a Mountain Dew bottle. One had a hole in the floor that was the only way to access the basement and I felt sure I'd fall through it one day and break my neck. And one had a "bedroom" that was the size of a pantry.

And at each house, we were one of half a dozen couples looking to buy and were told that if we wanted the house, we'd have to make an offer within hours and hope no one else beat us to it.

The idea of choosing the home where we might spend the rest of our lives within a matter of hours gave us both anxiety. Once again, we called off the search.

Six months later, Jon and I were lying in bed watching the water from the evening's rain run down the wall of our bedroom in yet another rundown apartment. A chunk of ceiling plaster hit the floor with a wet thunk.

"Let's look at some houses online," Jon suggested.

I gave him a look, already feeling anxious about what would go wrong this time. He scrolled away on his phone.

"This one looks good," he said, holding the phone out to me. It was a pale gray Cape Cod with a fresh coat of paint, original hardwood floors, antique crystal doorknobs, and a built-in bookshelf for our many books. Sizeable bedrooms, no peeling linoleum, up-to-date appliances, and no dungeon holes in the floor.

I felt my heart soften and let myself imagine how we'd arrange our furniture. When Jon asked if I wanted him to call the real estate agent in the morning, I surprised myself by saying yes.

The next day, I got a call from Jon around midday while he was at work.

"You didn't tell me you were calling the real estate agent! You must really like that house."

"I… didn't call her," I replied, confused.

"You're kidding," he said, incredulous.

After not having been in contact for more than six months, she called Jon out of the blue to tell him she might have found the perfect house for us — the very one we found online the night before.

"I've been so busy at work I haven't had a chance to call her, so I thought you must have called her and that's why she called me," Jon explained.

The serendipity inspired us to tour the home as soon as possible. When we arrived, we were the only ones there — no reason to be anxious.

Standing in the living room five minutes later, Jon and I looked at each other and said at the exact same time, "This is it."

We bought our house — our miracle house — and plan to live in it until they carry us out in pine boxes.

— Mandy Shunnarah —

New Chapter

I think that someone is watching out for me. God,
my guardian angel, I'm not sure who that is,
but they really work hard.
~Mattie Stepanek

I'd always thought that the way to start a new chapter in your life was to move. I was facing that new chapter with my young son as I purchased a fifty-year-old house just before Memorial Day 2011 in the quiet St. Louis suburb of Affton, Missouri. New chapter, new home, fresh start.

Old houses come with a laundry list of new responsibilities that didn't always make it onto my priority list. I was a single mom, working a full-time job, and halfway through my master's degree. If I wasn't at work, I was helping my son with homework, taking him to hockey practices and games, running him to guitar lessons, cooking, cleaning, paying bills, and somehow fitting my never-ending classwork into every gap in my schedule. Occasionally, I'd find a moment to revisit that to-do list and we'd squeeze in things like cleaning out gutters or painting a room. Slowly but surely, I'd eventually get it all done.

Spring turned into summer and summer turned into September. I continued my balancing act of work, kid, grad school, and all the other responsibilities. My list hadn't gotten much shorter as time went on.

September 29th started like any other day. I'd gotten out of bed at 4 A.M. to get ready for work and found a chunky pile of dog vomit. We had two rescue dogs and while it wasn't totally out of the question for this to happen, it wasn't a normal occurrence. Tired and now crabby, I cleaned up the mess and just kept going. I made a mental note to check with my son to see if he'd fed something weird to the dogs the night before.

The day continued as normal. About halfway through, I noticed that someone had left a Lowe's store ad on the breakroom table so I took it back to my desk. As I casually flipped through, one of the listings jumped right off the page and seemed to smack me in the face.

They were running a sale on carbon monoxide detectors and that happened to be one of my outstanding to-do list items. My tight budget had kept me from prioritizing this purchase but a nagging little voice inside my head now told me to "stop waiting." The sale ended the following day so I knew I needed to make time to run by the store. I shrugged, thinking the errand would delay dinner for a bit but it would feel great to cross off another item! I went on to finish my workday and made a stop for two detectors afterwards.

The detectors sat unopened on the table as I cooked dinner. I fiddled with opening them and inserted the batteries as I helped my son with his homework. Afterwards, we went outside to do some yardwork and play with the dogs while visiting with a friend who'd stopped by. As the sun set and forced us back inside, I popped the two detectors into place — one in our basement and the other in the main floor's hallway — before taking a shower.

As I exited the shower, I heard an unfamiliar screech. "What's going on?!" I yelled, still dripping wet.

"It's the detector downstairs," my son called back. "It's been doing that for ten minutes!"

I rolled my eyes, thinking "Of course! I bought the ONE dysfunctional detector in the entire store!" as I walked downstairs and removed it from its place. I pulled the batteries to stop the earsplitting screech, replaced them, stuck the unit back on the wall, and went upstairs. Ten minutes later, the screeching resumed.

"Maybe you should call someone," suggested my friend. "This may not be a bad detector."

"Who do I call?" I asked, as I'd never had this happen before.

Since my friend worked at the local natural gas company, he called an on-duty co-worker who promptly called 911.

"They're sending the fire department," he reported as he ended the call.

"Oh no," I replied, thinking I was wasting their time. "Please tell them this is NOT an emergency, so they don't need to run sirens and lights. My neighbors are going to think I'm already causing drama after living here only a few months!"

But much to my dismay, the Affton Fire Department was in full lights and sirens mode as they screamed into our quiet cul-de-sac.

"I'm so sorry," I began as the firefighters approached. "I didn't think the gas company would call 911!"

"Better safe than sorry," one reassured me, as our neighbors started opening their doors to survey the scene. "Now, please take everyone outside and we'll check things out."

My son, our friend, our two dogs, and I piled out of the back door and waited in the yard while the firefighters descended the stairs and into our basement. I waited, silently constructing more heartfelt apologies for wasting their time and the county's valuable resources.

After a few minutes, the back door opened and one of the firefighters stepped out.

"Ma'am?" he started. "Since it was your carbon monoxide detector that prompted this call, we took some CO readings."

"Okay," I replied, not sure what else to say.

"If I could explain something first — when we go into a building and the levels are higher than 90, we evacuate," he continued.

"Okay," I repeated.

"The levels in your house," he said, pausing for a moment, "are at 234."

I stood frozen, processing the difference between 90 and 234 and unable to respond.

"Ma'am, if you all would've gone to sleep tonight, you might not have woken up tomorrow morning."

The yard began to spin around me as I took in his last statement. The words "not woken up tomorrow" echoed back and forth in my head as I steadied myself against the dizziness. I looked over at my precious little boy, laughing and playing with our beloved dogs. Overwhelmed and overcome with the realization that we had come dangerously close to a silent death, I burst into sobs.

"Ma'am," he said gently. "It's okay—we know where the leak is coming from and the guys are turning the gas off now. You'll all be safe tonight."

"We've lived here since May," I choked out between sobs. "I only bought those detectors today!"

"Wow," he exhaled, pushing his helmet back. "You definitely had someone watching out for you then. Normally, the first sign of CO poisoning is your pets getting mysteriously sick."

"Yes!" I replied immediately. "One of my dogs threw up last night!"

"You're all very, very lucky, ma'am," he said as he put a reassuring hand on my shoulder. "Please take care and check your smoke and CO detector batteries monthly."

As we watched the firetruck pull away, I held my son tight and tearfully thanked whoever was watching over us and giving us another day to live. A new chapter in our lives was starting. Only this time, it wasn't because of a move. New chapter, new perspective on life, deeply grateful for every moment.

—Vicki Liston—

The Music Lady

Every day holds the possibility of a miracle.
~Author Unknown

When my first book, *Expect Miracles*, was published, I was invited to speak to the residents of a care home about an hour away. After the speaking engagement, the activities director enthusiastically said, "I think you would be best friends, actually 'soul sisters' with Sammie the 'Music Lady' who plays harp here every week."

She never said where the Music Lady lived. I assumed the kind woman lived near the residence. Making friends an hour away is difficult to cultivate, so I did not pursue the connection. The director had handed me a seed of friendship, but I never placed it in the ground.

Three months later, at Christmastime, I was sitting in a busy mall bookstore an hour and a half north from home. After signing books for two hours, I got a strong feeling that I should get up and leave immediately. I frantically packed up and headed to the car.

Initially, the plan was to go home. Leaving the crowded multi-level parking lot was not easy as many exits where blocked. I circled the lot looking for a way out. When I found the exit, I was behind a gray car that had an inspirational bumper sticker. I thought, "The driver must be a special person to want to share that message."

Because this exit was not in the direction of my home, another close by bookstore came to mind. I impulsively decided to stop there and autograph books to surprise their Christmas shoppers.

Four turns later, the gray car was still leading and when it pulled into the bookstore's parking, I got chills.

The driver was fumbling with something in her back seat. It was a harp! I asked if she was booked to play, and with her sweet smile, sparkling eyes and a heart that emanated a spiritual love she responded, "Yes."

I asked if I could help her and told her that I was there to sign books. Then, a light went on and I asked, "Are you the Music Lady?"

She answered and asked, "Yes. Are you Angel Scribe? An activity director told me there was an author who I would love meeting."

I replied in the affirmative as we stood in the cold-winter parking lot, stunned. Imagine! We had bumped into each other, but thankfully not with our cars.

As we unloaded her CDs, her sound system, harp, etc., Sammie explained, "I am here for the first time, I was late, got lost, and somehow ended up in the mall parking lot, and like you I was circling it. I was concerned about my lateness. Thank you for your help; your arrival and help is a blessing."

What miracle or voice had her turn into the parking lot and then lined her up with my car? Unexplainable… almost!

Apparently, months earlier, Sammie had phoned my home, based on the director's recommendation. The answering machine was broken, so I never got her message. Then she had e-mailed about us meeting, but I missed it in the hectic days of book tours and finishing up my second book, *A Christmas Filled With Miracles*.

Millions of people live in the Seattle area. What divine force propelled an author out of a bookstore and sent two cars in circles until they were following each other? It was an act of kindness that led me to walk up to a stranger. How did we intuitively know who each other was?

Our introduction happened in 2000 and the director was right, the Music Lady and the Angel Scribe loved each other immediately and we remain good friends.

An unusual connection is that we are both longtime friends with a woman in Canada. When our friend was ill, Sammie drove to Canada and played the harp in her hospital room, proving once again how kind and talented a music woman she is with everyone.

The next time you are stuck in traffic, or take the wrong road, or are delayed for any reason, take a deep breath, blow out your frustration and note that a miracle may be in the making.

— Mary Ellen Angelscribe —

Miracle in the Desert

Christmas is the day that holds all time together.
~Alexander Smith

His name was Benjamin Adair. His friends knew him as Bud and he owned a truck stop just outside Wickenburg, Arizona, "the dude ranch capital of the world."

The truck stop included a motel and restaurant. It was actually located in a tiny town called Circle City. Bud had converted the place into a ranch. He had built a corral and kept half a dozen horses in it for his own children and the neighborhood kids to ride.

I met Bud while working as a reporter for the *Phoenix Gazette*, Phoenix's former afternoon daily newspaper. Bud was a colorful character who loved to dabble in politics. He never won an election, but he ran for sheriff of Maricopa County, Arizona. and even once tried for the governorship.

Bud loved living in the desert, and he liked his neighbors. Each Christmas he would truck in a towering Christmas tree, decorate it lavishly with bulbs, lights, and ornaments, and invite the neighborhood kids in for a special celebration. The area supermarket managers would provide him with turkeys and Bud would dress himself as Santa and provide everyone who showed up with a plate of hot turkey and trimmings, as well as gifts.

The local news media liked Bud and we gave him ample publicity to make the Christmas party work. But one year it looked like it wasn't going to happen. Three days before Christmas, Adair called me and said, "We're not getting our turkey donations this year and I might have to call off the Christmas party."

I knew the previous year Bud had served turkey dinners to just under 2,000 children and adults. But the supermarkets he dealt with had made some changes in their policy and had placed a hold on any large-scale donations.

"So where do you stand, Bud?" I asked.

"Well, we've got the Christmas tree and hundreds of wrapped presents beneath it," he said. "But no turkeys."

After hanging up the phone I drove out to Circle City. Bud greeted me with a hot meatloaf dinner — he was famous for his meatloaf — and we sat down to discuss his gloomy prospects. Just as the sun was setting. a large semi pulled onto his parking lot. Steam was hissing from the truck and the driver stepped out and shook his head.

"My air conditioning isn't working and I've got a load of frozen turkeys that are going to spoil," he said.

Bud looked at me. I looked at him. We smiled.

We did some fast talking for the next hour or so. When we were finished, he called his boss. Then he shook Bud's hand.

On Christmas morning, Bud served more than 2,000 turkey dinners. He gave each of the kids a wrapped gift. And the truck driver — you guessed it — played Santa Claus.

— Geno Lawrenzi, Jr. —

Divine Intervention

Keep Steering

Never drive faster than your guardian angel can fly.
~Author Unknown

Darkness had fallen early that November evening. I was driving on Interstate 95 in Northern Virginia. The rush hour traffic was heavy, but I had almost reached my destination. I moved into the far-right lane, preparing to exit.

WHAM! An explosion rocked the car. It sounded like a bomb.

Before I had time to think, my little Honda was airborne, hurtling sideways across I-95. Headlights rushed toward me. I was going in the wrong direction! My body stiffened, bracing for a crash.

It didn't come.

But now a huge concrete barrier loomed in front of me. I was about to slam into it!

This is my death, I thought. I felt strangely at peace. *It's okay. I have lived a good life.*

Then a voice spoke in my ear, as clear as if someone were sitting beside me. "Just keep steering."

So I did. I gripped the wheel and pulled right as hard as I could, my shoulders tense and knuckles white with the effort. I felt the car begin to turn.

A different voice spoke in my other ear. "Don't overcorrect!"

I knew that voice — it was my dad. He'd taught me to drive.

I eased up on the wheel and gently applied the brakes. My car slowed and came to a stop — mere inches from the concrete wall. It was now pointed in the same direction I'd been driving, but in the center median. I had flown sideways across three lanes of heavy traffic without hitting anything.

I sat there, clutching the wheel, my whole body trembling. All the airbags had deployed, covering the windows and coating everything, including me, in fine dust. An acrid smell filled the car. I couldn't open my door.

The passenger door opened and a young woman peered in. "Are you alright?"

"I think I am." My voice was shaky. "But what happened?"

She told me that a double semi had slammed into the side of my little car. "I saw it happen," she said. "The driver pulled into your lane too soon — I could tell he was going to hit you."

A huge truck hit me. And I was still alive. I couldn't take it in.

"What's that burning smell?" I asked.

"It's the airbags," she said. "We need to get you out. It's not good to breathe that stuff."

I started to climb over the console, but someone banged on my door. A man with a long beard wrenched it open and helped me out. "I'm really glad you're alive," he said, his voice filled with compassion. "I didn't think you'd survive." He shook his head. "That was a heck of a piece of driving you just did."

In spite of everything, I smiled. It wasn't really my driving. I had help.

I stepped into the cold dark night and surveyed the scene. The driver's side of my car was a mangled mess. There was a giant dent just behind my seat.

Across the roadway, the huge semi blocked the right lane. Debris littered the highway. Traffic was at a standstill.

I fumbled for my phone to call my husband. My fingers shook so much I could barely press the buttons. Stammering, I tried to tell him what happened. I couldn't describe it.

When I hung up, I saw a young woman slumped over her steering wheel in the lane next to me. Heart hammering, I walked over and opened her door.

"Are you okay?"

She looked at me through tear-ravaged eyes. "I was sure I would hit you."

My own eyes welled. "I was, too."

I glanced behind her and saw a baby seat. My heart constricted. She was a young mother. What if I hadn't kept steering? I sent up a prayer of gratitude that our lives had been spared.

Sirens wailed, and then the police were there, directing traffic, asking questions, interviewing witnesses.

The accident had stopped all northbound lanes of traffic on I-95. Witnesses all described it the same way. Several drivers said they were certain they would hit me as I careened across the roadway.

But no one did.

I believe a miracle happened that night. And the lesson I learned is etched on my soul. "Just keep steering."

We never know what's going to hit us. We're driving along minding our business when out of the blue, something slams into us and knocks us sideways. That night, it was a truck. But it could be a tough diagnosis, a call in the night, or an unexpected death. Whatever it is, we're meant to steer through it. One day, one hour, one minute at a time.

Just — keep — steering.

— Julie M. Phend —

Is It You?

Remember that although bodies may pass away, the energy that connects you to a loved one is everlasting and can always be felt when you're open to receiving it.
~Doreen Virtue, Signs from Above

My father and I were never close. If not for my mother's presence, I would have barely spoken to him at all. So, when my mother died, I was presented with a dilemma. How in the world would I relate to this stranger who I called my father?

I grew up with what might be described as a bully for a father. He was quirky and volatile, and it was difficult to feel any genuine affection toward him. But there I was, a grown woman, aching from the loss of my mother and feeling as if I were meeting my father for the first time.

As the years went by, twelve to be exact, my resentful heart never budged. I felt the burden of our difficult relationship. His increasing frailty, combined with his stubborn disposition, made me both sympathetic and annoyed. I was raising my own family and working full-time. I was overcome with resentment that I had to care for him, but I had promised my mother.

His care became so time-consuming that I had to quit my job. I was increasingly resentful and frustrated with him and this obligation.

During one of his medical incidents, I felt that I was at the end of my rope. In the wee hours of the morning, once again I sat in a hospital with him. Feeling overwhelmed, I excused myself, heading for the nearest exit. Hoping that the cool night air would calm me down, all I could feel was rage. Standing there alone, I resisted the urge to scream aloud and somehow managed to call out to God.

"Why are you doing this, God? This man is unhappy and has so little life, and he is making mine impossible. Why is he still here?" I asked. I was so full of anger and hurt. I had prayed many times over the years, but this time I knew that God was talking back to me. An awareness came over me, that could only come from Him. The voice inside me said, "You are hurt because you believe that he doesn't love you—but he does."

A calm came over me as I stood in the quiet night air and heard God say, "He is here because you have something to learn." For the first time in years, I felt peace.

Three more years passed before my dad—who my children called Poppy—left this world. But in those remaining years I had learned to give him grace. I spent time with him, asking him about his youth, trying to understand his unfulfilled dreams and his love for my mother, my brother and myself. I came to appreciate his talent and passion for music and the honor that he felt serving in World War II. As I watched him succumb to the effects of Parkinson's and dementia, I observed a poise in him that I had never noticed before. He accepted the end of his life with courage and dignity.

With his favorite big band music playing, I spent the last visit with my dad, talking and singing to him. As I choked back tears I whispered to him, "I love you." No longer able to speak, he mouthed back to me, "I love you too."

Two weeks after the funeral I found myself sitting in the pickup line at a fast-food restaurant. I looked up at the sky and asked the questions that had been hanging over me since his death. "Did I please him? Did I honor him? Was I a good daughter?"

I suddenly found myself aware that I had been sitting in line for quite a while. I looked at the car in front of me and wondered why it was taking so long. Then I saw it! The license plate on the back of the car said "LUV POPY." I thought I must be misreading it, but I wasn't.

The sweet name that all the grandchildren called my father was right in front of me.

Despite my faith, I am a cynic—a "Doubting Thomas." But I couldn't find any way to read that license plate except as "Love, Poppy." To this day, I have never seen that license plate again. I have accepted that seeing it was a gift from God and possibly my dad telling me that I did a good job. I like to think that perhaps the grace that I had finally given my father had been given back to me.

—Angela J. Bonomo—

Miracle on the Highway

There are two ways to live: you can live as if nothing is a miracle; or you can live as if everything is a miracle.
~Albert Einstein

I used to think that "miracles" were just coincidental events that happened to produce a beneficial outcome. I didn't believe that an unseen outside force kept watch over us and swooped in when necessary. Until it happened to me.

I was driving my Mini Cooper down a steep, narrow, curving four-lane highway through a canyon just north of Edmonton in Alberta. The late Sunday afternoon traffic was heavy with vacationers returning to the city.

The speed limit, because of the danger of the twisting road, was only thirty miles per hour. But the road was tightly packed with speeding vehicles as people tried to get home before dark.

My three passengers were all chatting happily, excited about the good time they'd had at the weekend retreat. I, however, was nervous about the speeding traffic and was concentrating on the sharp turns on this unfamiliar road. There was no way to slow down without being hit from behind.

My car was in the left lane, next to the concrete divider, and the right lane was packed with vehicles next to us. Suddenly, even though I held the steering wheel in a death grip, the car moved. A lot. An unseen force picked my car up in the air and slid it one car width to the right. Now we were driving down the middle of the dotted line between the lanes. In that same instant, a large truck appeared out of nowhere and occupied the place to my left where my car had been a split second before.

I was now speeding along, matching the traffic flow, with a truck towering very close to me on my left and fast-moving traffic to my right — three vehicles abreast on a narrow, curving, two-lane downhill road.

A stunned silence filled the car. We all held our breath. After what seemed a very long time but was probably less than a minute, some kind person in the right lane slowed enough to let me fully enter the lane in front of him. We all began to breathe again.

What had just happened? None of us could believe what our eyes had seen. But we couldn't dispute the fact that our car had floated through the air and avoided colliding with a truck. Why had that truck deliberately moved into our space? Didn't he see us in front of him?

I surmised that because my car was only four feet, five inches tall, perhaps the truck driver who pulled up so abruptly, hadn't seen us. The car that had been directly in front of him had moved into the right lane to get out of his way. We were too short to be seen until he was practically on top of us!

My heart was pounding, and I was shaking like a leaf the rest of the way home. I knew we had narrowly missed being in a tragic multi-vehicle accident. Somehow, we were saved by an unseen force.

And yes — now I believe in miracles.

— Christine Clarke-Johnsen —

My Diamond

Love recognizes no barriers. It jumps hurdles, leaps fences, penetrates walls to arrive at its destination full of hope.
~Maya Angelou

It was a beautiful August day in Colorado, just weeks before school resumed for my middle child, Rochelle, and my son, Ben. We were sitting in our front yard, along with our Collie and our two cats, enjoying the afternoon shade of the honey locust tree. My husband, Carl, was also at home, working in his basement office. As we lazed outside, we watched as two girls came toward us on our side of the street; one riding a bicycle and one holding onto the back of it as she roller-skated behind.

Just as they passed by, the skater lost her footing and went down on the street, right in front of our neighbor's house. I jumped up quickly and ran toward them to help the fallen skater, and my foot caught on an uneven section of the sidewalk. Down I went... scraping my knees, my palms, and the final contact point—my chin! Ben came running up to me and I managed to croak the words, "Go... get... your... dad!" Meanwhile, Rochelle was checking on the skater, who was okay.

The two girls continued on their way, and I lay there on the sidewalk, bleeding. Ben and Carl came running, and Carl carried me into the house. He set me down on a kitchen chair and got busy cleaning my wounds with a wet washcloth. He started with my knees, then my chin, and on to my hands. As we washed the dirt and blood off, I noticed my wedding ring had turned on my finger. I spun it around, only to notice that several of the gold prongs of the setting were bent over, and the diamond was missing. It was gone!

Ben and Rochelle ran outside to look for the missing diamond. The place I fell on the sidewalk was bordered by small rocks — it was like looking for a needle in a haystack. They had no luck. I went out and searched as well, slowly, on my sore hands and knees. The boys who lived across the street saw us and came over to ask what we were doing. After hearing what happened, they joined in the search.

Many people spent many hours searching the area over the next several days, to no avail. My wedding ring, although not fancy, was priceless to me. We had twenty-five years of marriage under our belts, and to lose it was like losing a dear friend. I sadly tucked my unwearable ring away in my jewelry box.

The summer heat gave way to autumn, and autumn to winter. Our neighbor, Mike, was a good friend — and had a business buying and reselling cars. He would park them in his driveway, do a bit of work on them, then flip them to another owner. We bought several cars from him over the years because he was so good at it.

One mild winter day, Mike came over to see Carl. He wiped his muddy work boots on the doormat just inside the front door before heading downstairs to Carl's office. After their meeting, I said goodbye to Mike, and as I closed the door behind him, I noticed the dirt and mud around the front door and on the tile entryway. I got out the whisk broom and dustpan and swept up — and as I carried the dustpan toward the kitchen garbage can, I noticed a slight glimmer in the midst of the debris. I reached into the dirt, and picked up a little rock, rubbing it between my fingers. I couldn't believe it. The mud wiped away to reveal my diamond!

I started yelling at the top of my lungs as I ran downstairs to Carl's office to show him. It was unbelievable. As Mike had walked between his yard and ours, he had stepped in some mud that contained the stone, tracked it into our house, and wiped it off on our front doormat — months after I had lost it!

Carl had the diamond reset in my wedding ring, and we are

approaching our thirty-third year together. Although he has asked about getting me a larger stone, there is no way I would ever replace this diamond that was returned to me in such a miraculous way.

— Gina Gronberg —

The Road to Connection

Life is magical, and the synchronicities continue
to fill me with wonder every day!
~Anita Moorjani

His hair was the color of the black and white cow he bent over to feed. In his faded jeans and knee-high work boots he hunched beside his Ford pickup. I had a feeling we should talk to him, but hesitated.

"We better turn around," I said to my husband as the man uttered something in Portuguese. "I think we're trespassing."

Our rental car sat heavy on the muddy road with three kids in the back seat, and surfboards and fishing poles strapped to the top. A map and our family history journal lay across my lap.

The man glanced at us as we turned the car around. As he hopped into his truck a feeling struck me.

"Follow him," I said.

The man turned onto the narrow main road of Camino dos Regatos, stopped his truck and got out.

I asked him in my best Portuguese if he spoke English.

"No, but my wife does. She's coming soon," he said.

It was apparent that we were interrupting his workday, but we needed to ask someone for clues to help us find my husband's family before we drove back down the hill and gave up our quest.

When my husband's father died several years earlier, I was drawn to finding out more about his Azorean roots. I had found Portuguese genealogical records, but because I could not read Portuguese, I decided that we needed to go to the Azores. Ironically, within weeks of booking the trip I met a man who was an Azorean genealogist specialist. He taught me to read the records, and within months I had found many family names.

A few minutes later the man's wife arrived. We showed her our family tree and a copy of Grandfather Teotónio's birth record. We hoped that they knew someone, perhaps a neighbor or a friend, with our family name. Angelina said something about an uncle with the same middle and last name. As they spoke to each other, I thought about how much João looked like a younger version of my husband's father, Joe. In his life, Joe had never been on this road, the road of his father's childhood. His parents Teotónio and Magdalena had left this island as young adults to go to the farming communities of the Central Valley of California where Magdalena's brother lived.

That morning, with only days left on the island, we had set out in search of family. Driving along the ocean-lined road from Angra do Heroísmo through the seaside village of São Mateus, we headed inland to the farmland of São Bartolomeu. Turning up a narrow road we found typical Azorean traffic: a dozen cows covered the road followed by the herder, a teenage boy. After they passed, we saw the church that overlooked the small town square; white with brown trim and turrets. This was the boyhood church of Teotónio.

Past the town square was a sign reading Camino dos Regatos, the road written on the birth record of Teotónio. Church bells chimed as we climbed it, looking at each house's name plate tiled to the exterior wall. About two miles up, the road narrowed and we turned back. We had seen no nameplate for "Família Martins." It felt as if everyone that had ever lived on this road had left with Teotónio. Several of the houses we passed were crumbling and uninhabited. We drove back down the hill, disappointed, It was then that we had decided to turn down the muddy road where João stood with his cows.

Angelina and João continued to converse in Portuguese. My husband and I looked at each other, hopeful. It seemed as if they knew someone by our family name.

"How many brothers did you say your grandfather had?" Angelina asked.

I grabbed my journal from the car to check my records. "Eight. And two sisters."

She turned back to João. He smiled and nodded. Angelina said, "It wasn't an uncle. His grandfather was an Ignácio Martins!"

A grandfather? Could this very man be the relative we were seeking? Within the next few minutes, we came to the conclusion that my husband and João did indeed share the same great-grandfather.

Having discovered our relation with this one lone man, suddenly the road came to life. Several men walked out of a corner store, so small that I had not noticed it on the drive up. Another herd of cows passed by. A woman with a child waved in passing. A truck holding milkcrates rumbled down the hill.

João motioned for us to get into our car and follow him. His open bed truck, full of hay, led us further down the hill to the home where Teotónio was born. A tall two-story home sat on a small piece of wet pastureland. The white house with dirt-stained stucco and peeling paint still stood solidly, representing connection: connection to a grandfather, connection to generations before him, connection to this island.

These people were not my blood relatives, but through marriage I was a part of this family too. I was connected to not only the living, but to those who had passed before. A piece of my heart was in this green land dotted with lava rock that stretched into the sea.

A few days after meeting João and Angelina, we went back to spend time with them in their home. Again, I was reminded of Rick's father as I listened to João speak. He spoke a different language, but I knew what he was saying through his expression and tone. "I never want to leave this island. And next time you come back you'd better know how to speak Portuguese." He was a man who loved the simple life.

As we sat in their living room, adorned with family pictures, a couch, two chairs, and a view of the setting sun over vast fields of green that fell into the ocean, I too, longed for the simple life. A life rooted in the land, bare feet sunk deep in the earth, standing solidly like this old family home.

A few days later, as our plane gained speed on the runway, so did my tears. With my face fixed to the window, I strained my neck to look behind me until the green turned to brown and became a speck on the horizon. I was leaving something that I needed behind. Part of me still stood in the field of cows, still swam beside basalt cliffs, still sat with newly found relatives beneath orange-tiled roofs. That part of me will remain on the island of Terceira.

—Emily Avery Martin—

The School Miracle

When positive attitudes meet with faith, courage,
consistency and perseverance, miracles tend to happen.
~Edmond Mbiaka

I was surprised to get a message on social media from Robert. We had not seen or talked with each other in more than forty years, but he was asking how I was doing. I let him know that I was married to a lay pastor and working at a small Christian school. He told me that he owned a profitable security company and was married as well. We messaged a bit and then went on about our lives.

Two weeks later the school I worked at was having major money issues. They were going to turn off the gas. That meant no heat or hot water in the dormitories and the school would have to shut down. We were all praying.

Robert called me and asked how we were and then asked about the school. I found this odd because he had told me that he did not go to church. I told him about the money dilemma. He asked how much we needed, and I told him around $12,000.

He said, "I'll give it to you."

I thought he was joking. He told me that he had to talk with his wife about it but he felt "called" to help. The next day his wife called me to get the routing number of the bank account we wanted $12,000 deposited into. I was stunned as was the principal of the school.

I have only heard from Robert once since that time. We have

never talked about why he felt compelled to give $12,000 to a school he had never been to.

Miracles do happen.

— Shannon Hurley —

My Lucky Break

The guardian angels of life fly so high as to be beyond our sight, but they are always looking down upon us.
~Jean Paul

I was on my second date with Richard, the man who would eventually become my husband. That late winter day we drove to Mount Baldy, a towering mountain peak just outside Los Angeles, for a day of fun in the snow. The radio blasted our favorite songs, the latest from Ed Sheeran, Bruno Mars and Taylor Swift, and we sang along as the car worked its way up the winding highway.

Richard and I had met on a blind date a few weeks before. My mother and his aunt had joined forces to set us up. As co-workers, they chit-chatted often and had decided that the two of us would be a match.

The last thing I wanted was their meddling. As a college student I had a busy class schedule and a full social life. Even though I was less than enthusiastic, I decided that one date would not be the end of the world. And then, when I saw Richard standing on my doorstep, tall and handsome with his dark hair and deep blue eyes, I found myself believing in love at first sight. Soul mates from the start, we shared the same values, laughed at the same jokes, and enjoyed the same activities, from tennis to going to see the latest movie.

The air changed to cool and crisp as we ascended Mount Baldy. The landscape changed, too, from scrubby brush to a thick forest of trees. Patches of snow dotted the ground. Nearing the top of the mountain the snow became denser, sparkling under the intense blue sky. Opening the window, I filled my lungs with the fresh, pine-scented air.

When we came across a sleigh rental shack, set up at the base of a steep, icy hill, Richard asked if I would like to try a toboggan ride. I nodded my head in enthusiasm. I had never been on a toboggan and the prominently displayed "At Your Own Risk" sign did nothing to deter me. I always did gravitate to the fastest roller coasters at Magic Mountain.

Richard suggested that we take the run on the lower part of the hill. But I had another idea. I pointed to the highest course, a vertical incline that was sure to thrill. Richard reluctantly agreed and began to lug the toboggan to the top of the hill as I tromped through the snow behind him. I looked around and noticed we were the only ones attempting the steepest path.

When we reached our destination, we settled onto the toboggan. Richard sat behind me and held me tightly around my waist, making me feel secure in his arms. Seated in the front, I stared down at the sheer drop and held my breath. If I were on a roller coaster I would have been screaming, hands up in the air.

We scooted the toboggan forward and — whoosh — in an instant we were gliding downward. I shrieked with delight as we picked up speed, the rush of cold air pressed against my face. I didn't want this exhilarating ride to end. We were almost to the finish, when, out of nowhere, the toboggan smashed into a rock and we were airborne, flying out of control. Then, with a thud, we crashed onto the hard ground. I panicked, unable to catch my breath. The air had been knocked out of me, as if someone had punched me in the gut.

Richard was concerned and asked if I was okay. Even though my stomach hurt and I felt a little nauseous, I didn't think I was seriously injured. I took in a few deep breaths and assured Richard that I was ready to get back on the toboggan. The last thing I wanted was to be a killjoy.

At the time, I had no idea that I had broken my back, a fracture to a mid-line vertebra. I must have been in shock, because I have no memory of our hike back up to the top of the hill. Once again, we positioned ourselves back on the toboggan, poised at the precipice. It was at that moment that I heard a voice urging me to get off the sled, as if an angel from above was whispering in my ear of imminent peril. The warning echoed in my head, but I sat as frozen as the ice beneath me, determined not to heed that voice. Richard leaned forward with a push to set the toboggan in motion. Unexpectedly, it stuck in a patch of snow. I swallowed hard and suddenly I heard my own voice shouting out to Richard to stop.

I still wonder at the forces in the universe that had transmitted a cautionary message into my head and then when I didn't pay attention, had caused the toboggan to miraculously stall. All I wanted was to have Richard wrap his arms around me and once again experience the heady thrill of speeding down the slope. Like a typical twenty-year-old, I didn't think past the immediate moment to the dangers that can befall us when making impulsive decisions.

As we walked back to the car I still did not feel pain in my back. It was only after we began the trip home that a severe throbbing set in. By the time we arrived at my house I was in agony, the slightest movement causing me to gasp. Still in denial, I thought it was nothing more than an acute sprain. I went to sleep with a heating pad on my back. By morning the pain was so staggering I could barely maneuver myself out of bed. Somehow, I managed to get into the car and have my mother drive me to emergency care.

When the doctor showed me an X-ray of my back, I was shocked to see an obvious fracture. He told me I was one lucky girl, because I had come a millimeter away from severing my spinal cord and causing permanent paralysis. If I had sledded down the hill again, I would have done irreparable damage.

I often think of how different my life would be if divine forces had not intervened. I think of the guilt Richard would have had to carry for the rest of his life, even though it would be unfounded blame, if I had become paralyzed. Most every day I say a prayer of thanks for being spared from an injury that would have changed both our lives forever. I am eternally grateful for the simple acts of dancing, morning walks and bike rides.

—June Weiner—

A Miraculous Departure

Out of difficulties grow miracles.
~Jean de La Bruyère

Parkinson's ravaged my wife Joan's body for four years. By the end she weighed eighty-five pounds, couldn't speak or move a limb, and could only communicate by blinking her eyes. She was also in excruciating pain. I called Hospice in to make recommendations on pain control and to aid with Joan's end care.

As was my habit for the two years of her nursing home residence, I arrived in her room at 9:00 A.M. and greeted her with a kiss. Then I massaged her rigid legs, and sat beside her to read. I had no idea whether she heard me reading to her or not, but I chose to believe she did.

The hospice attendant called me aside to tell me she believed Joan was very near the end and that I should call the children in to see her.

Our three children gathered around their mother's bed. Hearing their voices bidding their mom goodbye and declaring their love for her gave me a sense of finality—and profound sadness. They tried to be strong for her, but the tears on their faces told the truth.

Mrs. Deaver, the hospice assistant, was reading scripture aloud: II Corinthians 5:17: "Therefore, if anyone is in Christ, he is a new creation; old things have passed away; behold, all things have become new."

I lay beside Joan on the narrow hospital bed, held her as close as possible, and prayed for the Lord to receive her. My heart was breaking; a significant piece of me for fifty years was about to be taken from me.

What would I do? How would I go on without her? I was experiencing total helplessness and gut-wrenching loss.

I noticed there was movement in Joan's rigid body; she raised both arms upward and was whispering. Mrs. Deaver and I exchanged looks of disbelief because Joan had been paralyzed for six months. But now she seemed to be greeting someone and welcoming that person. Her face glowed with joy.

"Joan, honey, what are you doing? Who is here?" I was stunned.

"I am talking to Jesus. He is here to take me to heaven, but first, I need to talk to you. Please do not interrupt me—just listen."

I sensed someone had placed me in a surreal suspension of time, place, and dimension; a profound sense of calm enveloped me. The experience was frightening yet beautiful, euphoric. And for the next twenty-five minutes, Joan reviewed our life together. She spoke of the good memories, accomplishments, the challenges we faced together, why she loved me, and what she expected of me after she went home to be with Jesus.

Then–she went home!

"Praise God," Mrs. Deaver and I declared in unison. We knew we had witnessed a genuine miracle.

I fell on my knees next to Joan's bed and thanked the Lord for His miracle. What a beautiful end for us both.

—J. Ross Archer—

Do the Possible

Anyone can be an angel.
~Author Unknown

The October court date for my divorce was looming ever closer. Honestly, I was so scared about testifying that I began to think that I would just stay married but live a separate life.

September rolled in and so did the beginning of the new school year. My new eighth grade students were a nice bunch, and I thought I was lucky to have them—especially my honors class. They were amazing. Honors students are dream students. They always have their homework, they're prepared for class, and they live for school.

About two weeks before the court date, one of these students was crying at the end of class. She was sobbing. I asked what was wrong. When a student gets like this, teachers go into counseling mode. That's what I did.

"Did something happen before school or here at school?"

"I—I can't leave class today," was her response between sobs.

"Is it your next class? Is there a problem with someone in class or the teacher?"

"No. I just can't leave class."

I didn't know what to think. I couldn't seem to calm her down and she kept crying. I offered to send her to the counselor for some help. She refused.

"Can you tell me why you can't leave class?"

"I have something to tell you, but I don't know how to say it."

Trying to break the tension I replied with a laugh, "I teach middle school. I have heard everything. I don't think you can scare me." Finally, I got a smile.

She said, "I have a message for you."

"You have a message for me?"

"Yes. While you were teaching, God spoke to me and told me that I could not leave class without delivering a message to you. But I don't know what it means. I don't know how to explain it or tell you what it means."

Now, I have heard about everything as a middle school teacher, but this was a new one on me. I said, "You have a message for me from God?"

She started crying again as she responded, "Yes, he told me that I couldn't leave class without giving it to you, but I don't know how to tell you."

I hugged her and said, "If the message is for me, I will know what it means. You won't have to explain anything. Just tell me what you need to say."

Her message was simple, "God said that I need to tell you that you need to do the possible and let him handle the impossible."

Now it was my turn to sob. And I did. This precious girl who I had known for about two weeks had no idea what I was going through. She had no clue that I was treading water so deep I felt like I would drown any moment. She did not know anything about my divorce struggles. I had never mentioned them once while teaching.

The message was clear on what I was to do. I knew exactly what it meant. I had to go through with my divorce. I had to face my husband in court and finish it.

The next week my attorney had me come in so that she could prep me for the hearing. While we were going over the details of many of the issues within my marriage, she apologized to me for letting it drag on for four years. Something I said to her must have unnerved her and she realized how tumultuous my marriage, separation, and divorce really were.

I remember looking her in the eye and saying that it was okay because I had received a message from God. Now, she was unnerved. She didn't know how to take this information at all. I sat back and told her exactly what had happened in my classroom that day. I told her that no matter what, I knew we were going to get closure to my case. I was sure of it.

The message delivered by that eighth-grade student restored my faith. I needed it. I was broken and tired of the years of trying to get my husband to agree to anything that would end the marriage. Those few words, "You do the possible and let me handle the impossible," were life changing for me. It was my miracle.

October arrived and so did my court date. Was I nervous? Of course! Did I still have faith that something amazing would happen? Of course!

It did. God showed his amazing hand that day in that court of law. My lawyer and I were speechless at the end of the session. We entered the elevator together and she looked at me and said, "I have never tried a case where God told my client that the impossible would happen, but it did. I don't even know what to think." I just hugged her and thanked her for supporting and helping me. I walked her to her car and loaded the boxes of files into her trunk.

The next day at school, I pulled my "message delivery girl" into the hall. I explained in a few words what had been happening in my life and what had happened in that courtroom. We cried together this time. I told her that her message had been exactly what I needed to proceed with my divorce. I also told her that it was time to renew my car registration and I was going to get custom plates with an abbreviated form of the word "possible" on them. She cried again. So did I.

Now, when people stop me and ask me about my license plates, I give them this story and the message that "You do the possible and let God handle the impossible." They usually cry. I smile and look toward heaven and whisper a thank you.

—Amy Mewborn—

Answered Prayers

Prayers for a Stranger

I believe that prayer is our powerful contact with the greatest force in the universe.
~Loretta Young

"Folks, if you're heading west on Lincoln Highway, be advised that there's an overturned vehicle in the right lane near the Mt. Joy exit and traffic has come to a halt. We'll keep you posted," the broadcaster announced.

That's just great! I thought. I prepared myself for bumper-to-bumper traffic for the next mile or so until I passed the crash site.

Our boys would be getting home from school any minute and I didn't have anything ready for dinner, so it was going to be another pizza night, or worse—leftovers! I knew our boys, ages sixteen and eleven, would be scrounging around in the kitchen to find something to eat and probably already ruined their appetites.

As I approached the crash site, I did what I always did, I prayed for the victims and their families. There was an overturned car lying in a ditch—close to the highway. An ambulance was already on the scene, but I feared the worst. How could anyone survive an accident like that?

The traffic picked up after the accident, so I took the Marietta exit to enjoy the spectacular fall foliage. It was my favorite time of year. As I drove up the driveway to our home, I realized that Jake's Subaru wasn't there. That was odd. We had a policy that he would call if he was going to be late. We'd have to review the rules again.

I entered the side door of the house and laid my things on the kitchen island. "I'm home!" I shouted upstairs. No answer. Jake and Josh weren't home yet. I wondered if Jake had picked up Josh from school, but he would have told me; I was sure of it.

Just as I opened the refrigerator door, my cell phone rang; it was my husband. I jumped right in before John could speak and asked, "Do you know where the boys are? The house is empty and it's almost suppertime."

There was a long pause and then John blurted out, "You need to come to the emergency room at Lancaster General Hospital — right away."

"What are you talking about?" I asked. As soon as the words left my mouth, a shiver ran down my spine.

The phone dropped out of my hand. And then I instinctively grabbed my purse and headed for the car — with my coat trailing behind me. To this day, I don't remember driving to the hospital, but I found myself turning into the ER parking lot and running toward the entrance. John was waiting for me and I collapsed into his arms — sobbing. "Please tell me they're going to be okay," I pleaded.

John held me close for what seemed like an eternity and then said the words I dreaded, "I don't know anything yet."

For twenty awful minutes the only thing we knew was our boys were involved in a car accident and were taken by ambulance to this hospital. The nurse would let us know when we could see them.

Finally, the nurse told us we could go back to see our boys. I spotted Jake's tennis shoe splattered with blood on the green tile floor in the small cubicle. There was a police officer standing outside the drawn curtain.

"Are you Jake's parents?" the police officer asked abruptly.

"Yes!" we said in unison.

"Well, I'm not citing your son for any violation of the law. It wasn't his fault."

The officer went on to explain that Jake swerved to miss a large box that fell off the back of a flatbed truck. When he did so, he hit some gravel and flipped the car upside down — landing in a ditch.

I froze. The officer noticed my face turned ashen and asked, "Do you need to sit down?"

"No, I'm fine... I just need to see my boys," I replied, as I entered Jake's cubicle. His face was bloody and bruised, but the doctor who examined him told us he only had some contusions and lacerations and would be fine. I heaved a sigh of relief.

As I approached the bed, Jake opened his eyes, "Mom, please don't cry!" I grabbed his hand and cupped it over mine — not wanting to let go.

"Mom, you need to see how Josh is doing!" Jake demanded. The nurse came in and said that Josh was in the adjacent room, but Kelly was still having X-rays taken.

"What?" I shrieked. "All three of them were in the car?"

"Yes, I believe they were traveling together. Kelly is your son's girlfriend — correct?" the nurse asked, politely.

I nodded my head. The nightmare kept getting worse; our two boys and Jake's girlfriend were in an accident. How could this happen?

John went to be with Josh while I waited for word on Kelly, who had been sitting in the passenger seat of the car. I was shaking my head — not wanting to believe any of it.

As it turned out, our boys escaped with only minor injuries — contusions and lacerations. And Kelly had a broken nose, but nothing life-threatening. The officer on the scene filed his report and said, "Your boys are very fortunate. I've never witnessed a car so badly damaged where there wasn't loss of life!"

I've never forgotten those words. The accident that occurred on Lincoln Highway, just miles from our place, was the one that I passed on the way home from work that day. The family and victims that I prayed for were my loved ones — Jake, Josh and Kelly!

To this day, John still keeps the key to the Subaru in his wallet as a reminder of the day that God spared our boys from serious injury or death.

— Connie K. Pombo —

A Moose

Today… I am grateful for God answering my prayers…
In His own beautiful way…
~Author Unknown

Sheila and I were best friends and former neighbors. We stayed connected for more than four decades through all the ups and downs of life. Through our handwritten weekly letters, we shared parenting tips, hopes and dreams, and our innermost thoughts. When her letters stopped coming, I phoned.

Brain tumor. Malignant. I'm sure she said more, but those are the only words I processed. During Sheila's treatment period, when her letters were nonexistent, I wrote faithfully. Two years later, in remission, suffering from short-term memory loss, she resumed writing weekly, repetitive letters.

We took a trip to Maine together then. We climbed the stairs to the top of a lighthouse. We walked along the Atlantic shoreline. Not once did we mention her fleeting thoughts, vacant stares, or repetitive questions. When I mentioned Alaska, where we originally met, Sheila's eyes flickered with recognition. She laughed with delight when we reminisced about the baby buffalo that scratched its back on one of our trailers, and the moose antlers lying all over the woods during rutting season. Alaska memories remained fresh in her long-term memory. We recalled the herds of caribou, moose, and buffalo that pounded down our gravel road.

As Sheila's memory faded and it was obvious her days were growing shorter, we decided to take one more vacation — in northern New

England. Hiking was out of the question, but I hoped a scenic drive through miles of forest, as desolate and uninhabited as Alaska, would jog my dear friend's memory.

"Let's take a day trip through Moose Alley." Her husband volunteered to drive the winding roads up Route 3 into Pittsburg, New Hampshire, the northernmost town at the Quebec border.

"Guaranteed to see moose," said the gas station attendant. "They lumber along the edge of the forest, onto the highway, and root through beaver dams for aquatic greens. Have a nice drive, folks."

Mile after mile, we scanned the woods along the road. We drove for two hours without any sightings. Cramped in the car and disappointed, we decided to turn around and stop for a late lunch.

"I so wanted to see a moose." Due to her short-term memory loss Sheila didn't realize she'd been complaining repetitively and wishing over and over for a moose sighting.

While we were stopped at a red light in a small town, I prayed silently, "Lord, my dear friend's body and mind are rapidly aging, and our time together is short. Her wish is to see a moose like we used to see when we lived in Alaska. If there is any way You could allow us a sighting on our way home…"

Then we watched in disbelief as a nearly 1,200-pound moose with a huge rack of antlers lumbered out of the woods to our left.

"Sheila, look!" I whispered and tapped her shoulder.

The bull moose moved hesitantly across the road and halted right in front of the car. Then he turned and looked directly at Sheila. She sat spellbound. Speechless, and motionless, we all watched as that heaven-sent moose stood there for ten seconds staring directly at my friend. When it loped off into the woods to our right, we laughed, squealed, and collectively rejoiced. "Amazing! Unbelievable! Sheila, that moose was heaven-sent, just for you!"

Some might consider our moose encounter a coincidence. I believe in my heart it was a miracle for my best friend.

— Linda O'Connell —

Faith and Warmth

We must remember that the shortest distance between our problems and their solutions is the distance between our knees and the floor.
~Charles Stanley

My three children were at their father's house but would be coming home that evening to a very cold house. Our tiny one-bedroom cottage was heated by a lone fireplace, but I had no money to buy wood. So, I knelt in the tiny front room and began to cry out to God.

Almost immediately, I heard a quiet knock on the door. Drying my tears, I cautiously went to see who was there. I opened the door to a young boy with a very dirty face. "May I help you?" I asked.

Straightening his shoulders, he proudly told me that he had been chopping wood with his father down the street. They didn't have a fireplace so his dad wanted to know if I could use some wood.

Hello? An answer literally minutes after the prayer!

After my incredulous and excited "Yes!" I didn't have to do anything. He ran back to his father and the two of them brought load after load after load of wood. They stacked it neatly against the house, and by my rough calculations there had to have been at least two cords of wood. The father and son had declined my offer of help, so I could only stand there and watch with amazement the tangible answer to my prayer being fulfilled before my very eyes.

With their act of kindness completed, they smiled and left.

Still in a state of astonishment, I gathered up stray pieces for kindling and loaded my arms with the wood. With much joy I built that much-needed fire. Usually, fresh cut wood is hard to get started. But not this time. It ignited right away.

This miracle of grace gave me renewed joy and strength. With a light heart I prepared two loaves of fresh bread, baking one at a time in our miniature oven. My children arrived home to the delicious aroma of fresh bread and the coziness of that incredible crackling fire.

All that I thought was going to be hopelessly wrong, was now abundantly right.

— Brenda M. Lane —

The Healing Service

Prayer does not change God,
but it changes him who prays.
~Søren Aabye Kierkegaard

I had been preparing to put away an armful of folded laundry when I caught the toe of my slipper on the corner of our bed. I slammed headfirst into the wooden doorframe of my bedroom closet.

And now, after four years had passed, the crushing pain that had begun with a concussion had become too much for me to handle. I couldn't make it through a day without a migraine, dizzy spells, losing everything in my stomach. I no longer felt comfortable meeting friends for coffee, dining in a favorite restaurant, or even grocery shopping.

My husband now purchased most of what we needed. There were mornings when I couldn't get dressed. Instead, I'd wrap myself in my warmest robe, slowly enter the kitchen, sit by the fire, and listen while my husband read from his devotionals and Bible.

In addition, though I had for years enjoyed inviting friends to our home, my new rule was no guests, no noise, no radio, no commotion. I never knew when I might end up in bed with agonizing pain.

My primary care physician prescribed more than one medication, but to her dismay and mine, nothing had worked. She'd referred me to a physical therapist, a speech therapist, and for more than one CT scan and MRI. My husband had even driven me to the ER more than once.

Meanwhile, my daughter and granddaughter had flown in for a

surprise visit, but in less than twenty-four hours they were leaving because I couldn't get out of bed. Burying my head in my pillow, I screamed that I would never again be me! "I can't go on living like this much longer," I'd written to my closest friend.

Every morning began with a sense of dread. I wondered if I would ever again be able to write or meet friends for coffee or even prepare a supper for myself and my husband. I was at the end of my rope. I didn't really want to keep going. I wondered if God even existed, or was I simply crying out and praying to an unfeeling, empty room?

Nevertheless, I got on my knees and prayed. With my face on the bedroom carpet, I felt these words: "Healing service." I hadn't exactly heard a voice, but I'd heard something and instantly understood I was hearing from God.

Healing service? Where would I find such a thing in small-town Montana?

The following day, my coffee group would be meeting at a donut shop that was everyone's favorite. For the first time in days, I'd opened my eyes to a morning without pain, so I dressed and grabbed my purse. I would meet friends and hopefully get through the morning without having to leave early.

I arrived before the others, stepped to the counter to place my order and then, without thinking, I began to blurt out what I'd heard about a healing service and—

"My church. Sunday morning. Nine-fifteen," Margie the shop owner said, as she found a slip of paper and began to scribble directions to the place where she worshiped.

"Your church?"

Smiling, Margie nodded and handed me the donut I'd ordered. "Be there. You won't be disappointed."

The following Sunday, my husband drove us to the church Margie attended. I feared I wouldn't be able to explain my situation to strangers.

"What do you have to lose, Babe?" Scotty whispered.

We'd barely made it into the entryway when I was greeted by warm smiles and hugs from several women. And they'd barely said, "Welcome" before I was blurting out the reason I was there.

Instantly, one woman took my hand. Another gently touched my shoulder. "Those of us who pray will be meeting in there," she said, pointing to a room across the hall that was already filling with men and women of all ages.

I entered the room, dropped into a chair, squeezed my husband's hand and, head bowed, wondered if I'd made a foolish mistake. Maybe, I thought, while the others are bowing heads with eyes closed, we could leave — except, now one and then another member of the gathering began to pray and praise out loud! I wouldn't look up; I couldn't speak. Instead, I considered bolting from my chair. I would explain on the way out that I'd made a mistake; I needed to leave; I didn't have it in me to show or tell without crying. Only now, without warning, I'd begun to weep. Silently but with tears spilling into my lap.

I don't know how long I sat in that room. I do know I heard one person quietly enter and then another and then several together. Allowing myself a quick glance while barely lifting my head, I could see the circle had grown to maybe twenty members. Each praying, raising hands, humming…

And then the music in the sanctuary began to fill the room in which I was sitting, and one by one, each praying member began to leave. One woman, as she stepped away from the chair beside mine said, "You'll be okay. God has heard your prayer."

I began to feel filled to overflowing with a sweet peace.

We didn't stay until the end of the service. We had other plans that meant we needed to go home, but as we walked to the parking lot and I shared with my husband that I hadn't "felt" anything, he smiled. "That's okay, Babe," he said. "God knows, and He still does answer prayer."

Not until a week had passed did I begin to realize something had definitely happened in that service. No, I hadn't "felt" anything happen as the others prayed; I'd only wept. But I'd now gone a week without a migraine. In fact, I hadn't even experienced a minor headache.

Two weeks passed.

Then three.

And today I count on my fingers nearly ten months without a

single migraine. I no longer wake up fearing the day. I do sometimes wonder, though, "Why me?" — because I have more than one friend whose migraines continue to be a significant problem. But my question hasn't yet been answered. I only know that my plea with my face buried in the carpet and the prayers of the friendly strangers at that church were heard — and I received a miracle on a Sunday morning in May.

— Nancy Hoag —

Good Intentions

I believe in miracles... prayers
that are answered and healing hands.
~John McLeod

I was lying in the bed watching television when my six-year-old daughter ran in, hysterically sobbing. She was saying something about her fish, Petie, who she had only had for two months.

As soon as I saw the fish tank, I knew what had happened. You could hardly see the green plants or the ceramic castle through the hazy water, and there were several bottles of scented body spray lined up next to the tank.

Petie was floating on top of the water looking quite dead. "Oh, Petie," were the only words I could find. I pulled my daughter into my arms as she repeatedly said, "I didn't mean it."

I calmed her down and escorted her from her bedroom. Back in my bedroom, we talked and she explained that she had wanted her fish to smell pretty. She didn't know it could make Petie sick.

Then she grabbed my hands and squeezed them tight. "It will be okay, Mommy, because I'm going to pray for him," she declared. I watched my six-year-old leave the room, drop to her knees, and pray such a fervent prayer that I began to cry. She called out to God and begged him repeatedly to save her fish. She confessed to her mistake and asked for his forgiveness. My daughter believed with her whole heart in a God that could do anything, including resurrecting a goldfish from the dead.

For several hours I kept her out of her bedroom, careful to avoid the reality that Petie was gone. We went for a walk, ate lunch, and devoured our favorite dessert. I placed her in front of the television to watch her favorite cartoon while I snuck upstairs to dispose of Petie's remains. This time I felt prepared as I entered her bedroom with a fish net in one hand and a garbage can in the other.

I didn't even realize I had dropped the garbage can until I heard the large clang it made when it hit her bed frame. The closer I came to the fish tank, the more surreal it felt. It simply couldn't be. Petie was darting around the tank like nothing had ever happened.

I ran downstairs and grabbed my girl as excitedly as she had grabbed me earlier. "You gotta see this!" I yelled like a child opening a gift on Christmas Day. Petie was alive, and so was my faith.

—Bobi Gentry Goodwin—

God's Dollar Bill

In times of trouble, be strong. And wait patiently for God to rescue you.
~Lailah Gifty Akita, Think Great: Be Great!

Sand entered the car along with Bob as he rushed to get out of the sandstorm. His calves were bright red from the abrasive wind.

"I can't see what's wrong," he said. "Everything looks okay, but who can tell in this storm? I don't want to leave the engine open too long and get sand in it."

We were on a belated honeymoon: a cross-country camping trip to California and back. Bob's orders to report for active duty in the Air Force arrived on our wedding day so we'd waited years for this trip. Now we were three plus a dog; our two-year-old daughter, Rachel, sat in her car seat, watched over by our Sheltie, Bonnie. But instead of enjoying the wide-open vistas and blue sky of the Sonoran Desert, we were stopped on the shoulder of I-10 and our car and trailer were enveloped in a brownish cloud of desert sand.

The sandstorm had appeared on the horizon, approaching us head-on as we zipped along, then suddenly engulfing us. At first, it seemed no different from a blinding rainstorm. Bob slowed a bit because of the poor visibility but kept going.

"There's an exit up ahead," I said. "Maybe we should get off and wait out the storm." I was worried about Rachel; the sand was infiltrating the car even with all the windows up and the air-conditioning going.

No sooner had I spoken than our car slowed suddenly and then died. Bob had managed to coast onto the shoulder where we glided to a halt just below the green exit sign I'd spotted. Cars and trucks rushed by as Bob attempted to restart the motor. Without the air-conditioning running, the passenger compartment quickly grew uncomfortably warm. It was 101 degrees outside. We didn't dare crack the windows; there was enough sand getting in with them closed.

We sat there for about ten minutes while Bob periodically attempted to restart the engine. No luck. I wet a cloth to wipe Rachel's sweaty face while Bonnie panted in the back seat. The temperature inside had gone up about twenty degrees and it was hard to breathe with the dust.

"Bob, we can't just sit here; it's getting too hot. Can't we make a run for the exit?"

"We'd have no skin left by the time we got there." His scraped legs were evidence of that. "Besides, we wouldn't be able to breathe. I could barely hold my breath long enough to check the engine. And what would we do with Rachel and Bonnie?"

We both went silent with worry.

Then Bob said, "We should have thought of this before: let's pray."

He grabbed my hand and bowed his head. I don't remember exactly what he said but I do remember how worried he sounded. He told the Lord he didn't know what to do. His final words were, "So, Father, please make the car start so we can get to the exit. In Jesus's name, amen."

We looked at each other. Bob squeezed my hand, then put his hand on the key. I think both of us took a deep breath before he turned it. I know I did, and I silently repeated, "Please, Father, please!"

Bob's hand turned, the engine caught, and our Skylark started right up.

"Thank you, Jesus!" Bob exclaimed, immediately putting the car in gear and heading up the ramp only a few hundred feet in front of us. At the stop sign, we noticed a gas station and store on the corner; Bob pulled the car in under the awning.

We sat there for a minute, hardly believing we were safe. Then we got Rachel out of her car seat, put Bonnie's leash on, and ran for the shelter of the store, passing a state trooper's car on the way in.

The store was wonderfully cool. We stopped to catch our breath and look around as the store clerk greeted us, "Howdy, folks."

"Can we bring the dog in?" Bob asked.

"No problem in this storm."

The trooper, who was leaning against the counter, said, "You folks are lucky you made it in. It's bad out there."

Bob agreed. "We were stuck on the shoulder just short of the exit. I didn't think the car would start again."

The trooper nodded in agreement. "Yeah, the silicon from the sand gets in the engine and melts onto the ignition points. You have to get in and actually rub the silicon off."

"Well, our car just restarted after we let it sit for a few minutes."

The trooper snorted. "No way. Not possible."

"But it did!"

"Look, son," the trooper said patiently, "unless you rubbed the points with something slightly abrasive—we usually use a dollar bill—there's no way your engine could restart."

"But... but, I didn't do anything except open the hood and shut it. I couldn't see through the sand, and I didn't know to use a dollar bill. I'm not a mechanic." Bob sounded both amazed and insistent.

I added, "Bob got back in the car, we prayed, and the car started. Just like that."

The trooper was unconvinced; so was the store clerk, who said, "You're not from Arizona, are you?"

We shook our heads. "No, we're stationed in Virginia, but we're from Michigan."

The trooper asked, "That's your Buick with the trailer and Michigan plates?"

When we nodded, he said, "Well, all I can say is God must have reached down and rubbed your points Himself, because there's no way your car could have started otherwise."

He tossed his drink cup in the trash can and nodded thanks to the clerk. "I'd better get out there and see if there's anyone else who's really stuck. The storm looks like it's passing. You should be good to go soon." He nodded courteously and went out the door.

We stayed until the sandstorm passed, then loaded everyone back in the Skylark. I'll admit we both held our breaths while Bob turned the key, but the engine started right back up and we continued on our way.

We've shared our story several times, and most mechanics agree: there was no way, with the ignition system on a '71 Buick Skylark, that our car could have started by itself. As the trooper said, it was impossible.

But it did.

We call it the miracle of God's Dollar Bill.

— Renny Gehman —

Praying for Bea

Hope is like the sun, which, as we journey toward it,
casts the shadow of our burden behind us.
~Samuel Smiles

I suddenly woke up in the middle of the night with Bea on my mind. I could not seem to shake her name or her face from my thoughts so I decided to pray for her. I had no idea why but I knew that I should pray.

Bea had been my son's kindergarten writing teacher three years earlier. We were just acquaintances. I didn't understand why I had such a strong urge to pray for her.

The next morning, I had my usual Bible study group to attend. It was at the church where my son had attended kindergarten.

I arrived early, and as I entered the meeting room a friend called out to me to come quickly to see this woman who had to decide whether or not to undergo a heart transplant. She needed it badly, but her husband had just died and she worried about who would raise her four young boys if she didn't make it through the transplant.

The woman was Bea. In shock, I told my friend: "I have been praying for her all night."

I had no idea that Bea had been on the waiting list for a heart transplant at UCLA. And now here I was looking out a window at Bea sitting in her car making that decision.

I have often wondered since that night how many other people might also have had the same wake-up call to pray for Bea.

Bea decided to get the transplant. She told me later that she had asked God if He could please make that transplant last for ten years so that she could raise the boys before it wore out.

God answered her prayers and the new transplanted heart lasted eleven years. This brought the ages of her sons to eighteen through twenty-eight years of age. They were well past the age of needing to be raised.

Bea received yet a second heart transplant and is currently doing very well, enjoying her family and her grandkids. And the bonus is that we ended up becoming good friends!

— Lu Scannell —

Somehow I Knew

Prayer is a joy and a privilege, available to all of God's children. The Lord longs to hear all of our concerns.
~Corrie ten Boom

With a sudden knowing, I spun toward my husband. I could only hope I hadn't disturbed the people seated behind us. I felt as if I'd literally been shaken, but there was no reason. "We need to go home!" I whispered. I was already slipping into my coat, with my heart racing. "We need to leave right now."

I didn't know why we were going, and I also didn't understand why it had to be "right now" but I did feel—even though this was a film we'd been wanting to see for weeks—that if my husband didn't move, I would be leaving without him.

But my husband did move and, together we felt our way up the darkened aisle and into the intense lights that filled the theater lobby.

This was before cell phones, so we raced home still not knowing why. I just knew that something wasn't right, and I knew it was our daughter Lisa who was in trouble. Even though I couldn't imagine what kind of trouble it was, because she was safely at home with a sitter we trusted, I was convinced this was not some ridiculous whim.

We'd only just pulled into our driveway when our young sitter threw open the front door and exclaimed, "I'm so glad you've come home early! Lisa's been sobbing and screaming, because she's in terrible pain and—"

I ran up the stairs toward our daughter's room and found her balled up in the middle of her bed. She was sobbing. "It hurts! It really hurts, Mommy!"

"What hurts?" I asked, as I touched my daughter's clammy forehead and silently prayed, "Dear God..."

"My legs...my legs," she wept — as I dropped to the side of her bed and saw, with her tiny nightgown pulled up above her knee, hard golf-ball sized knots in her calf muscles. Knots I might have massaged, had I been there before the pain had become so awful. Knots I might have tried to deal with by applying a hot water bottle. Instead, I scooped my daughter onto my lap, thanked our pale sitter, and asked her if she would stay with our other two children while we took our youngest to the hospital.

In the ER, the doctor examined our daughter and said he knew exactly what had happened. He didn't know why, but the knots — or cramps — could be taken care of with medication right then. Within minutes, our little one, who'd been sweating profusely from both the fear and the pain, began to relax.

When we took Lisa home from the hospital that night, the sitter said, "Her pain seemed to become worse when she feared you wouldn't be coming home. I didn't know how to let you know... and I could only pray to God."

She'd "only" prayed, and I smiled. Because of course she would have. She was a pastor's child and the one teen we had been trusting since before our youngest was born. And although she'd had no way of contacting us by phone, she'd found another way, through an all-knowing intermediary.

— Nancy Hoag —

A Heavenly Recipe

Be an angel to someone else whenever you can,
as a way of thanking God for the help
your angel has given you.
~Eileen Elias Freeman,
The Angels' Little Instruction Book

"Okay Lord, you've got my attention." It didn't sound like much of a prayer, even to me, after the miracle of us getting a home when we'd been so in debt. But I knew that God understood.

I'd promised when we moved in yesterday that I was going to live on what we had. No more charging things and then challenging God to provide the payment a month later. He apparently intended to take me at my word, and he was doing it through Laurie, our first grader.

Out-of-breath and distraught, our little girl had run back a block because she'd forgotten to tell Mommy that it was her turn to bring cupcakes for the class—today! With two days to payday and not even change in the house, I'd answered her pleading brown eyes with an extra kiss and a promise to be there at noon with the cupcakes. She bounded off the stairs again, happy, and I giddily called after her, "Don't worry; it's no problem."

But there *was* a problem. Two minutes later, imagining Laurie's trusting smile when I delivered on the promise, I rummaged in the unpacked boxes for baking tins and the mixer. I confidently set them on the counter; then opened the refrigerator, only to discover there were no eggs! No eggs? How would I make cupcakes without eggs?

I tried to figure out how I could fix the problem. A little voice inside me whispered, "Trust me. Pray!"

Pray? For eggs? I looked at the clock. It was after 9:00. I was running out of time, and I was mystified. Mystified because a peace had settled over me. One word had brought that peace — "Pray." "Okay," I surrendered, "I promised to take you at your word, Lord. You have surely shown me by getting us into this home that you can deal with little things like eggs. Please help me keep my word to my little girl and also keep my promise to you not to spend what I don't have."

The next step was an act of faith. I turned on the oven and measured all the ingredients as our preschooler lined the tins with paper cups. We'd just finished making — and sampling — the frosting when I heard the mailman close the box on the front porch. Of course! God could send us a refund check or something in the mail! I rushed to the porch to get the mail and was flabbergasted by what I found. There, neatly stacked under the mailbox, were two cartons of eggs!

I laughed, as our little preschooler joined me on the porch chanting "Eggs! Eggs!" We looked up and down the street and saw no one.

Leaving the egg mystery for the moment, we raced into the house and got those cupcakes finished, cooled, frosted, and delivered shortly before noon.

"They look homemade," the teacher said as she greeted me at the door. "Yes," I said. "It's, um, a heavenly recipe." Laurie waved and smiled as the teacher closed the door, and Cheri and I walked back home wondering about the mysterious eggs.

The baking utensils were still out, and I had the luxury of two-dozen eggs, so I decided to make one of my husband's favorite desserts: gingerbread. In fact, I decided to make a double batch so some could go in lunches the following day.

The phone was ringing when Ken walked in the door from work. "What smells so good?" he called out.

I answered the phone and heard my friend Bonnie asking. "Did you find some eggs on your porch?"

"Was that you?" I exclaimed. "I looked and didn't see anyone — why would you leave eggs on my porch?"

"Well," she said, in her typical one-breath paragraph, "about 8:00 or so this morning I got the strongest urge for gingerbread... and well, you know I can't bake, but I thought of you and how much I like gingerbread. I know things are tight for you just getting into your new house, and I thought maybe if I bought the most expensive ingredient, you would make me a batch of..."

"Gingerbread?" I croaked in shock.

She continued. "David offered to go to the store before school to get the eggs and he was supposed to ring your bell and give them to you, but he just got home from school and informed me that he left them on your porch without telling you!"

I sucked in my breath as she finished her tale with, "Desperate, huh? So would you consider making..."

"Gingerbread? No problem." And I told her the story.

—Delores Christian Liesner—

Everyday Miracles

Unbelievable Odds

There are no miracles for those that have
no faith in them.
~French Proverb

The ski trip was off to a bumpy start. Tumbleweeds blew across the road and the SUV shook from gusts of wind. The storm had arrived shortly after my sister Robin and I landed at the Reno Airport. Our brother Russ had driven down from his home in Lake Tahoe to pick us up. Before returning, he planned to retrieve two paintings he'd left for framing at a Carson City art gallery.

Russ owned a business and set his own hours, so he could ski whenever he wanted. But it was a treat for my sister and me to ski in Tahoe for a few days without our husbands and kids. While we chatted about our flights and family gossip, the vehicle rocked like a boat on rough water.

"This stretch of road is known for funneling crosswinds through the Washoe Valley," Russ said. "Sometimes it's shut down for trucks and sometimes it's closed to everyone. No barricades today, so it's safe."

That sounded reassuring but didn't stop the roaring wind, rattling windows, and sand blasting against the car. The sandy air obscured the view of the Sierra Nevada Mountains. There was only dirt and sagebrush as far as the eye could see, with an occasional farmhouse. The highway divider was a sunken patch of earth between two asphalt lanes.

A huge blast of air hit and suddenly both windshield wipers popped up, frightening us. They wobbled with the gales but stayed stuck straight ahead. "Arrgh," Russ growled, "I can't drive like this." He pulled over, cut the engine, and struggled to open his door.

Eye squinting, he forced both wipers into place. Back inside he said, "Hope it doesn't happen again, that blowing sand really stings!"

We continued our turbulent ride, though the winds were calmer when Russ parked at the gallery. He reached into the driver's side door pocket and gasped. "My wallet! I tucked it in here after paying the airport parking, but it's gone now." He poked deeper. "The picture frames are already paid for, but they'll want the receipt."

We searched under and between the seats without any success. Finally, Russ said what we all thought. "I bet it fell out when I stopped to fix the wipers."

Robin sighed. "It's lost somewhere out there."

Russ nodded. "I had it when we left the airport, and our only stop was on the highway. Guess I didn't push it down far enough, so it dropped out when I opened the door. I'll go see if they'll let me have my pictures."

He returned smiling and carrying two large rectangles wrapped in brown paper that he placed in the rear on top of our luggage. After he jumped into the driver's seat he said, "When they heard about my missing wallet, they didn't give me any hassles. I'd planned to drive up the mountains from here, but we'll head back the way we came to search for my wallet. Not sure of the location though, all I noticed then was the wipers. Do you remember anything about where we stopped?"

"No," I said. "I was watching you."

"Me too, and we don't know the area," Robin added. "But we'll keep our eyes peeled."

"It's in the middle of nowhere," Russ said. "It'll take a miracle."

"The odds are long," I agreed, "and we didn't come here to gamble, but this is one risk we ought to take. I hate the idea of starting our visit with you losing your wallet."

"Thanks." Russ grinned. "It's an ordinary black wallet. We'll be going in the opposite direction, so it should be lying on the other side of the road, at least ten minutes back, closer to twenty. We'll start checking around ten."

At the ten-minute mark, Russ slowed down and pulled over. We scanned the other side of the highway. The wind shrieked as more tumbleweeds blew by. Nothing resembled a wallet. Russ steered back onto the road. A little while later he pulled over again.

We did this repeatedly. Each time, a disappointment. After many attempts, I felt it was almost time to quit, and knew the others did too.

Russ shifted in his seat. "It's only a wallet." His voice sounded resigned. "It had some credit cards and cash. I just wish I didn't have to spend the first part of your vacation time calling credit card companies and the motor vehicle department. But it'll be okay. Like I said earlier, finding it here would take a miracle."

Ahead in the distance, something small, square, and black shimmied in the dirt divider and then popped up. Then, the mysterious object began cartwheeling on its edges across the asphalt. As it tumbled ahead of us. Russ drove closer and started braking. "Could it be?"

"Maybe," Robin said.

"Possibly," I said.

Russ stopped the SUV. "Definitely!"

What was now obviously a black wallet took its final somersaults across the lane and then fell flat, directly in front of us, as if waiting. Russ yanked open the door, leapt out and grabbed his wallet from where it had landed. He raised it tightly in his hand, his jacket billowing. "Whoopee!" he shouted.

We cheered and laughed.

Russ got into the SUV and I patted him on the back. "That was amazing!"

"Incredible!" Robin agreed.

Russ flipped through his wallet. Nothing was missing. It wasn't even dusty. He refolded it. "That was impossible! Almost like a religious experience."

"Well," Robin said, "the chances of us being in exactly the right place at exactly the right time were astronomical."

"Only seconds earlier or later," I added, "and we would have missed it. We were even looking for it in the wrong spot, on the other side of the road."

Russ displayed the wallet atop a flattened hand. "It's as if it were resting in the highway divider and knew the perfect moment to appear."

Robin grinned. "And just when we were thinking about quitting, it arose from a divot between the roads. That's miraculous all right!"

"Yep," I said. "Felt extraordinary to me."

Russ shrugged. "Well, I said it'd take a miracle."

Robin and I laughed. "And you were right!"

The winds no longer felt threatening. I was calm and happy.

For the rest of the ride to Tahoe we chatted about the "miracle wallet." All the little pieces that had to fall into place for its dramatic return, and how much we wished we'd been able to capture proof on video. Although this journey had gotten off to a rough start, it had turned into an unforgettable event that defied all our expectations.

— Ronda Ross Taylor —

Just a Hug

Don't believe in miracles — depend on them.
~Laurence J. Peter

Miracles surround us every day. The sun rising and setting, the beauty of nature. Even waking up each morning. Then there are the big miracles — premonitions that save lives, the miracle of Lourdes.

Well, a miracle happened to me on a beautiful spring afternoon. It started and ended within a few moments. A bystander wouldn't even have noticed.

After all, it was just a hug. But to me, it was nothing short of miraculous. In fact, it was mind-blowing! I savor every moment of it as I relive it in my mind almost daily.

The hug came from Zachary, my thirty-four-year-old son. He was diagnosed with autism at age two. It has been a long road, filled with many challenges. The fact that Zack is nonverbal complicates matters immensely. However, we have always found a way to stay in tune with one other and get our message across.

Autism involves persistent obstacles in social interaction and communication. Many parents, like me, yearn for spontaneous signs of affection from their child. I was blessed to get one on a day when Zack and I had just taken a walk around the neighborhood. We always hold hands and talk on these walks. He listens, and I talk. Popular topics of conversation are Huff, the horse he rides each week; his siblings, Danni and Lexi, who constantly watch over him; and Tivo, his best buddy. The dogs we encounter along the way are one of my favorite parts of our excursion because they usually make Zack laugh. His whole face lights up when he sees a dog.

Routine is important to Zack. We always watch a movie after our walk. That day we watched one of his favorites, *Lady and the Tramp*. He had loved that movie since he was a toddler. I always take his hand, and he allows me to hold it during most of the movie. His autism prevents him from offering his hand to me first.

Snack time followed. Zack beat me to the kitchen, as usual. His eagle eyes scanned the cabinets, countertops, and refrigerator, searching for potato chips or pretzels.

Before Zack had a chance to sit at the table, I stood in front of him and started to serenade him with a favorite chant that I often use. I sing "Mommy loves you, Mommy loves you, yes, I do, yes, I do," to the melody of "Frere Jacques."

In the middle of my song, I noticed that Zack was intently observing me. Suddenly, he took a step toward me and held his arms out. Another small step followed, and then, it happened! He wrapped his arms around me in a big bear hug. A feather could have knocked me over as I realized that, for the very first time, my son was spontaneously hugging me! Swiftly, I wrapped my arms around him, too, luxuriating in this miraculous moment.

He took a step back with a little smile on his face. Then he sat down as usual to wait for his snack. I stood there in shock for a moment. This magical hug ended almost as quickly as it had started, but the impact it had on me will be eternal.

On an ordinary spring day, the extraordinary occurred in a small kitchen in an average little house. That hug is one of my greatest blessings. It belongs to me, filling me with joy every day.

— Gail Gabrielle —

The Wading Pool

How beautiful a day can be
When kindness touches it!
~George Elliston

A forty-five-inch plastic wading pool wasn't ideal for a family with five kids, but for several years that was all we could afford. I would tug it out of storage at the beginning of each summer and fill it with a hose. Then our boys would strip down to their shorts and take turns jumping inside. With their ages ranging from two years old to eleven, there wasn't room for them to do much of anything besides hop around and cool their feet, but, thankfully, they never seemed to mind. And the pool served as a refill station for water guns, too.

Then, one summer day I overestimated its strength.

We'd decided to have a few friends over for a playdate. The kids spent the afternoon outside, eating a picnic lunch and splashing around in the water. When one of them hoisted their old Little Tikes slide over the edge of the pool, I probably should have seen what was coming. But everyone was enjoying themselves and I didn't feel like disrupting the fun.

So, the kids slid down the slide and into the water for hours.

And a day or two later, I discovered the hole. The slide had punctured the plastic.

I was more upset than I probably should have been. But we didn't have the money for another pool and so much of summer remained!

Fortunately, I didn't have to grumble for long.

As I was cleaning up the yard and discarding the damaged pool, I got a text message: "This was given to us today." The message was from my husband and his text included a photo. A co-worker had given our family an eighteen-foot water slide. It included built-in sprinklers, and, if you can believe it, a small pool at the end.

—Erin Eddy—

The Lost Engagement Ring

I think miracles exist in part as gifts and
in part as clues that there is something
beyond the flat world we see.
~Peggy Noonan

I was looking forward to my son Scott's visit and our morning trip to the Collingswood Flea Market. It was a typical November day, chilly in the shade and warm in the sun. A perfect day for outdoor shopping.

Scott and I walked up and down looking at the many tables covered with Christmas decorations along with the usual clothes, attic treasures, CDs and jewelry. We bought a few small items, but it was a window-shopping morning at best. Nothing called out to me.

After an hour of walking with the wind blowing and a nip in the air, we decided to call it quits and go home for lunch.

On our way, we made a quick stop at Wawa for those delicious soft, salted pretzels. Scott ran into the store while I waited in the car. Sitting alone, I was rubbing my cold hands together when I noticed that my engagement ring was missing. I knew I'd been wearing it when we'd visited a jewelry stand earlier, and I hadn't taken it off. My heart was racing now.

When I informed Scott of the missing ring he couldn't believe it either.

"Mom, if you had worn gloves, it wouldn't have fallen off your finger. Look in your pockets and handbag!"

We searched the car and I searched my clothes, too. No ring! It must have fallen off my finger in the cold.

We headed back to the flea market and parked in the same spot as before. We checked that area, and then began walking up and down the maze of tables while looking at the ground. Leaves blew in the wind and people were everywhere. Hundreds of feet passed by and I began getting lightheaded as I intently looked at the ground. I shuddered at the thought of someone finding my ring and wearing it home, not knowing the sentimental value and its history. It was an expensive engagement ring my now deceased partner had given me twenty years earlier. I had never lost or misplaced it in all that time... until now.

We gave up, cold and hungry. I was furious at myself for having lost the ring. We drove home as I tried to hold back my tears.

After lunch, which I had no appetite for, we decided to return to the flea market. If we were going to find it, it was now or never. Time was of the essence.

And so, for the third time we parked the car in the same spot. Because it was later in the day, most of the vendors had packed up and left.

We went to the manager's office and told him my sad story. I left my name and phone number hoping that someone would find the ring and turn it in.

After that, I took a deep breath and we set out on our mission. It was much warmer and not as windy. I took the left side of the paths and Scott the right. We walked and walked and walked. There was broken glass that glistened like a diamond ring. There were shiny soda can tabs that caught our eye. There were silver coins. Finally, we reached the far end of the flea market. There were a number of empty tables because the vendors had already packed up and departed. And there, under one of those tables, I spotted a shiny little circle in the dirt.

"I found the ring!" I shouted to Scott.

"No way. Really?"

It was truly a miracle. Three hours after I lost it, with hundreds of people walking by, my ring waited for the person meant to find it... me!

— Irene Maran —

The Water Bottle

Impossible situations can become possible miracles.
~Robert H. Schuller

I work on a military base in Florida, situated on the Eglin Air Force Base Reservation, which consists of 250,000 acres of natural beauty. Every day after work, I go for a run on one of the many trails there. Bright green moss grows on the trunks of the trees, the ground is covered in sea foam–colored deer moss, and honeysuckle and wildflowers grow throughout.

Every run is beautiful, peaceful, and full of new sights due to the various twists and turns. The trail options really are endless! I have run as few as two miles and as many as thirteen without backtracking. Trails appear on the left, the right, and occasionally there are intersections leading in four different directions.

On the more popular trails I will see someone walking their dog but on the more distant ones I am the only soul. My curiosity as to where the next trail leads can keep me on a running adventure for miles, and that is exactly what happened on one particular day.

After work I'd headed out for an easy 1.5-mile out and back run. Not too short but also not too long for the first day of the run week. It was a warm seventy-four-degree sunny day but the trees were providing adequate shade. I was maintaining a comfortable pace, enjoying the beauty that was surrounding me, and before I knew it, I was at the 1.5-mile turnaround mark. I was not quite ready to head back so I decided to continue. The trail I was on runs parallel to another trail so I decided to take this trail back up and then take a connector on the left. That would allow me to return to my starting point.

When I got to the connector, I saw something that piqued my curiosity: a sign with a red arrow pointing straight ahead. I was intrigued as to where this option led because it looked like it pointed to a ten-mile path that the military guys use. I would follow the remaining bit of their route. I figured it would connect me back to my original trail or deliver me back to the base. In my mind, it made perfect sense, as do all my great ideas.

After a mile or so the GPS on my watch said I was 3.29 miles away. I knew I needed to turn around and go back the way I came before it got too late. I began pressing the left button on my watch to access the "Take Me Home" feature and that is when it all went wrong. I had pressed the button one too many times and accidentally closed out the session.

My heart dropped. I knew once I closed the session the "Take Me Home" feature was no longer an option because the map that was tracking me no longer existed. My watch didn't know where I had started. The best option now was to continue following the arrows.

After nearly another hour of twists and turns, nothing looked familiar. I was hot, thirsty, and very turned around. I needed to hydrate and for a while that was all I could think about. The heat and distance had taken its toll on me. I had run three more miles yet was not any closer to where I had originally begun. The trails kept moving me south, but I needed a trail that would take me straight east. The sun was beginning to set and I was beginning to panic. I had to keep moving if I wanted to make it out of the trail before it was dark.

Then, after another mile or so, I saw something lying in the middle of the trail. I slowed down, keeping my eyes straight ahead as I continued toward it. Just a few more steps and then, right in front of me lay a bottle of water, in the middle of nowhere, completely out of place among the dirt, leaves, and moss.

I looked around trying to determine how it got there. I did not see or hear anyone. The forest was completely silent. I had not passed anyone in the seven miles I had completed. There were no tire tracks and the only footprints in the sand belonged to me, yet still, I was hesitant. Should I drink it?

I bent down and picked it up; to my astonishment, it was unopened. I was so hot and thirsty. I had been silently pleading for water and now I held a new bottle of water. How did the bottle of water get there and how, in the exact moment of need, did I stumble across it? Feeling my dad's presence with me, I whispered a "Thank you" and with that little boost, I pressed on. Four miles later, eleven miles in total, I finally had made it back to the original trail and back to my vehicle. I made it out just before sundown.

To this day, I have never seen another person on those trails. I have run thousands of miles out there, and never before that day or since, have I come across another bottle of water.

—Aubrey Summers—

Basset Hounds

Mothers hold their children's hands for a short while,
but their hearts forever.
~Author Unknown

Basset Hounds are known for many things, but being easy companions is not one of them. They stink no matter how much you bathe them, howl at all hours of the night, and they are one of the most stubborn breeds out there. Perhaps that's why my mother loved them so much, because they were the only creatures that gave her stubbornness a run for its money.

She grew up with dogs her entire life, mainly boxers and lost mutts, but her great love was her male Basset Hound named Luke. As a little girl, I would beg to see her pictures of Luke and listen to her retell her adventures with her dog. I guess it was no surprise that we ended up with our own Basset Hound, Ginger.

To say that Ginger was my mother's soulmate was an understatement.

My mother developed cancer years later and started spending more time with doctors than with Ginger. She would lie on the couch, too tired to move, and Ginger would lie beside her faithfully. Her health was deteriorating as well, and she seemed to prefer resting beside my mother, the two a comfort to each other.

I feared the worst. What if Ginger died while my mother was sick? I couldn't stand the thought of my mother mourning for her deceased pet while in her condition. I bought her a male Basset Hound puppy, one that could maybe help her transition after Ginger's death and also remind her of Luke.

I had bought him for her, but somehow, he became mine and I named him Scotty. Surprisingly, Scotty gave Ginger back her vitality. She was puppylike again, chasing Scotty around until he lay down exhausted.

My mother had always wanted to breed Ginger but had been told that she couldn't have puppies. She did, though, with Scotty. But the two puppies she had only lived for about two days because she couldn't feed them properly.

Both Ginger and my mother then worsened over the next few months. My mother's family lived in Picayune, Mississippi, and she would spend the weekends there sometimes. It provided her with a place to get away from it all: the treatments, the fear of leaving her husband and child, the fear of losing herself. She never admitted this, but she didn't have to.

It was on one of these weekends that Ginger peacefully passed away.

And then my mother tired of her three-year battle and stopped her treatments. She switched to an all-natural approach she'd heard about. It didn't work for her.

The funeral was long and packed with people I barely knew in Picayune. I stayed quiet at the front, listening to the words said about my mother—her love of Jesus, Jerry Lewis, and Basset Hounds. There was nothing about her humor though. Her stubbornness. Her contagious laugh. Nothing about the funeral screamed "Anna."

And then there it was, after the funeral, sitting on the side of the road at the end of a gravel driveway. It was watching the long procession of cars roll past to the cemetery for the burial. A pair of droopy soulful eyes, four stubby legs, and long ears dangling as its head followed each car. A lone Basset Hound, sent from God to pay its respects to the woman who truly understood what it was to be a Basset Hound.

As the dog focused its gaze on me, I let the tears flow freely and smiled. My mother may have been gone, but I felt her there all the same.

—Lauren Signorelli—

Make-up and Miracles

Sometimes, reaching out and taking someone's hand is the beginning of a journey.
~Vera Nazarian,
The Perpetual Calendar of Inspiration

Vera sat with her shoulders hunched, withdrawn and silent. In all my years working with Alzheimer's patients, the hardest part was bearing witness to the isolation that it imposed. Vera was definitely isolated, and my efforts to involve her in the social life of the facility that was now her home were only met with a haunted, lonely stare from the diminutive woman with the pixie haircut.

She had no immediate family left and had never married. What her life had been remained a mystery, her files containing little hint of her background. As an activity director, I had learned to walk a fine line between a resident's past and the present they now faced; with Alzheimer's disease, each day might present an entirely new set of circumstances where things like a personal history, something we all take for granted, is suddenly meaningless.

In a case like Vera's, if I had been able to discover a little of her story, it might have made her present a bit more bearable. But there was nothing, no guiding clue. And the one person who held within her heart all the secrets that I was trying to decipher could not provide me with anything.

But she was one among many who needed whatever distraction

I could manage to provide. What I tried to do, with varying degrees of success, was help the residents connect with each other, and in so doing form their own support systems. Vera needed someone who found themselves dealing with the same illness, the same challenges, and who would be there for her... and who she could, in turn, be there for.

The days passed, however, with Vera remaining as she was when I first met her. She remained withdrawn and uncommunicative and, sadly, mostly ignored by the other residents and even some of the staff. Her physical needs were taken care of, and she had plenty of good food and good care, but for all of that, she might as well have been invisible. Alzheimer's disease had robbed her of companionship.

***

It was the beginning of the holiday season and such times for people like Vera were a mix of good and bad. The luckiest residents had family members visit, or perhaps even got to leave the facility to spend part of the holidays with their family. The facility would also be hosting a Thanksgiving dinner, and family members were invited to attend. I always enjoyed these special events, and I especially enjoyed seeing the families reunited and happy, with Alzheimer's disease temporarily forgotten, drowned out by laughter and football.

Because she had no family to look after her interests, Vera was one of several individuals who had a professional care manager, a wonderful lady named Melodie, who hosted an annual holiday dinner for the residents without family members. Vera had always attended these dinners, but Melodie told me that she remained silent and withdrawn.

One year, I was drafted to help get Vera ready for Melodie's dinner. We were short-staffed that day and I was asked to do her make-up. Now, I really had little experience with make-up, but I had attended art school, so I bravely agreed to try. I tried to quell my nervousness as I drew on eyebrows and applied blush, eye shadow and lipstick. I even parted Vera's short hair and sprayed it so that it held. The final touch was a pair of large earrings set with rhinestones.

When I finally finished and stepped back to have a good look, I was completely astonished. We all were. Vera was more than pretty.

Vera was stunning. I am not exaggerating when I say that she could have passed for a grand star of old Hollywood. Isa, one of the nurses on hand, ran to get a mirror for Vera to see. And presented with her beautiful self, the miracle I had waited for happened before all our eyes. Vera was beyond delighted. She smiled and laughed. She was radiant!

Vera was the belle of the ball at that evening's dinner, and although she still didn't say a word, her entire demeanor changed. Suddenly, she was the most popular of all the residents and became the acknowledged leader of a group of women who always sat together, not actually talking, but always there for each other. That one glance in the mirror unlocked a vivacious spirit, someone who showed joy with every smile that now lit up her face.

Sometimes a person has to have that look in life's mirror to see themselves in all of their beauty. Perhaps Vera saw in that mirror the person she had been years before.

On that day, I learned that, with God's help and a little make-up, a miracle can be made.

—Jack Byron—

The Cardigan

I believe that tomorrow is another day,
and I believe in miracles.
~Audrey Hepburn

"Why did I ever get rid of that cardigan?" I asked myself when I received word that a cardigan I had sold to a customer had gone missing. "That was the stupidest thing I could've done."

A cardigan is just a cardigan, right?

I thought so too. But apparently, little things can become big things when we're not paying attention to our gut. And when it came to my gut, I had ignored the thought of keeping it. And sold it anyway.

My gut was now telling me, "I told you so."

I'm a vintage clothes seller. I've been selling (re-selling, really) vintage clothing online for more than a dozen years. It's not only one of the best hobbies turned income producer I've ever had, but it's something I can't give up.

One day, I sourced a gorgeous vintage 1950s cardigan that was dark gray, made of wool, and of course, made with care and quality that just isn't found today.

I took photos of this piece, drooled over the fact that there were no holes in the fabric, and tried it on. As the saying goes in the world of vintage sellers, "Don't try on the vintage." Because once you do, inevitably, it will fit or could fit, and you think, "Maybe I just need to hold on to this one for a little bit longer."

This cardigan was just that. I tried it on. It fit me perfectly. But I decided to list it for sale. "I have plenty of cardigans," I thought. "There will be more of these."

"Sure, there will be more, but nothing like this one," my gut said to me.

I pushed that thought out of my mind and listed the piece. It sold almost instantly to a lovely lady in Germany. And at that very moment, I regretted selling the cardigan.

So, with a heavy heart, I shipped it off to Germany.

If you sell what you love, you have to regularly say no to keeping items. But with this cardigan, I wished I'd listened to my gut a little more and kept it.

You know that adage "Set free what you love and if it's meant to be it'll return to you?" For whatever reason, the cardigan package was returned to me. Of course, this twisted the knife deeper in my heart. I had to ship it again to Germany where its rightful owner awaited it.

Then, for a second time, I received a notice telling me the item was being returned to me. Only this time, I never got the package. We waited months to see if it would come so that I could, yet again, reship it to the most amazingly patient woman I've ever worked with.

But it was gone.

I always ship with insurance, so the buyer was refunded. But we never knew what happened to the cardigan. And a part of me was frustrated that I had decided to sell it in the first place. If I hadn't listed it, I wouldn't have had this problem, and instead, I'd have a gorgeous cardigan. Of all the things I've loved and sold over the years, this was the one that had to permanently disappear?

Ten months passed and then one day I found myself thinking of the cardigan. I remember thinking to myself, "If that cardigan ever shows up, I'll know miracles do happen."

Not a week later, guess what appeared on my doorstep? I tore open the package and stared at the cardigan in disbelief. "You came back to me!"

Would the cardigan have manifested without me thinking about it? I don't know. But there was something miraculous in just thinking about the miracle of it coming back to me.

What I do know is this miracle cardigan is mine. This is the third time I've had her in my hands and I'm going to hold onto her this time. This is a miracle I can hold on to; something to remind myself on days when I'm looking for miracles that anything is possible.

— Heather Spiva —

Dreams & Premonitions

Dream Man

You don't find love; it finds you. It's got a little bit to do with destiny, fate and what's written in the stars.
~Anaïs Nin

In my early twenties, for several years I had a recurring dream. In my dream, I was walking down a road when a man appeared by my right side and gently took my hand. At his touch, my whole being filled with peace. I felt like I already knew him deeply, as if my soulmate had come. I turned to look at him but his face remained in a mist, his image erased from the shoulders up.

I would wake from these dreams filled with a mix of love and frustration. Why was I never able to see his face? How would I recognize him if he finally appeared in my life?

When I was twenty-five, I moved to Edmonton and began a relationship with a very nice man. One day, as I was climbing the stairs to enter a building, I almost collided with a tall, attractive young man who was leaving. I had never met him before but when our eyes met, I felt a sense of deep recognition. Then I had an alarming thought. "Omigosh! I am dating the wrong man. This is the man I am supposed to be with!" We muttered apologies and went our separate ways. A few months later, I left on an extended trip to Europe and never returned to live in Edmonton.

Three years later, I was living in Toronto with my girlfriend. In the evenings after work, we would go to our friend Gene's home to relax and play board games with other friends. One night in February,

Gene told us someone he knew was in town briefly for business and was coming over later. When he arrived, I was pleasantly surprised to find it was the same man I had bumped into on the stairs in Edmonton years before. He introduced himself as Greg.

That night we all decided to go to the movies. Everyone had different ideas about what they wanted to see and, as fate would have it, Greg and I ended up together alone. It was just an accident of circumstance but we enjoyed watching the film *Close Encounters of the Third Kind* and chatted like we had been friends forever.

In March, as we were all sitting around playing games, Greg visited again.

At ten o'clock, when I got up to leave, Greg asked if I would like to go for a walk. It had been a very strange day for me. Cupid must have been on the hunt. Amazing as it sounds, three men had asked me if I would marry them earlier in the day! I gently rejected each request. I was still waiting for that man in my dreams to show up.

It was mid-March, and frozen snow lay on the ground as I ventured out into the frigid night air with Greg. Although he was as handsome as any movie star, Greg wasn't vain. He was gentle, soft spoken, down to earth and natural. I felt safe with him even though I had only met him a few times. We walked along for a while without speaking and then Greg said softly, "We're going to get married."

"What?" I couldn't believe my ears. He might as well have thrown cold water in my face for the shock I received. I looked at him in amazement.

Without a trace of annoyance, Greg replied, "It's the truth. My intuition is always right." I was at a loss to know how to answer him. I felt very comfortable with Greg but marriage was a huge decision and I hardly knew him.

Just then we hit an icy patch on the sidewalk. Greg was on my right side and quickly took my hand to support me while we walked. The moon was full and bright, lighting up the snow with millions of sparkling ice crystals. I was overcome with a sense of wonder at how romantic this scene was when it suddenly dawned on me that this was the scene from my recurring dream only this time it was real! Could

Greg be… him? My soulmate?

The next night, Greg invited me to sit on the couch with him. He proceeded to try out Plan B. He asked me if we were friends. I was delighted that he would consider me to be his friend so I said, "Yes."

Then he said, "Good. So you're my girlfriend then."

I started thinking that perhaps I had misjudged Greg. He was certainly a fast talker! Nevertheless, I had never forgotten that encounter on the stairs three years earlier when my heart told me he was the man I was supposed to be with, so I consented to be his girlfriend.

Then he asked me, "What happens when a man and woman become girlfriend and boyfriend?"

My mind ran up a red flag of warning. "What?" I asked.

"They either break up or get married. Do you want to break up?"

"I just became your girlfriend one minute ago!" I said with exasperation.

"Well, then we should get married." he said, smiling.

He picked up a calendar from a nearby desk and flipped through the pages. It happened to open at April. I felt a flood of relief. "You want to get married next April?" I asked. That would give me a year to get to know him.

"No. This April. Let's call our parents and make the arrangements." Then he closed his eyes and slid his finger along the days until his finger stopped on April 9th.

I sucked in my breath as I counted the days. If Greg had his way, we would be married in just sixteen days. My mind was shouting, "No way can I do that so fast!" However, my heart left no room for doubt… so I agreed. We made the arrangements.

Our friends were flabbergasted and some advised against the rush. We were married on April 9th, the day he chose, in a friend's home in Unionville, a little town just north of Toronto.

In two months we will celebrate our forty-fourth wedding anniversary. When I look back over our happy years together, the shining magic of it all strikes me — ours has truly been a marriage made in heaven.

— Christine Clarke-Johnsen —

A Dead Tree Saved My Marriage

A dream which is not interpreted is like
a letter which is not read.
~The Talmud

My husband and I were having difficulty managing our blended family. He had two children and I had two; the four of them ranged in age from eight to thirteen. Things came to a head and we separated. After eight weeks of that, I decided that I'd had enough of the conflict and stress; I just wanted to be done.

On the Friday before Father's Day, we had a very difficult, emotional talk. I let him know that although I loved him, I didn't see any way we could solve our problems. I felt we should cut ties and move on. We had no children together, and we had been unsuccessful at integrating our two families after almost three years of trying.

The next day, Saturday, I tried my best to limit conversations and contact with my husband, thinking that it would help us to "move on" and accept our situation. He had asked to see me several times and I declined, thinking the interaction would be too hard. I was closed off, emotionally and physically exhausted, and I didn't want to talk about it anymore. We'd been driving ourselves crazy for months with indecision and constant conflict, trying solutions that failed time after time. I went to dinner with some ladies from work as a distraction, then came home and went to bed.

That night I had a strange dream about the eighteen-foot tree that was positioned right outside my sunroom, which was basically a room made of windows. I had realized the tree was dead that spring when it didn't bloom, and I was worried that it might fall over in one of the strong spring storms, which often came with powerful gusts of wind. I could see it falling through the glassed-in sunroom and into the house, a terrifying thought.

In my dream, I had come home from work and my husband had cut down that tree! He had left me a note that said, "Even if we're not together, I want to make sure you and the kids are taken care of and safe." I woke up thinking what a selfless act of service that was. Acts of service just happen to be my "love language" and although my husband would do anything for me, usually I felt like I had to ask. So, when in the dream this worry of mine was just taken care of, I felt loved, cared for, and relieved.

After a few minutes of looking out my window at the dead tree and thinking about how strange it was to dream about it, I went to get my coffee and get ready to see my dad for Father's Day. When I sat down with my coffee and checked my phone, I saw a text message from my husband. It read, "I know you'll probably be going to your dad's house today for Father's Day. If it is ok with you, I would like to come over and cut down that dead tree while you're gone."

I was in shock. What are the chances that I would dream about a dead tree and the very next morning he would text me about it? After a while, I told him he could come cut down the tree, and we could talk afterwards. I couldn't ignore this strange coincidence, and I had to tell him about it.

When I got home, there he was, in ninety-degree heat, buzzing away with a chainsaw. He took a break, and I got him some ice water. We sat on the porch, and I told him about the dream. He then told me that the weekend had been the hardest he had ever had. He told me that he felt very low, and he was angry with God for allowing his life to fall apart and make him lose his family. He said that he prayed for three days for God to show him what he could do and woke up on Sunday morning unable to get that dead tree out of his head. I told him that if it weren't for the dream I had the very same night, I wouldn't have seen him because I didn't want to prolong the pain.

I am not one to ignore signs, however, and ours came at just the right moment. Everything that seemed impossible was now fixable. After we had a long talk and agreed that it was a sign to try again, he got back to chopping wood. I found a round disk of wood from the tree lying on the ground and snuck it into my pocket. I took it into the house and hid it away. I plan on making a keepsake out of it, painting it with the word, "Hope." That should make a good third anniversary gift for my husband and serve as a reminder to both of us that sometimes when it seems like there's no way out, God can use something as insignificant as a dead tree to bring two people back together.

—Jennifer M. Starr—

Reaching Down from Heaven

Pay attention to your dreams — God's angels often speak directly to our hearts when we are asleep.
~Eileen Elias Freeman,
The Angels' Little Instruction Book

My life's journey has never been a straight road. Instead, it has been full of twists and turns, wrong ways and dead ends. And months ago, I was confronted with yet another path I had to take. I was told the house I had been renting for more than twenty years was going up for sale. I would need to find another place to live.

My daughter, from across the miles that separate us, encouraged me to buy my own home. I couldn't afford it, I didn't want to paint walls and make repairs, and I wasn't sure about my credit score. "You can try," she told me gently. She suggested I meet with a mortgage broker to begin a preliminary mortgage approval. I dreaded the possibility I wouldn't be approved. After all, I don't own a single credit card.

The first day I went to view the listings, the houses in my price range were as mediocre and disappointing as I had imagined they would be. My sister, an interior decorator and real estate agent, went with me that day, and after walking through several houses, she could sense my despair. When there was one last house to view, I told my sister that I didn't think it was worth the drive. I assumed it would be in disrepair, as were all the other houses I visited. Besides, the asking price was more than I could afford. "We're going to look at it anyway," she said.

I saw my sister smile as she pulled into the driveway. The home was picture perfect. Hopeful, I told her and the universe and myself that this was the house I wanted. Once inside, I stood for a moment taking it all in as she wandered from room to room, calling out to me that every room was move-in ready. "Just beautiful. You deserve this home," she concluded, so happy and excited for me. I made an offer on the house, a ridiculously low offer, but the most I could afford.

Later that evening, I described the home to my daughter. She knew that I had made an unreasonable offer and reassured me that there would be other homes to look at. I told her that this was the home I wanted. I had to smile — it reminded me of my mother once saying to my broken heart, "There will be other boys to date."

She would have loved this house, this picture-perfect-for-me home. My father would have looked around, turning on faucets, examining its structure. In my mind's eye I saw them visiting with me in the living room, eating Sunday dinner at my dining room table, planting gardens with me. My parents created such a sanctuary of strength, love, and family in my childhood home that I pictured them doing the same in this house.

And that very night, I experienced a dream. I was in my parents' kitchen, feeling a calmness I had not felt in weeks. My mother was making my favorite dinner, and my father was sitting next to me at the kitchen table, slouched in his chair, nodding off to sleep. The aroma of meatloaf and scalloped potatoes filled me with happiness. I breathed it in. I saw precious treasures — the furniture my father had built, the artwork my mother had painted.

I reached out and put my hand on my father's hand. He startled. My mother sat down, and she put her hand on mine. She smiled. "We will help you with the house," she told me so vividly I forgot I was dreaming.

Most of my dreams fade over the course of the day, but this dream remained with me. It felt so real. It blanketed me with comfort, it hugged me with peace. I knew then that no matter what happened I would be okay.

I bought the house, and the process was indeed full of twists and turns and wrong ways. Through it all I felt calmed by my parents' love, their hands reaching down from heaven to bless this home and make it mine. It was just a matter of time before I stood at the door, walking inside to a brand-new beginning. I think of the dream often and always will. I feel the miracle of my parents reaching down from heaven.

And I know that my mother would like this little tidbit of wisdom: Sometimes you must let go of questioning why your path was so challenging—and just walk on the road in front of you—to fully appreciate your journey.

—Katherine Mabb—

The Promise in Goodbye

He was a father. That's what a father does. Eases the burdens of those he loves. Saves the ones he loves from painful last images that might endure for a lifetime.
~George Saunders

Nothing but darkness came through the kitchen windows on that St. Patrick's Day, eleven days after my fourteenth birthday. I didn't want to be awake yet. I'd planned to sleep in late since Grandma was staying with us. Mom was in Chicago, sitting by my dad's bedside. She assured me they'd be back in Omaha soon. As soon as Dad healed enough to travel.

I couldn't understand why Grandma woke me so early or why Dad's best friend was waiting to talk to us. Maybe my older brothers had figured it out on their way down the stairs but not me. Not until I heard him say, "I'm sorry to bring the news that your dad passed away early this morning."

I ran upstairs back to my bedroom. But I soon learned I couldn't outrun grief. It became my constant companion.

I still idolized my dad. And for good reason. Where I couldn't ever seem to please my mother, I could easily please my father. He loved me even though I'd been a chubby, awkward kid. He never cared that I was indecisive, trying out three instruments — with lessons — before settling on the flute. Or that I flunked out of after school ballet, jazz and tap. Dad accepted my "B" and "C" grades with the same enthusiasm he did my brothers' "A" report cards. He didn't mind my drama. I knew he liked me as well as loved me.

I became obsessed with the fact I hadn't been able to say goodbye to him. I'd said goodbye to him as he left on his trip to New York, a trip he never came home from, but not goodbye for all time. I fretted, cried and avoided school for as many weeks as I could. When I did go back, I couldn't manage the assignments.

All I thought about day after day, night after night was hugging my dad one last time and saying goodbye. I knew it would never happen; he was dead after all. But my grief was unrelenting. And I had no one around who could help me.

I have no memory of my mother during this time but one. Every night, after her martini glass was empty, she'd pour coffee and sit in the breakfast nook and cry. I began to join her, thinking I could comfort her. And hoping she could comfort me. After a few nights of burning my tongue on black coffee, Mother asked me to leave. She preferred her solitude.

Alone in my room I filled notebooks with sad poetry. I sneaked into Dad's closet and lay there for hours, drinking in the scent of Old Spice that still clung to his suits. I soaked my pillows with tears. Day after long day, I couldn't find peace or manage my way out of the sorrow.

After a few weeks of this, Grandma came over for a visit. She held me as I poured out my broken heart. She listened as I said that I needed to say goodbye to my dad. I needed to see him one more time. I had to tell him I loved him.

"Emmy, ask God to let you say goodbye," Grandma suggested. "Ask him every night before you go to bed. God can do anything."

I grabbed onto the hope Grandma offered. The last few weeks, I'd felt abandoned in a hard world without my father's love. I hoped, if there was a god, he would hear me and grant my wish. So every night before I slept, I begged, "If anyone can hear me, please let me say goodbye to my dad. Please. I just need to say goodbye one last time."

I wasn't sure what I expected. I had no idea how any unseen deity would grant my prayer. I didn't believe I was all that special. Every night for what seemed like weeks I petitioned the silence. Sweetly some nights. Amid gulping sobs on others. Until one night I had what at the time I thought was a dream, but one so real and so different from any dream I'd ever had. Even decades later, I've never again experienced anything like I did that night. I think it was more than a simple dream. It felt as if my consciousness went somewhere.

I found myself on what seemed like a high mountain, but it wasn't cold. I saw green all around me, up the mountain and in the valleys. The light was brilliant, but I saw no light source. It was as if the light emanated from the grass and trees and flowers that surrounded me. I twirled around to see what I could about this magical place. When I came back to center, Dad stood directly in front of me. My wonderful father stood before me looking healthy. That gray-looking skin color, gone. The pain behind his eyes, gone. He was happy, smiling and well.

After launching myself into his arms, I wept on his shoulder. I clung to him, begging him to come back.

"Daddy I need you so much. I can't live without you. Please come home."

He peeled my arms from around his neck and stood me on the grass in front of him. He bent down so we were eye-to-eye and he smiled at me with deep love and care.

"Emmy, I can't come back. You know that. I just came to say goodbye."

I kept crying and through my sobs I told him I couldn't live without him. But he assured me I could. "You will be fine. Life will work out for you," he said, standing. "But I need to go now. I just came to say goodbye."

He wiped my tears and gave me one more hug. And in that hug, I found the peace I'd been seeking.

When I woke, I found my pillow wet with tears. After my heartbeat slowed, I realized I felt lighter. Just a bit, but enough for me to believe I really had said goodbye. Something shifted in me that night. I could see my way to living without my father, even though I didn't want to.

Decades since that "dream," I can still remember it in fine detail. It's never left me. It's a gift from somewhere I can't yet comprehend. But I will one day when I greet my father once again.

—Emily Allen—

What I Saw of Heaven

It's time to say goodbye, but I think goodbyes are sad, and I'd much rather say hello. Hello to a new adventure.
~Ernie Harwell

I call out to Kay in the next office, "Kay, I'm going home for an early lunch. I need to call Joyce, so I can visit with Norman after noon at the nursing home."

Kay replies, "Okay. I'm leaving at 12:00. I will see you at 8:00 in the morning."

I get in my car that is parked by the church office and fellowship hall. As I drive a few blocks to the parsonage, I realize that I have a bowl of chicken noodle soup waiting for me.

After lunch I get ready to leave for the nursing home. I start thinking about the past two years that I've been visiting with Norman and Joyce. For most of the two years, Norman was at home in a wheelchair with Parkinson's. He has been suffering with it for years. He's built big but not overweight. I would guess that his height is six feet or more. He's ninety now, and I have always been impressed with how sharp he is.

At his home he told me he fought in the Battle of the Bulge during World War II. He said he got frostbite during the heavy encounter with the German troops fighting their last offensive battle. They fought for over a month from December 1945 to January 1946, in the dense forests between Belgium and Luxembourg.

As I pull in front of the nursing home, I'm guessing that Norman has been here for three months. It's sad to see his strength waning.

I walk up to them in the dining room and say, "I never get tired of admiring this good-looking couple."

They both smile. Norman has a sparkle in his eyes, and Joyce says, "Good to see you, Pastor Bill." I ask them how they're doing.

Joyce says, "We're both doing well." (Norman has had difficulty speaking since he came to the nursing home.)

I ask, "Do both of you want to listen to a Bible reading today?"

Norman nods his head and Joyce says, "Yes. We're almost done here. Let's go to Norman's room and have the reading there. We'll be all set in about five minutes."

Norman is able to drive the electric wheelchair to his room. As Joyce helps him get situated, Norman is able to control the wheelchair to the right height, forward and backward, and almost any position he wants.

I sit down with my Bible and say, "We usually don't think about a romantic story in the Bible. I want to read some passages from Genesis about Isaac and Rebekah."

I read about how Abraham sent his servant to the town of Nahor to get a bride for his son Isaac. After the servant met Rebekah, he stayed with Rebekah's family and was allowed to escort Rebekah to her prospective groom. Isaac went out to the field one evening and saw camels coming.

Rebekah looked up and saw Isaac. I look up at Norman and Joyce and say, "They lived happily ever after!"

Joyce says, "That is a romantic story! You're right; I haven't thought about the Bible in relation to romantic stories."

We talk about several things, even about the different songbirds that come to Norman's feeder outside his window. I remark, "I love songbirds and birdwatching."

When we finish visiting, Joyce asks me to pray. After praying, I get up and shake Norman's hand, and he smiles and still has that sparkle in his eyes. I say goodbye and tell them I always look forward to visiting.

Before dusk that evening, Joyce calls me and says, "Pastor, I'm with Norman at the hospital in the ER."

I reply, "I'll be right there." It's a fifteen-minute drive and when I walk into the ER, the receptionist directs me to Norman's room. I wait while the nurse checks him. His legs shake at times. The nurse is still working with him when Joyce motions to me to go outside the room.

After we walk into the hall, Joyce says, "The person on duty at the nursing home guessed that he pressed the wrong control on his chair, or he held the forward control too long. It probably pushed him out of his chair."

After I pray at Norman's bedside, I'm told that they are taking Norman to a hospital in Indianapolis. When I go out, it's almost dark. I ask Joyce if I can follow the ambulance.

She says, "We'll be alright, pastor. You go home. I will call you later."

At home, I fix some decaf coffee, and get my notes ready for the next day. I'm in bed just after 9 P.M. I fall asleep while I'm praying for Norman.

I'm sound asleep, when suddenly, I see myself at a beautiful country estate. It's a very pleasant day. People are visiting and laughing on a huge lawn. There are long tables covered with cloth and food and drinks. I'm standing near the edge of a big porch that is in front of a large, elegant home. In front of me and to my right are a set of eight or nine very wide gray steps. About fifteen feet from me and about halfway down the steps is a big, attractive man who appears to be in his late thirties. When I see his profile, I realize it's Norman!

It seems like the dream ends after I recognize Norman. I get up and start getting ready for work. Shortly after, I get a call from Joyce. She is very somber and says, "Pastor Bill, Norman passed away."

I know in my heart that God was telling me that everything is okay, because I saw Norman in heaven.

—William Clark—

A Message from the Deep

You may be gone from my sight, but you will
never be gone from my heart.
~Henry van Dyke, Jr.

When I was a junior in high school, I was stunned by the beauty of a new girl named Joyce. She was striking, with long, thick blond hair and an open face. I memorized her schedule and when possible I would station myself in the high school corridors and gaze at her with longing as she passed by. This went on for months until I found out that she was quite religious, attending the after-hours Christian meetings on campus.

I joined the group and finally initiated some clumsy conversation. More conversations ensued. For me, it was almost a miracle to look at her, much less speak, yet we exchanged ideas and laughter, and I felt the warmth of her growing friendship.

Our first "date" was biking to a nearby park to play Frisbee. A revelation: Joyce's willowy limbs belied her sinewy strength—she could fling a Frisbee a marvelous distance, and would madly dash, long legs wheeling to catch one in extended flight. Better yet, she would laugh with mad abandon at the disc's carry, whether she'd thrown it or caught it. She was splendidly uninhibited and natural, a sweet soul. I was in love.

I knew her first as a beautiful athlete, then discovered that she was a fine photographer, a lover of literature, a friend to animals, and an early environmentalist. My love deepened; she constantly amazed me with her fresh outlook, her unselfconscious grace, her humor. We were together for almost two years before I betrayed her with an earlier girlfriend. When I confessed, she was shocked and said, "I don't know you." I had fallen so far, for a cheap act that baffled her in its incongruity. She took me back, but there was distance between us.

Still tenuously together, we went to different colleges, separated by several hundred miles. We wrote and saw each other on long weekends, but when I got the inevitable "Dear Tom" letter, I wasn't that surprised. I remember a line from the letter: She said she had felt for the longest time that I was merely "floating on the surface," a sham of sorts, a person without depth. The acuity of that remark pierced me like an arrow.

We still saw each other occasionally over the ensuing years, uncomfortable friends, me with an unyielding longing, her somewhat removed. She had a college boyfriend for a couple of years. Later, she took up with an adventurer, a fellow photographer, with whom she deeply connected. They lived together for a bit, and then decided to go on a photographic venture down an obscure river in Colombia. They disappeared, and were never found despite repeated visits there by both sets of parents.

I was living in Seattle when a mutual friend sent me a newspaper article about her disappearance. The friend was someone I would eagerly grill when I saw her: "How's Joyce? Is she still with that guy? Does she seem happy?" Though I'd been in a few relationships since our breakup, Joyce was still the woman I loved. Reflecting on the course of our relationship had never felt like an ignorant obsession with me; I felt her to be my soulmate, and that I'd asininely squandered something precious.

More time passed, but memories of Joyce stayed. I still thought of her frequently, longingly. It seemed clear that she wouldn't be found — she was gone. And I never had the chance to tell her I still loved her.

But one night, after a day when I hadn't even thought about her, I had a dream. It was a dream unlike any I'd ever had: shockingly real in every tactile sense of sight, sound, and touch. I was underwater, and those waters were gently moving. Maybe a lake, or a river? The water was crystal clear. I looked ahead of me, and there she was: Joyce, her long, blond hair moving with the current.

She was looking at me, and she raised her hand in greeting. Then she pointed to the water around her. "This is what happened. We both drowned in the river." But I didn't exactly hear the words; I felt them in my mind. Joyce was communicating directly to my heart. It was both terrifying and exhilarating. She told me that it was fine, that it was over, that things were okay.

We faced each other in the water, calmly, affectionately. I told her in the same way that she communicated with me that I missed her, and that I loved her. She smiled and nodded the same to me. And then I woke up — and that was as startling as waking up in the river.

I had a profound sense that indeed she had drowned in the river. That she knew how I cherished her, and that she wanted to tell me what happened, to give me a final goodbye, and to wish me well. I am not much given to otherworldly incidents, or belief in ghosts or even an afterlife, but I believe that message came from Joyce, from her sweet soul.

— Tom Bentley —

Midnight Rider

God pours life into death and death into life
without a drop being spilled.
~Author Unknown

On weekend nights I drive the safe-ride shuttle at a liberal arts college in Maine—taking students to different places off-campus in the first half of the shift, cross-campus in the later hours.

At 1 A.M. one Saturday night, a student climbed into the van asking to go to her residence hall.

After less than a minute the student, a girl from India, asked: "How is your mother?"

I gave her a quick glance, then asked how she knew my mother.

"My freshman year, I volunteered at the D'Youville Home and knew her, and I often saw you visiting there. How is she doing?"

I couldn't remember ever seeing her, but politely replied, "Anita passed away two years ago."

"Oh, I'm sorry to hear that."

"She had a wonderful life... she was ninety-eight," I added.

But her next question surprised me: "How did you feel afterwards?"

Taken aback by her directness, still I heard myself say, "It was hard at first, I'll admit that. But on Thanksgiving morning, a month to the day after she made her transition, I had an incredible dream, involving her and my dad, and it took away the sadness."

"What was the dream?"

"In the dream I was driving a British Mini Cooper inside a series of connected warehouses. They had elegant wood beams and tall wide-plank walls. My elderly father was in the seat beside me. He had been confined to a wheelchair in the last years of his life and had predeceased my mother by twenty years.

"We traveled through the linked warehouses until we came to a stop before a wall with two tall oak doors. I got out of the car, pulled a wheelchair from its trunk, and got my dad into the chair to wheel him toward the doors.

"As we neared them they quietly opened, and two men who knew my dad stepped forward. One said, 'Ed, you have to come downstairs, and see our new workspace,' and they pointed to stairs leading to a large room whose function I couldn't make out from where I was.

"At this invitation, my dad, for the first time in many months, got up without assistance and began going down the stairs, which had elegant handrails I couldn't imagine belonged to any 'workspace.' I immediately rushed up behind him to offer any support he might need.

"But as he descended each step, he became younger and younger until he was in his early thirties, with an erect posture and the handsome appearance I recalled.

"From there we looked out over the scene: a magnificent ballroom, with an extensive buffet at one end, and an elegant bar at the other, with people chatting at tables filling the room.

"To the right of this landing was a table with friends of my dad who had predeceased him, all of them known to me and all now returned to their more youthful thirty-something appearance.

"Then, comically, instead of taking the last few steps to the floor my dad leaped over the handrail and landed in a chair at their table. No one seemed surprised, as if it was expected.

"And it was then, still smiling, that I looked out and saw my mother, now in her early thirties again, with her long hair pulled up as I'd often seen it as a child. She was wearing a white gown and going from table to table, giggling—inquiring what people were eating, and were they having a good time—and it was then I awoke.

"It was also at that moment the burden of her passing lifted for me instantly. It has never returned, because I knew with certainty that my parents are in a better place now where old age, illnesses, and infirmities do not exist for anyone.

"It's something I know with every particle of my belief, every essence of my being," I said to the student.

Then without hesitation she asked another surprising question, "Was it a dream that happened during the day, or at night?"

"It was night," I answered.

"In the Hindu Faith," she said, "night dreams like that are messages from God." She stepped out of the van and, thanking me, walked into the night.

I had never seen that student before, and I never saw her again, and rarely have I had one-time passengers.

—Paul Baribault—

Love Between Namesakes

Goodbyes are only for those who love with their eyes.
Because for those who love with heart and soul
there is no such thing as separation.
~Rumi

"Alice, come to the phone. Your oma in Germany wants to talk to you." I gripped the heavy black receiver in both hands and placed it against my ear. I could hear crackles, and a disembodied voice said, "Hello Alice, I am your oma. My name is Alice too." I pushed the receiver away, too young to understand why this voice said she had my name. I was four years old and didn't know that "oma" meant grandmother in German.

Two years later, my father and I traveled from Canada to Germany to visit my grandmother. When we stepped onto the busy train platform in Augsburg, a slender woman with brown hair and a big smile waved and walked toward us. She kissed my father and spread her arms open to me. Not recognizing she was the voice I had heard on the phone, I hid behind my father's legs. He laughed, embarrassed, and pushed me toward her, "It's your oma, Alice. Hug her." I recall the smell of her soap and the warmth of her embrace.

My father and I stayed at his sister's house. Oma was an executive secretary on the American military base in Augsburg and could only see me on weekends. One Saturday morning, when I walked into my aunt's dining room, Oma was there to greet me. She said, "*Guten morgen*, I brought you something." She gave me a pencil case filled with colored pencils, handed me some paper, and sat me down at a table to draw. When I drew a cow, she sat next to me, placed her arm around my shoulder, and said, "My, you are an artist!" On another day, she gave me a children's book, sat with me, and read it. No one ever encouraged me to draw and admired my artwork or sat and read exclusively to me at home.

Our Name Day (a Catholic celebration) took place during my stay in Germany. The family, my father and me, his sister, her family, and Oma and her second husband gathered around my aunt's wide polished dining room table. I can still hear the chatter and clink of plates and the smell of German dumpling soup, sliced cold cuts, and bread. I can still see Oma smiling at me from across the table. My Name Day gift from Oma was a children's accordion. It was bright red with a row of colored keys. In retrospect, it is evident that she dearly wanted to discover what talents and traits I had inherited from her family.

After that trip, Oma and I corresponded via letters. At first, I could only send her pictures, but as I learned how to write, I wrote her cards for all the holidays we shared, Christmas and Easter, on our Name Day and birthday. In high school, I studied German and started writing my letters in my rudimentary German. She wrote me back in German and insisted that I only write her in German from then on. Our correspondence made me feel I had a special bond with her, but I couldn't prove it.

Dreams are significant in my family. My father, aunt, and other family members have all had dreams that, on occasion, came true. They are called precognitive dreams, prophetic dreams.

In late March 1978, when I was seventeen, I dreamed of attending a funeral in a church. At the end of the center aisle, there was a casket. People were crying, and as I approached the coffin, I woke up. I wondered who had died but put it out of my mind and went to school. Then, after returning home from school, I found my father sitting in the dark in the living room. His face had a sad expression. He said, "Your oma has liver cancer. The doctors say she might have only six months to live."

"Oma has cancer?" I repeated, absorbing his words. It was then that I recalled, "I had a dream last night that I was at a funeral." My father stood up and walked out of the room.

In August, on a Sunday afternoon, while my father spoke to Oma on the phone in the kitchen, I sat in the living room, listening to him. I desperately wanted to see Oma one more time and prayed intensely in my head, "Oma, please ask Dad if I can go to Germany for three weeks." Then, all at once, I heard my father say, "Yes, well, I think Alice could go to Germany for three weeks." I could not believe my ears. I assumed Oma and I must have been thinking the same thing. But days later, she went into the hospital, and my hopes to visit her disappeared.

On a Monday night in November, as my father drove me home from a doctor's appointment, he asked me, "Would you like to fly to Germany with me on Thursday?"

"Yes, of course, I would," I said, staring at him in disbelief. That night, I kneeled and prayed at the side of my bed. I visualized Oma lying in a hospital bed and repeated, "Oma, I'm coming to see you. Please, stay alive so that I can see you."

The following day, I went off to school, and at 9:30, my father received a call from my aunt, "Walter, I can't get Mom to relax. She keeps shouting Alice is coming, Alice is coming! Is this true?"

I remember the evening my father and I arrived at the hospital—the steps we had to climb, the pungent smell of sanitizers. On reaching the hallway, Oma was there. She rushed to me in her white hospital robe and wrapped her arms around me. We stood together that way for a while. I knew then it was true. All those feelings of closeness and bonding with her were not my imagination. Oma truly loved me.

The week I spent in Germany passed quickly. She was still alive when I left. What happened afterward has remained with me all my life.

Two days after returning home, I was in bed studying a book with the bright ceiling light above me. I was interrupted at ten by the shadow of a person standing over me, but no one else was in the room. I looked around me, and there was nothing wrong with the lights. I looked at my watch and noted the time. Then, it occurred to me: *Oma's just died, and she's come to say goodbye.* For a moment I felt her love around me again and I prayed for her. An hour later, the telephone rang in the kitchen. I answered and recognized my aunt's voice. She was crying and could not speak. "Oma has died?" I asked her in German.

"Yes, an hour ago."

—Alice G. Waldert—

Delivered from a Devastating Dream

Oh, I have passed a miserable night, so full of ugly sights, of ghastly dreams, that, as I am a Christian faithful man, I would not spend another such a night...
~William Shakespeare, Richard III

A devastating dream shocked me awake in late 1969 in Da Nang, South Vietnam during the Vietnam War. I was a U.S. Army captain and a medical evacuation helicopter pilot, in addition to being unit operations officer and, later, commander of the 236th Medical Detachment (Helicopter Ambulance) located at Red Beach on the southern shore of Da Nang Harbor.

In this dream, my four-man flight crew had received a mission to evacuate wounded Americans from an enemy minefield. As I landed next to our patients, one of our UH-1H ("Huey") skids came in contact with an undetected mine. Our aircraft was blown up in a violent and fiery explosion, along with those patients on the ground. That's when I sat straight up, still trembling in my bunk.

Perhaps my mind created this nightmare because of what had occurred previously to a fellow medevac pilot, flight school classmate, and friend who was stationed near Saigon to the south. He was copilot on a mission when his aircraft commander unknowingly landed on a similar mine. One crewmember was killed, one of the aircraft commander's legs was blown off, and the blast separated their cockpit from the cargo compartment. Incredibly, my friend had not been injured, but his traumatic story still replayed in my mind for weeks.

Starting in July 1969, for an entire year, the war became very deadly and dangerous for us. Our air ambulance loss rate was 3.3 times that of all other forms of helicopter flight. A third of our aviators, crew chiefs, and medics became casualties. We were always front-row-center for the action.

Medevac flying demanded a rapid response, and enroute care could mean the difference between life and death for wounded soldiers and civilians. Our crews encountered enemy fire and other dangerous situations so often in our *unarmed* aircraft, each mission was like knowing you're about to be mugged as you walk down an unlit side street in a rough neighborhood, but you don't exactly know when or how bad.

This was especially true of a mission in early January 1970 southwest of Landing Zone Hawk Hill, thirty-two miles south of Da Nang, where a battalion aid station was located. Flight crews from our unit used it as a field site to cover our 5,000-square-mile operational area.

After hundreds of missions, that long white mission sheet our aid station radio-telephone operator (RTO) would hand an aircraft commander had the capability of creating serious trepidation. This was especially true if it indicated "insecure landing zone," "ground troops surrounded and in heavy contact," or anything involving a "minefield and booby traps."

That's how it made me feel when I was handed a mission sheet a number of months after my friend's mine incident, that read "Infantry platoon walked into an enemy minefield. Seven urgent U.S. WIA [wounded in action]." We quickly scrambled. That's when a gut feeling, a sixth sense, alerted me that this would be no routine mission. There wasn't a choice, though. Seven Americans weren't going to make it without us. It was our responsibility and we had to go. There was nothing else to do but pray.

Enroute to the eight-digit ground coordinate approximately six miles away, I made initial contact with the infantry unit on our FM radio.

"We've got seven people who need evacuation right now!" their RTO shouted into our headsets, obviously agitated. "We walked into booby traps and anti-personnel mines."

"Roger. Understand seven wounded," I replied. "We're about a minute out. Have you made a recon of the area where you want us to land to make sure it's clear?"

There was a distinct pause, "Uh... yeah. It's all clear."

I'd flown over 800 missions to that point. This included having seven birds shot up by enemy fire and being shot down twice in eight months. That's when I felt the need to give him my "emergency reality-check speech."

"Okay, Brave Victor One-Four, just remember that if we sit down on a mine, it's going to be a long time before another crew can get out here to help any of us. And I don't like loud noises, so I recommend having that area checked again where you want us to land."

I prayed silently, as I always did before a tactical approach, for our protection and that of those we were called to evacuate.

After being assured for the second time that the *exact* spot where they wanted us to land was clear, I began a rapid descent from 1,500 feet toward the red smoke from a grenade they'd thrown out to mark the spot.

I planted our skids on either side of the billowing smoke that enveloped our aircraft, making it hard to breathe. Our medic and crew chief helped load the seven ravaged bodies, most with their packs still on their backs. Only a minute or so elapsed before I "pulled pitch" and headed back to the Hawk Hill aid station.

About a week later, I was in operations in Da Nang making out the pilot flight roster when an infantry first lieutenant and his driver walked in.

"Sir, does Dust Off 6-0-5 fly out of here?"

"Yeah, that's me," I replied.

He introduced himself as the platoon leader of the seven wounded troopers in that minefield the previous week. After graciously thanking us for evacuating his men, and informing me that all seven had survived, he provided further information.

"The grass was a couple of feet high where you landed," he continued, "and it was hard to visually check. So after you took off, we went over the area again… and discovered the triple prongs of a 'Bouncing Betty' mine sticking out of the ground. Your left skid landed on it and mashed it down," he added. "But it didn't detonate. We laid down some C-4 (plastic explosive) to blow it in place. When it blew, the whole top of the hill came off. I'd estimate there was at least a two-hundred-pound anti-tank mine buried under the 'Bouncing Betty.'"

The Viet Cong had obviously captured American mines and used them against us. We'd landed on top of both mines and still survived. If that lieutenant hadn't taken the initiative to drive nearly thirty miles in an open Jeep over an often-mined road to locate me, I'd never have discovered how I believe God had protected us.

Perhaps my previous devastating dream was a foreshadowing of the possibility of what was to come… a warning of some sort. Or maybe it was God's way of proving to me that His hand was already primed to protect us, even before I'd prayed.

— Robert B. Robeson —

Just as Close

The bond between friends cannot be broken by chance;
no interval of time or space can destroy it.
Not even death itself can part true friends.
~Saint John Cassian

Pam's cancer didn't stop her. She was still there for her family and friends, always available to help anyone at any time. She would offer light when times were dark or offer words of encouragement to keep you strong.

When the doctor told her in the fall that she only had a few weeks left, Pam decided that she had too much to do. She would need a year.

The first goal was to focus on her children. Her daughter was pregnant and she wanted to meet her first granddaughter. She got to hold that baby before she died. The second goal was to watch her son, who was a high school senior, perform in a spring musical competition. He did an outstanding job and Pam was able to sit in the audience and watch him amaze the judges.

Her next goal was to make her own funeral arrangements so her children wouldn't have to. Pam knew I was caring for my mother with Alzheimer's and needed to learn how to make funeral arrangements as well. Together we learned what we needed to do. It was so much easier making decisions together. We were there for each other and when the arrangements were in place, I promised Pam that I would be at the cemetery to watch the sun set on our incredible friendship.

Eleven months after the doctor's diagnosis, Pam was ready to complete her final goal. As a long time, talented artist, she created her final pen and ink drawing, titled "Celebration." Pam wanted her last piece of art to show that life provides many reasons to celebrate. In her drawing, an 1881 Queen Anne home sports window boxes brimming with summer flowers. The front yard contains a lace-topped picnic table set with a vase of sunflowers and plates of sweets and treats. You feel the coming excitement of a grand event as you see the back of a young girl climbing up a chair to hang the last bow on the ribbon-wrapped pole. It is left to the eye of the observer to decide what the celebration might be.

On a bright Friday afternoon, while Pam sat with me in her small kitchen, she told me that she had finished her piece and had met all her goals. God had blessed her with nearly a year to complete her list and she was ready now. She was grateful and felt she had lived an abundant life.

That night, I dreamt of Pam. We were in a car. Pam was sitting in the front seat and I was in the back. We were casually chatting when I suddenly realized that she had her beautiful long dark hair again, her eyes were shining, and her skin was radiant. She was dressed in a sky-blue dress that took my breath away. I knew that it was a dream and I told her that I couldn't imagine life without her. She smiled warmly and said, "We don't do life alone. Don't forget that I will always be with you. I will always be as close to you as I am here in the front seat of the car."

I suddenly woke to the phone ringing. It was Pam's daughter letting me know that she had just passed.

It has been years now, and I still smile every time I look at her "Celebration" drawing in my bedroom. Pam, my personal angel, reminds me to pay attention and to celebrate all things in life. She will always be with me and when I need her, she will always be as close to me as she was in the front seat of that car.

—W. Bond—

Angels Among Us

An Angel on Assignment

Make yourself familiar with the angels and behold them frequently in spirit; for, without being seen, they are present with you.
~Saint Francis de Sales

It was August 30, 1966. I was twenty-two years old and working the Wilshire Division of the Los Angeles Police Department. With only ten months on the job, I was assigned to uniformed patrol and on this day, I had been involved in clean-up activities in areas impacted by the August 1965 Watts Riots.

Tired after a long, hot day, I walked slowly up the short hill from the station to the employee parking lot that was located east of the facility. After opening the car door of my new red Volkswagen Bug, I slid my off-duty gun under the seat and drove out of the parking lot. Because the weather was warm, I drove with both the driver and passenger windows down. I also wasn't wearing a seat belt since they were not standard equipment at the time.

Driving home, I noticed that freeway traffic was heavy, so I decided to change my route and drive down Fulton Avenue which ran past Los Angeles Valley College. After exiting the Ventura Freeway, I traveled north toward the intersection of Fulton and Oxnard streets. Where the two streets bisected, a tri-light signal controlled the traffic.

Proceeding down the slight hill toward the intersection, I watched as the signal for my direction changed to green. As I entered the intersection I glanced to my left and saw a white Cadillac racing toward me. Instantly, I knew that he was going to run the red light and collide with me broadside. I also knew that I was going to die.

I felt a tremendous impact as the Cadillac slammed into the side of my car. The force was beyond description, but with the impact, I felt something else. There was tremendous pressure being exerted on either side of my neck as if large and powerful hands were gripping my shoulders.

I was ripped from the driver's seat and pulled up and over the short gearshift column. I found myself flying in the direction of the open passenger window. Next I felt the large hands under my back and realized that I was in a prone position traveling down a long, dark tunnel at a high rate of speed.

Then the warmth... the incredible all-encompassing warmth. Like electricity, it permeated my entire being and was accompanied by a peacefulness I had never known. I recall thinking that it was much like the feeling experienced just as the anesthesia for an operation became effective, but multiplied a thousand times.

With the warmth came the realization that I was standing directly over my physical body. I lifted my arms, examined my hands, then turned my hands over and saw that my spirit form was identical to my physical body.

I looked at my physical form that was just in front of me and saw that my eyes were closed, my arms were at my side, and I appeared to be sleeping. As I looked just beyond my body, I saw a man who stood quietly with his arms outstretched and his hands under my back. I knew immediately that he was the angel who had pulled me from the car and was now transporting my body down the long black tunnel toward a brilliant light. As we travelled, the light grew in brightness and size.

His body and garment were a glistening white color. He neither smiled nor frowned. It was as if he was on an assignment and his being here was all business. As I looked into his face, which felt very familiar, I felt more an observer than a participant. As we continued down the tunnel, I again looked to my right at the brilliant bright light that seemed to be drawing me toward it.

As we travelled, I suddenly realized I could comprehend and see all that surrounded me. I was totally aware of everything without moving my head in any direction. All 360 degrees around me was open to my view and all at one time. It was as if I was standing in a transparent bowl and there was no front or back, no up or down.

The light drew nearer. The peacefulness increased.

Then the voices.

"He's dead; cover him up," one said.

My mind raced. Don't do anything we'll all regret, I thought.

Then I heard the wailing of a siren.

That must be for me, I thought.

As suddenly as the experience began, it ended. My spirit reentered my body through my head and easily slipped back into place. There was no pain, and no discomfort. I was just suddenly awake, lying on the sidewalk.

I sat up.

The crowd gasped.

The blanket that covered my head and chest slid to the ground.

"I'm a police officer," I whispered. "I need to get my gun out of my car."

I stood and walked to the Volkswagen, which was lying on its side. I climbed onto the passenger side, slipped through the window, found my service revolver and then climbed out, walked to the curb and sat down to await the ambulance.

When the distance I had traveled through the air was measured, it was determined to be 125 feet from the point of impact to where I had been placed on the sidewalk. I had traveled across four lanes of traffic to get there. The Volkswagen was thrown approximately sixty feet and landed at the northwest corner of Oxnard and Fulton Avenues.

I was told that I had been on the sidewalk dead for nearly fifteen minutes before I sat up.

At the hospital the doctor examined and released me, finding no broken bones or internal damage. Physically, I suffered no injuries except for a few minor abrasions on my back, but following the accident, I felt as though I had been in a violent street fight. The windbreaker I wore was not damaged, but my white cotton T-shirt was shredded.

This experience had a tremendous impact on me and I later spent a great deal of time on my knees seeking a better understanding of what had happened and why I was spared.

One night, as I knelt in the dark in prayer pondering the experience, I was permitted to see the accident. I saw the angel pull me out of my seat, across the gearshift column and through the open passenger window, all before the car flipped and careened across the street.

With the passage of time came the realization of the miracle that occurred. I also received a testimony of the fact that someone I recognized had been sent to protect me; a protection that has been my gift throughout my life and one I will never take for granted.

— Richard B. Whitaker —

Riding with an Angel

Angels represent God's personal care
for each one of us.
~Andrew Greeley

About 8:00 in the evening, the phone rang. "Is Paul there?" my mom asked me, referring to my eighty-two-year-old stepdad.

"No," I replied, "I haven't seen or talked to him all day."

"Well, he had a doctor's appointment at one and he's not home yet."

This was a serious concern for both of us. Paul's doctor was less than a mile from their house, so he should have been home long ago. And Paul was starting to show some signs of dementia, although he was still functioning pretty well. He had left his cell phone at the house, so that was no help.

I lived less than ten miles from my parents' house, so I told Mom I'd run over and we'd drive around their small Kansas town, to the coffee shops, relatives' houses and grocery stores. Surely, we'd locate him.

After picking her up, it was going on 9:00 P.M. and we both knew it was far too late for Paul to be out alone. We checked every location we had thought about to no avail. Paul is the sweetest, good ol' boy you'd ever want to meet and can visit to no end, but at this point, all the "visiting places" were closed. With a feeling of panic, we drove to the Augusta Police Department to report a missing senior citizen.

After all of Paul's information was relayed to them, the police officer told us to go back home. They'd keep us updated and he'd surely show up. We went back to their house and two officers showed up, just to look over the house and talk to us some more. I felt like I was in the middle of a police crime drama that I had no desire to be a part of.

One of the officers suggested that we call the local hospitals to see if my stepdad was there. As soon as they left, we started that task. My mom talked to the ER nurse at a small hospital about fifteen miles from their house and gave the nurse a full description of Paul. Silver hair, blue eyes, eighty-two years old, and a diabetic. "No one of that description has been brought here," the nurse informed her. My mom left her phone number.

The night wore on. I tried to rest on the couch but was too fired up to relax. I prayed: "God, please don't let something happen to Paul and to our family again so soon."

We had just lost my cousin's thirty-two-year-old son Derrick in a car accident. He was a gorgeous, successful young man, who had the world in the palm of his hands, but lost it all that hot, summer night just two months earlier in that tragic accident. He adored his entire family, just as we adored him, and it had been a massive blow.

Paul had been my stepdad since I was eighteen, after losing my father when I was eight. I could not have asked for a better, kinder man to step into those shoes, and we had always been as close as if he were my biological dad. My nickname for him had always been "Brownie." Losing Paul this soon after losing Derrick would be another blow that would be hard to overcome.

Around 7:00 in the morning, a highway patrol car pulled up and two officers got out. My heart sank. The first thing they said when entering was, "Do you have a picture of Paul?" I grabbed my phone and swiped to the latest picture I could find.

"Why?" I asked, fearing they needed it to identify his body.

"Well, it's been long enough now that we are going to put him on the 8:00 A.M. news under a Silver Alert."

That was good news but still, he was missing, so back to the waiting game we went.

Two hours later, we heard another car in the driveway. I looked out and saw one police officer get out. He took his time and was talking to someone on his cell phone, and then on his car radio. He walked up to the porch, I opened the door and looked him in the eye, and he said, "We found him and he's okay." I took three steps backwards and dropped down like a lead balloon on a chair sitting by the door.

"Where?" my mom asked.

The officer said, "Well, it's a rather odd story."

About an hour earlier, the police station had received a call from a lady who said she had just gotten home from work and there was an elderly man sitting in his truck, in her driveway, out in the country. Keep in mind this was another town about twenty miles from their home. She said she went out to him, and he appeared to be groggy and very confused. She asked him "Is your name Paul and are you lost?" He nodded yes and as a nurse, she recognized that he needed some orange juice for his grogginess and low blood sugar.

How did she know all this about him? Amazingly, she was the nurse who my mom had talked to the night before, in the hospital ER. She knew all about Paul and that he had been missing and what she needed to do.

After a few tears of relief, my mom and I rushed to the hospital where Paul was being observed. I walked into the ER, only to see him sitting up in bed and smiling and as happy as could be! He had a snack and the attention of all the nurses around him.

"Brownie!" I said, "Where have you been?"

"Well, I got kinda lost last night and was driving all over town, when suddenly, this good ol' boy that kinda reminded me of Derrick was in the truck with me. He pointed different ways to drive around town and we had a good visit. But I started to get tired, so he pointed me out of town to a house in the middle of the country and told me to park there and I'd be alright. The next thing I knew, a lady was helping me and brought me some juice. It was quite a night!"

Derrick and Paul had always been great friends, and as we discussed the incident over the next few days, we decided that our family angel, Derrick, saw that Paul was in trouble. As friends do, he showed up to lend a helping hand.

— Kathy Thompson —

Through the Eyes of a Child

Unable are the loved to die. For love is immortality.
~Emily Dickinson

When our children were small, my husband Dan and I lived in Tampa, Florida for several years. My mom's brother Bernard and his family lived in Florida also, so when my mom visited from her home in Connecticut, she got to see all of us.

On one of those visits, she brought her older brother Arthur along. We always had a good time when he visited, as Uncle Arthur was a professional magician and he put on shows for us.

One day when we were laughing raucously at Uncle Arthur's tricks, Mom received a phone call. We could tell from the expression on her face that it was something tragic. She hung up the phone and turned to us.

"That was Aunt Eleanor. Uncle Bernard passed away last night," she said, her voice shaky.

I was going to miss Uncle Bernard. He flew a plane in World War II, and really enjoyed the feeling of freedom it gave him. Sometimes we'd be riding along with him when we were going out for ice cream or a snack. Suddenly, he'd swerve and we would grin, knowing he was looking at some type of aircraft flying overhead.

He also had a wonderful sense of humor. This is best described by the inscription he requested on his tombstone when his time came: "What a revolting development this is!"

Seeing tears on my mother's face snapped me out of my memories.

I went to her and put my arm around her shoulder. "At least you're nearby so you can attend his funeral," I told her. "I know he'd have wanted you to be there, and Uncle Arthur, too."

So, we quickly made reservations for a rental car to take Mom and Uncle Arthur to Uncle Bernard's, to help with the funeral arrangements in Jacksonville, and spend a couple of days with Bernard's family.

I didn't want to miss the funeral, so I decided I'd drive up that day, but one problem cropped up. Our older kids were in school all day and they would get home around the time Dan returned from work. But our youngest, Helen, was in nursery school and there was no way I could drive from our home near Tampa to Jacksonville and be back in time to pick her up after the half-day morning session. And all our regular babysitters were in school themselves, so we were stuck. I had to bring Helen with me.

I was a bit uneasy about bringing Helen to a funeral at her tender age. She didn't remember Bernard from the one time she saw him as an infant. So, for Helen, it was just a fun trip with Mommy. We sang songs, played the alphabet game, and listened to the radio.

We arrived in Jacksonville and expressed our sympathy to the family, then headed to the church. After a moving service, everyone began to file out. We had been in a special room for family members, and because I couldn't see where the line was heading from our vantage point, it was only then I realized that everyone was filing right past my uncle's open casket. I was concerned it might frighten Helen to see him, so I snatched her up and carried her past the casket as quickly as I could.

There was a reception afterward back at my uncle's home, and we stayed for a while. But it became obvious the meal wouldn't be served any time soon, and since we had a long drive ahead of us, we left and headed for home.

That drive was memorable because I had a full tank of gas, but I hadn't counted on paying for supper—I only had a few dollars in cash. So, we went to McDonald's and got one drink, one small French fries, and a four-piece Chicken McNuggets that we split. If you ask Helen today about the most memorable part of the trip, it would be that tiny meal we shared.

Luckily, Helen hadn't been scared at the funeral. In fact, she said she especially liked the man who smiled at her. Since I knew very few of the attendees, I just said, "That's nice," and changed the subject. Before long, she was asleep and the rest of the drive home was uneventful.

Some years later, the topic of Uncle Bernard's funeral came up. "Do you remember you told me there was a man at Uncle Bernard's funeral who smiled at you when we were lined up to exit the church?" I asked her.

She said, "Yes, Mom. It was the man standing behind the coffin."

I was puzzled. "I'm pretty sure there was no one standing there," I said.

"Yes, there was," Helen insisted as she scrunched up her eyes, trying to recall. "He was standing there quietly, watching people as they walked past him. He nodded at some people and he smiled at me. But he didn't talk to anyone so I thought maybe he worked at the church."

I shook my head. "You must be confused, honey."

"No, Mom. I DO remember. There was a light all around him," she said at last. "He had a glow. He was shiny."

Still curious about this little mystery, I described my uncle to her, what he looked like and what he was wearing. Then I got out our family picture albums that showed pictures of my mother's family — brothers, sisters, aunts, uncles, and cousins.

As we flipped the pages in the album, Helen said suddenly, "That's him! That's the man who was standing behind the coffin. I'm sure of it."

I gasped. It was Uncle Bernard.

I realized at last it must have been him saying goodbye to his friends and family.

We'll never forget our kind, amusing uncle who wanted to see his beloved friends, family and loved ones one more time. If anyone loved his family as much as Uncle Bernard did, it was certainly believable he'd take the opportunity to say goodbye to them all. And it took the innocence of a child to see that, to see him.

— Elizabeth Delisi —

Emergency Dispatch

All God's angels come to us disguised.
~James Russell Lowell

One summer's evening, I was returning home very late from work by way of a commuter train. To get from the train station to my house, I had to walk through a lovely park that had several footpaths which wound under a lush canopy of trees and hanging vines. The sweet fragrance of honeysuckle clung to the humid air.

My only distraction from fully enjoying my walk was having to pay attention to my footsteps, because the footpath was unpaved and poorly lit. I was in full business attire—complete with high heels, a skirt, a briefcase, and a pocketbook—all of which restricted my ability to walk at a fast clip. Still, I relaxed into the lovely environs and embarked on my mini trek home.

Suddenly, from behind, I heard bushes rustling and a stranger's voice angrily calling out to me. "Hey, come here!" I froze, unable to move a single muscle or make a single sound. I silently prayed, "Oh, God, help me." Then, a surge of adrenaline kicked in and I ran away as fast as my high heels would permit.

From the darkness behind me, I heard the man angrily yell again, "Hey, get over here!" Fear propelled me forward, and as I rounded a turn, I saw my house in the distance, across the road that ran alongside the park. But my panic only escalated as I realized it was too far away for me to get there in time.

At that moment, a white car that I'd never seen before suddenly screeched into the driveway of my house. A large man popped out of the car and spun around in my direction. I tried to yell for help but nothing came out, plus I knew despairingly that it was impossible for him to see or hear me anyway.

I heard the man behind me shift to a fast trot, rapidly closing the gap between us — he was going to catch up to me. But then suddenly the large man bolted across the street, running fast and hard in my direction. I desperately wanted to yell out to him, but I was still too panicked to cry out for help. He ran directly toward me with his arms wide open and swept me into in a bear hug, swinging my body away from the danger behind me. Having firmly established his large body as a safety barrier between me and harm, he then said loudly, "Honey, I'm so glad to see you! You're running so late from work, I was getting worried!"

This complete stranger was pretending to be my husband! Instantly, I heard the menacing footsteps from behind suddenly stop, then take off running away from us in the opposite direction. Only then did he release me from his hug and in the darkness I heard his kind voice say, "Let's get you home now."

I don't remember walking the rest of the way out of the park and crossing the road to my house — seemingly, we were both transported to my front door. Still riddled with anxiety from my ordeal, I tried to insert my house key into the door lock but could not do so because my hands were shaking so badly. Without a word, he gently cupped my shaking hand with both of his to steady my grip and guide the key into the lock.

Still shaking, I fumbled through my pocketbook looking for some cash, mumbling through my tears that I wanted to pay him for his immense kindness in saving my life. He gently responded, "Oh, I don't want your money, I just want to make sure you get home safely." For the first time I looked up at the large man and was greeted with a handsome face and a warm smile. I thanked him profusely and he patiently waited until I stepped inside my house and locked the door behind me.

As I watched him back out of my driveway and pull away, I realized that I had just had an encounter with an angel. I had never seen him or his car before or since, despite my searching for him every day thereafter. How did a complete stranger know where I lived, then screech into my driveway, no less? How could he have known I was in the park—and in grave, imminent danger? It was impossible for him to see me as he was driving down the road, given the significant distance and the thick canopy of foliage that enshrouded the dark, winding footpath I was on. He certainly didn't hear me, as I was unable to cry out for help. It was dark and the park was large—of all the available footpaths winding through the park, how did he know to run to the exact one I was on?

I am convinced to this day that the moment I prayed, this angel was dispatched to save my life. Why? Perhaps for no other reason than that someday I would put pen to paper and record my experience for others, so they can experience the same comfort and faith that I now have—knowing that prayers are answered, and we're never really alone.

—Pamela Dunaj—

My Personal Angel

Alone is impossible in a world inhabited by angels.
~Author Unknown

When I was pregnant with my first child in April 1985, my mother had a strange accident. To this day, we don't know what happened exactly, but she was painting the trim on our house when she fell and hit the back of her head. My father, who was also painting at the time, heard the clink of the paint can hit the cement. Upon calling out to my mother and not getting an answer, he walked around the house to investigate. Mom lay unconscious in the driveway. The neighbor called an ambulance, and it took my mother to our local hospital, where the ER staff stabilized her.

Still unconscious, she was flown by medical helicopter to a Pittsburgh area hospital, where she underwent surgery for a subdural hematoma. Our long wait began, and so did our prayers. Her surgeon told us only five percent of patients make it through the complex procedure.

Being a very strong woman, Mom survived the surgery and then was put in a medically induced coma. Her brain needed time to heal, and we hoped she would wake up after that. The doctors told us they didn't know what to expect.

I gave birth to a healthy baby girl that June and couldn't wait for Mom to see her. When she was two weeks old, I took my daughter to see her grandmother in the hospital. I was convinced that my mother would wake up once I placed the baby in her arms, but that didn't happen.

Mom was the glue that held our family together. We never gave up, hoping she would wake up from the coma and return to us. We spent many long days by her bedside praying and talking to her, trying to coax her to come back to us.

She never came out of the coma and passed away right after Christmas in 1989. By that time, I had two children whose only memory of their grandma was a pretty lady asleep in a bed whose hair they combed when we visited her in the nursing home.

In 1991, I became pregnant with my third child. The baby was due in late July, and I was miserable due to the summer heat. In early July, my doctor told me that the baby could come at any time. I was ready; however, the baby was stubborn and waited until July 29th to make his appearance.

Once my labor started, my husband took our two children to his parents' house a mile from ours. They would stay with Grammy and Pappy for a few days while I gave birth and got their new baby brother settled in at home.

When I got to the hospital, I was admitted and brought to a pleasant room. Soon after getting settled in and in between contractions, a nurse came in and asked if I would mind having a student nurse as part of my care team. I readily agreed, and the nurse left my room. About ten minutes later, she returned with a young girl dressed in a nurse's white uniform and introduced the girl to my husband and me. I don't remember her name, but I will call her Susan for the story.

The first thing I noticed about Susan was her eyes, which were brown with big golden flecks. They were my mother's eyes. Then Susan's hand touched my arm while I was having a difficult contraction and her touch was magic. The pain of the contraction fell away, and all I could think about was that my mother was with me. After that contraction, she left the room.

I turned to my husband and asked him if the student nurse reminded him of anyone. His answer stunned me because he said the girl reminded him of my mother. Every time Susan came into my room during the hours I was in labor, I felt an instant sense of serenity and peace. She always knew what to say, and whenever she touched my arm, the labor pains subsided.

I had asked to have an epidural, and soon it was time for the anesthesiologist to come and give it to me. When he came in with another nurse, they tried for a long time to insert the epidural but, for some reason, they couldn't. Another nurse came into the room and examined me, saying I was too late for an epidural because the baby's head was crowning.

The nurses moved my bed to a delivery room, and I quickly found myself pushing. The student nurse's calming words filled my mind even though she was not in the delivery room. Finally, the baby was born, a healthy little boy, and I was tired.

The next thing I remember is waking up in the recovery room. The nurses were kind and said I would be reunited with my husband and newborn son soon.

I asked to speak to Susan, the student nurse who had been with me during my hours in labor. They looked at me and at one another quizzically and told me I must have had a dream. I just shook my head and stated that I had a student nurse named Susan, who was very sweet and kind to me during my labor. I told them she reminded me of my mother, and I wanted to see her and thank her.

The head nurse came over to my bed and explained that I had to be mistaken. She said student nurses were not assigned to the labor and delivery floor of the hospital. At that point, I was so emotional I cried.

When I was finally taken back to my room, the first thing I did was ask my husband if I did have a student nurse caring for me during my labor. His emphatic yes was all I needed to hear. I knew that my mother, who had passed away two years before, had found a way to be with me during the birth of my third child.

When I think back to that day, I realize that Susan was always alone when she came into the room, and she never checked my vitals or hospital chart. She just stood by my bedside and comforted me. The other nurses came in to check my vital signs and the progression of my labor.

To this day, I can still close my eyes and remember the touch of her hand upon my arm and the peace and love she gave to me the day my youngest child was born.

My mother was with me as an angel in the form of a nurse. How appropriate, as it was the vocation she had always wanted me to choose.

—Joan D. McGlone—

An Angel in Uniform

The golden moments in the stream of life rush past us, and we see nothing but sand; the angels come to visit us, and we only know them when they are gone.
~George Eliot

I had said a prayer before going to bed, the same guardian angel prayer that I'd said since I was a child. When I finished, I had a strong feeling that someone I loved needed help but that somehow it would be alright. I looked at the clock. It was 11:00.

I awoke at 2:00 A.M. when my daughter Patricia called for me. She had just come in. "Mom. Mom," she called and I heard the anguish in her voice.

I jumped out of bed as she came in. "What's the matter?" I asked, wrapping my arms around her.

"I thought I was going to die," she said. I examined her.

"Was there a car accident? Are you hurt?"

"No."

"What happened?"

"The store was empty except for Theresa behind the deli counter and me at the register," she said. "A man wearing jeans and a gray hoodie came in. He seemed nervous. I watched him. He stood in front of the newspaper rack, picked up papers, and put them back without looking at them. He walked down the candy aisle and stared straight ahead. The untied laces of one of his sneakers dragged on the floor. He grabbed a package of chips and turned toward me. That's when I saw the handle of a gun tucked into the waistband of his pants."

I gasped and hugged her.

"I looked at Theresa," she said. "She'd seen it too and got down on the floor behind the display case. He thought we were alone."

"Don't you have an emergency call button under the counter?"

"Yes, but I froze."

We sat on the bed. I put my arm around her and wiped away a tear that trailed down her cheek.

"Go on," I said.

"He walked up to me, threw the chips on the counter, and put his hand on the gun."

I gasped. "You'll need to quit that job. It's dangerous for a young woman to work the night shift."

"Mom, I'm twenty-two. The job helps me pay for college."

I wanted to help. "Let me brew us some tea," I offered.

"No, Mom. I can't drink anything now."

We sat in weighted silence. I sandwiched her cold, damp hands in mine. After a while, I held her and rocked back and forth like I'd done when she was seven and awakened by a nightmare. After a few minutes, she continued.

"I can still see his eyes. They were filled with contempt. He hated me. I knew he could shoot me. I believed he would shoot me."

Tears ran down her cheeks. I rubbed her back. She dried her face on my shoulder.

"His eyes drilled into me. I couldn't move." She inhaled a jagged breath.

"You're home. You're safe," I said. "What happened next?"

"He didn't say anything. He opened his mouth like he was going to say something. Then the bell on the front door jangled. A policeman came in. I didn't recognize him. We give complimentary coffee to uniformed officers. I know most of them, but I didn't know him."

I exhaled a breath I didn't realize I was holding. "Thank God. What did you do?"

"It happened so fast. The officer walked up to me. He was so calm. He had the kindest blue eyes I'd ever seen. He had wavy black hair. I knew he was there to help. It even felt like he knew what was happening."

"What did you do? What did you say?"

"Nothing. I think I was still in shock. The man looked at him, pulled his jacket over the gun, and ran out of the store. A radio on the policeman's belt went off. He pushed a button, smiled at me, nodded, and walked to the door.

"Theresa jumped up and said we should stop the police officer and tell him what happened. So I ran to the door but no one was there. Theresa and I saw the taillights of the robber's car as he pulled onto the road but there was no officer. There was no police car."

I hugged her as she continued. "You know the store is set back from the road. It's a big parking lot. My car and Theresa's were the only ones there. Rob, who works the next shift, pulled into the lot. He didn't see a police car either."

"How could that be?" I asked.

"I don't know, Mom. We called the police. I've been filling out reports for the last two hours. The officers said no one from their precinct was at our store and none of their officers matched the description of the one we saw. They checked neighboring departments and came up with nothing. It's like he doesn't exist."

"The main thing is that you're safe. Do you think you can sleep?"

"I doubt it. Can we sit here for a while?"

"As long as you want," I said.

"You know, Mom, I almost missed the whole thing. It had just turned 11:00 so my shift was over."

—Judy Salcewicz—

The Midnight Piano

Music is well said to be the speech of angels.
~Thomas Carlyle

If you've ever moved from a small city to a mega-city, you'll understand the words "culture shock." My first seventeen years were spent in the warm embrace of a friendly, coastal city. It's the kind of place where you need to wear make-up when you leave the house, because you're guaranteed to run into someone you know. Family celebrations involved friends so close we called their parents "aunt" and "uncle." My passion was music, and my growing talents flourished in a supportive collective of choirs and bands.

I thought I'd spend my whole life in that close, loving community.

But my dad was amazing at his job. One winter, the headhunters came calling. He and Mom considered all the options and made the decision. We were moving to Toronto.

Toronto isn't Canada's capital city, but it's the largest and, arguably, the most influential. At that time, the population was 3.8 million—literally thirty-six times bigger than my hometown! I had no idea how I could possibly fit in to such a place.

For the first time in my life, I was lonely. I was surrounded by millions of people, and yet I felt completely alone.

The only saving grace was our new house. The stately gray home was well over 100 years old and steeped in history. It had warm hardwood floors, soaring ceilings, and detailed crown molding, thick with a century of paint. It was the first time I'd lived in a Victorian home, and I quickly fell in love.

But as summer turned to fall, my homesickness only increased. After graduating from high school that June, I'd decided to take a "gap" year to work before entering university. As everyone my age started the fall semester, I was left on my own.

Without classes to attend, I found myself staying up later and later. As my parents slept upstairs, I would sit alone in the darkened living room, watching TV, listening to music, and wondering what everyone was doing back home.

Then, one night, I heard something unexpected. I heard the piano playing.

The piano was in the dining room, down the hall from the living room. I thought I must have been hearing things.

But there were no other possible sources of sound. Our suburban neighborhood was tucked in for the night. Mom and Dad were upstairs asleep. The TV and the stereo were both off, and this was before the days of music players on everyone's cell phones.

It made no sense. There was no way I could be hearing music.

But then I heard it again—classical piano music. It was soft, but it wasn't coming from a distance. It was too clear.

It had to be our piano.

I held my breath and listened. After a minute, it stopped.

I couldn't believe what I'd heard and yet I knew exactly what I'd heard.

Something, or someone, had chosen to play the piano—for me.

There was no doubt in my mind that I was the intended audience. There was such gentleness in the music, and in the playing. For the first time in months, I felt a sense of peace wash over me.

I didn't tell anyone about the late-night serenade. After all, Mom and Dad were going through their own transition with the move. The last thing they needed was their teenage daughter proclaiming their new home was haunted.

As the weeks went by, I continued to struggle. No matter what I tried, I felt heartsick for the people and dreams I'd left behind.

But on nights when I felt particularly low, the piano music would come. Not every night — just on the nights when I needed it most. Not for very long — just long enough to calm my breathing and still my soul. It no longer shocked or surprised me to hear the piano playing in the dining room, because I knew it was playing for me.

As the winter melted into spring, things started to take a turn. I found a great job teaching music to young children. I learned how to take the subway and explore the city's vibrant multicultural neighborhoods. I joined a choir, where I sang challenging choral works and built easy friendships. I was finally starting to find my place.

And then one night, sitting alone in the living room, I realized that I didn't hear the piano. In fact, I hadn't heard it for over a month.

And I never heard it again.

Over the ensuing years, that piano became the centre-point of many beautiful memories. My best friend and I spent hours sitting side-by-side on the piano bench, singing together in harmony. Our family dog would jump up on a dining room chair to "listen" to my vocal exercises. My boyfriend-who-eventually-became-my-husband and I practiced a love duet over those keys. And every family party for years ended with a rousing sing-along of gospel songs, led by our choir director, with everyone belting out parts and laughing when they forgot the lines.

But that first year, when I felt so lost, someone knew I needed a home, and they knew the best way to welcome me was with a song on the midnight piano….

— Allison Lynn —

Angel in My Pocket

I guess I have never really doubted that
we are all born to our guardian angel.
~Robert Brault

Each time I visit my daughter in Rochester, New York I make it a point to shop in a charming gift boutique about a half-hour from her house. As a cancer survivor, my way of paying it forward is giving one-inch-tall pewter angels to friends and acquaintances. These are easily tucked into a pocket for comfort and encouragement during doctor's visits, chemo treatments, and hospital stays.

On this trip, I was thrilled to discover a new collection of "pocket angels." Some were colorful enameled figures etched with encouraging words, others had beautiful copper wings. Each came with a tiny card imprinted with a lovely prayer. I purchased a variety of tiny figurines.

I had spent more time than usual browsing and was surprised to see heavy snow falling outside the shop window. The weatherman hadn't predicted any storms so I had left the house under clear skies without a hat, scarf, gloves, or boots. In addition, I was driving my husband's truck, which I found difficult to handle under even normal circumstances.

For the trip back to my daughter's house, I decided to avoid the crazy traffic on the main roads and expressways. I chose the shortest route, a country road. I'm no stranger to driving in bad weather, having grown up in Buffalo, but I was a little out of practice since moving to North Carolina several years earlier. Hence, I forgot what a dangerous combination open fields and blowing snow could be.

Soon the wind gusts began whipping the fallen snow across the surface of that country road, causing white-out conditions. Creeping along, I regretted my choice of routes. I had zero visibility. Despite having the defroster on full blast, the windshield wipers were freezing over. My nerves were raw navigating my husband's big truck. I was terrified when I engaged the four-wheel-drive and the truck skidded as I hit drifts of deep snow.

Wind gusts continued to increase, making it difficult to keep the vehicle on the road. I rolled the window down and, with my head hanging out, tried desperately to see any landmarks or signs. Because I wasn't dressed for the freezing weather, I was shivering uncontrollably. It was a desperate situation but I had no choice except to continue inching along with my hazard lights flashing. Praying out loud, I struggled to keep the pickup under control.

All my life I believed I had a guardian angel. My thoughts went to the bag of newly purchased "pocket angels" sitting next to me and I prayed my real angel would help me now.

As that prayer crossed my lips, for a split second, there was a complete calm and I could see the road clearly. I gasped when I saw that I was in the left lane! As quickly as the storm abated, the white-out conditions resumed but, in that momentary reprieve, I was able to make out the headlights of three cars traveling toward me.

Just in the nick of time, I jerked the steering wheel and corrected my position. Realizing I could have been the cause of a multiple vehicle head-on crash, I trembled as I thanked God for sending my angel to protect me.

I let out a huge sigh of relief, and said a silent prayer as I pulled into my daughter's driveway. Before I got out of the truck, I grabbed a "pocket angel" from the bag and attached it to the visor. I figured a little added insurance couldn't hurt. I looked at it before I opened the door. A smile crossed my face when I read the inscription on the angel that said, "Watch Over Me," and I knew she had.

— Terry Hans —

My Army of Angels

Let gratitude be the pillow upon which you kneel to say your nightly prayer. And let faith be the bridge you build to overcome evil and welcome good.
~Maya Angelou

I was born into a grieving household—my father was killed by a drunk driver when I was only nine weeks old. My first memory, at three years old, is my grandfather suffering a heart attack and dying right before my eyes. On my eighteenth birthday, my other grandfather died. On my twenty-first birthday, my best friend Becky was killed by a drunk driver on her way to my surprise party. And on my twenty-fifth birthday my great-grandfather died. I always thought I was jinxed because of all the death around me, but that all changed in 1999, when I came face-to-face with death myself, after suffering a pulmonary embolism.

Someone asked me the other day if I believed in angels. I had to take a minute and collect my thoughts before answering. I never know how much of my personal experience to divulge because it was so incredible.

It was during the first couple days that I was in the ICU after my embolism. They all came to me—my father, my two grandfathers and my best friend, Becky. They surrounded my hospital bed and whispered words of love and encouragement. "You are not alone, we are always by your side," they said. "We will guide you, if you allow us—just take us with you." I felt their love and the warmth of their presence so strongly. They stayed right with me during those days I spent in the ICU. They spoke to me and inspired me to fight for my life. I don't think I'd be alive today if it weren't for them.

After a week in the hospital, I was released and returned to the world with a new, deeper appreciation for life. And for the last twenty-plus years, I have ended every day with a prayer of gratitude for the extra days I have been given.

Even though I haven't "seen" my angels since I left the hospital, I am constantly aware of their presence. And since then, more angels have joined them—a dear friend and true love I lost to cancer in 2001, my younger brother who passed away in July of 2018, a dear childhood friend who lost her battle with cancer in August of 2018, and my mother who died of a rare brain disease in 2019.

Life hasn't been easy, especially since losing my mother and brother, and there are times when I dissolve under the weight of fear and grief. That's when I whisper, "Are you there?" and immediately I feel the glowing warmth of my angels' presence. I hear their words of love and inspiration in the gentle breeze, I feel their encouragement in the mighty mountains that surround me, and I feel their love in the kiss of sunshine on my skin. They have stood by me through harrowing job interviews, painful breakups, admirable achievements and heartbreaking losses. They hold me up when I feel too weak to stand on my own. They remind me, every day, that I am not alone and that I am loved.

So, to answer the question, do I believe in angels? My answer is, unequivocally, yes! I travel through this world with an army of angels everywhere I go.

—Kim Carney—

Medical Miracles

Angel in the House

To me every hour of the light and dark is a miracle,
Every cubic inch of space is a miracle.
~Walt Whitman

After fifteen years working in a hospital, I stepped away and took an RN case management job with an insurance carrier. The Monday through Friday schedule allowed me to be more present as my daughter's interest in theatre grew.

Ten years passed and my baby went off to college.

I realized that I missed doing hands-on patient care, so with some trepidation I sent resumes to hospitals in my area. Within two months I had a job offer. So, there I was, forty-five years old and going back to bedside care.

My heart raced as I drove through the parking lot on my first day. It had been so long since I had done clinical nursing. Would I remember how to start an IV? Or do a sterile dressing change? My only comfort was knowing that my first week would be spent in orientation; I would be observing and hanging back.

My anxiety grew with each passing day, though. I hid it well, jokingly referring to myself as "the old-timer back for seconds." I felt lonely at work. More than once, I caught myself thinking I wasn't sure I could do this.

Monday morning arrived after my orientation week. My first patient rolled in from the fourth floor. There was already an IV in place and no dressings to change. All I had to do was a physical assessment and check that all consents were in order.

I took a deep breath and strode over to the bedside.

"Hi, I'm Susan. I'll be getting you ready for your procedure."

The bed swallowed up my patient's petite frame. From a distance she could have been mistaken for a child. Up close, though, deep wrinkles lined her forehead.

She nodded, with a slight smile.

I kept talking "Let's get this blood pressure cuff on. Then I'm going to look through your chart."

With the review completed, I returned to her side and double-checked the insertion site of the IV. It was appropriately covered with transparent tape, but the edges were loose. Securing the dressing would prevent it from loosening when she was in the procedure room. Over my shoulder I saw a roll of medical tape on the bedside table. As I turned to reach it, she curled her fingers around my hand.

"You're gonna be fine."

"Pardon?" I said.

Her voice, strong and clear, didn't match the delicate frame from which it came.

"It's good that you're back."

Goosebumps ran up my arms and what followed was a calm that went to my core. If it weren't for her doctor walking up to us at that moment, I might have forgotten why I was standing at her bedside.

"Okay, Susan, she ready?"

"Yes, sir."

The anesthesiologist and nurse took over. I watched as they rolled her toward the procedure room.

The strange thing was that when that lady had arrived, everyone else was with patients. There had been no conversation about my "new nurse" status in her presence. There was no way she knew I was a returning nurse.

Still, the words that came out of her mouth — they had a profound impact on me. I spent the remaining hours with a sense of peace.

The next day, when told to take my lunch break, I instead went upstairs. I wanted to see this patient and tell her how much she had helped me.

As I approached her room, I heard multiple voices inside. I knocked on the partially opened door before opening it.

"Hello, may I come in? I met your family member yesterday."

A gentleman sitting solo waved me in. Entering I saw that there were five more people in the room, all gathered around her bed.

I hesitated, feeling brazen for entering at a moment so obvious for family.

"Your mother here. She gave me words of encouragement yesterday that I'm so appreciative of. I just wanted to thank her."

They all stared at me as if I were speaking another language. Ashamed that I had interrupted their time together, I lowered my eyes until I heard someone clear his throat. It was the same man who had invited me into the room.

"Our mother here, she uh, well, uh, she had a stroke quite a while back. She hasn't talked since."

I didn't imagine it. It wasn't a case of someone coughing or mumbling and me thinking there was an "Excuse me" or "Sorry" blurred in the middle. She had spoken two full sentences to me.

Rooted to the spot, I opened my mouth but nothing came out.

The same man spoke again.

"Miss, our mother is a Godly woman. If she gave you words of encouragement, she got a little help from our Holy Father. You're blessed."

The other four present murmured and nodded in agreement.

"She had a stroke?"

"Miss, it's in her records. Happened at home. Little weak on her left side, but the talking, that stopped. Long ago."

I didn't want to cry in front of them, and I still didn't know what to say. So I simply walked over to the patient's beside and gave her a kiss on the forehead. The family, now all on their feet, gave me warm words of encouragement and wished me well during my shift.

With this experience, I went from feeling like a wilting daisy to a sunflower, absorbing sunlight everywhere. There was no more anxiety driving into work, just joy that I was able to work with patients and help people heal. And I never felt lonely again.

— Susan Bartlett —

An Unexpected Blessing

A new baby is like the beginning of all things—wonder, hope, a dream of possibilities.
~Eda LeShan

From the very beginning, my husband and I wanted a child. We longed for a child. We cried out to God and prayed for a child. We sought help from fertility doctors. We were tested for all sorts of medical issues. I took oral fertility medications. We kept trying.

We underwent a procedure called intrauterine insemination (IUI). We tried over and over.

After five heartbreaking, unsuccessful rounds of IUI, we moved on to in vitro fertilization (IVF). Though it was invasive, expensive, and wreaked havoc on my hormones, our IVF resulted in four fertilized embryos. Finally, something was working! Our dream of having a child was within reach!

On the day of the embryo transfer, the two strongest embryos were transferred from their cozy petri dish back into my body. The other two embryos remained in the lab under observation, to determine if they would be viable for cryo-preservation.

Within a few days, we received word that our embryos in the lab were no longer viable. We grieved that loss but remained hopeful about the two stronger embryos inside my body.

Two weeks later, I returned to the fertility clinic for a pregnancy test. The embryos we had worked so hard for—that I had been carrying inside me and trying to keep safe and snug—were no longer viable. My pregnancy test was negative. IVF had failed.

When IVF failed, we hit rock bottom. To top it off, my husband's father had just passed away. However flawed the logic, my husband believed that because his dad was gone, God would surely bless us with a child this time. One life for another life, if you will.

We wept. We mourned. We asked God why. The struggle to conceive had consumed our lives. By this point, we had endured years of shots, medications, hormones, high hopes and devastating heartbreak. Five long years of ups and downs since our wedding. I was ready to get off this roller coaster. My body, and my emotional and mental health, had suffered long enough. It had become too painful to bear. So, we stopped trying.

Nearly six years passed.

During those next six years, we slowly emerged from the dark shadows and gradually moved on with life. At some point along the way, we accepted that parenthood was not going to happen for us.

In early 2018, I began experiencing unusual and troubling health symptoms—heavy bleeding and severe pain and bloating, among other things. I thought I had uterine fibroids, ovarian cysts, or even cancer. As my symptoms grew worse, I grew increasingly fearful that something was terribly wrong.

I took the earliest doctor's appointment available on Monday, May 14. As the doctor examined me, her concern mounted and she decided to send me to Radiology that same day. I was convinced she was thinking the worst, just as I feared. When she finished my exam, she looked me square in the eyes and said sincerely, "We're going to figure this out."

Two hours later, I returned to Radiology. As the tech began my abdominal ultrasound, she looked at me, confused and amused. She hesitated a moment, then said, "You're pregnant!"

My heart skipped a beat. I was pregnant? How was this possible?

"Are you sure?!"

"Yes, you're definitely pregnant!" She laughed. "And it looks like you're pretty far along. Let me take some measurements."

If that wasn't enough shock, she then announced that according to the measurements, I was likely already a whopping thirty-two weeks along! I was going to have a baby in eight weeks!

My mind was spinning. I couldn't hold back the tears of utter shock at the news I'd just received, incredible relief that I wasn't dying after all, and sheer joy that after all these years, I was going to be a mother.

It had been six years since my husband and I had stopped trying. Nearly eleven years since our wedding day. Pregnancy was so far off my radar that I was bracing myself for a cancer diagnosis.

Of all the diagnoses I had imagined, not one had been a positive scenario. But I had just received the ONE positive outcome that I had considered impossible. Pregnancy.

Now aware of my situation, my doctor began to realize that many of my perplexing symptoms were actually serious pregnancy complications, including an excessive loss of amniotic fluid. I was admitted to the hospital immediately.

She explained that since I had lost so much amniotic fluid, the baby would likely come early. She hoped I could make it two more weeks before the baby was born. I was going to have a baby in TWO weeks? I couldn't wrap my head around it.

But only five days later, on Saturday, May 19th, I went into labor. By that evening, I was contracting every three minutes. My blood pressure and my white blood cell count were up, both things that had been in the normal range until that day. So, my doctor determined that the baby needed to come, and I had an emergency C-section.

Samuel was born that evening, at just under thirty-three weeks, and only five days after we even knew he existed. Oh, the joyful tears we shed when he heard his newborn cries!

It is only by the grace of God that this miracle baby came into the world. I received no prenatal care and I experienced what were such serious complications that, prior to my C-section, a neonatologist warned us that the baby's lungs could be severely underdeveloped and that he might not survive.

Samuel spent the first five weeks of his life in the NICU. He went home with us on our 11th wedding anniversary and he's now an active, healthy four-year-old.

—Jessica Hinrichs—

The Breath of Life

While we are sleeping, angels have conversations with our souls.
~Author Unknown

My husband was packing our belongings into the car for a thirteen-hour drive home from our road trip, and I couldn't breathe. Every time I inhaled it felt like a spear was going through my back.

I didn't say a word to him. I just thought I needed to get home to rest. Then I'd be fine.

When we got home, I went straight to bed. During my fitful sleep I heard voices. None of them was especially coherent. While I'd received messages in dreams before, this was different because it wasn't clear.

In the morning when I woke all I remembered was that the voices seemed to indicate I was in jeopardy and I should pay attention. Jeopardy? Pay attention to what?

Then I sat up in bed and not only was the searing pain in my back much worse, now it also felt like a long knife was going through my chest. Even tiny breaths were agonizing. My husband walked into the room to ask about the laundry and found me doubled over in pain. When I explained that this had been going on since the prior day, and it was ten times worse now, he said, "I'm taking you to the ER."

By the time we reached the hospital, my skin was ashen and I couldn't walk unassisted. I was getting so little oxygen that it was all

I could do to keep from passing out.

The ER triage nurse took down my symptoms and excused herself to speak to a doctor. She returned with a wheelchair, stating that they were putting me in one of the ER beds. The next few hours flew by as the ER personnel poked and prodded me trying to figure out what was wrong.

Finally, a young doctor determined that a CT scan would show them what was going on in my chest and off they wheeled me to the scanner. I don't remember much about it as I faded in and out of consciousness. Within minutes after returning from the imaging suite the young doctor and a nurse rushed into my room. He instructed her to immediately hook up an IV and begin administering a blood thinner.

"Why?" I asked feebly.

"You have a massive pulmonary embolism, a blood clot, that's stuck in your pulmonary artery right where it enters the lung," he said. "I'm admitting you right away."

I didn't question the doctor's judgment because through my work in medical communications I knew a great deal about this type of embolism; a lot of people didn't survive them if they didn't get immediate medical intervention. And even those who did go to the hospital sometimes didn't make it. I then realized that this was exactly what the voices in the dream were warning me about.

All I could do was let the doctors and nurses take care of me and hope for the best. A short while later a doctor from the floor where I would be admitted came to see me.

"Is it true that initially you weren't going to come in today?' he asked.

I nodded. It was a Sunday and I had originally thought that I'd wait and visit my doctor on Monday.

"It's a good thing you did because had you stayed home your husband would have woken up tomorrow morning to a dead wife lying next to him. You have one of the largest embolisms we've ever seen in this hospital."

Over the following days, I drifted in and out of sleep. I was on medication to keep me as pain free as possible and also to prevent me from moving around too much and dislodging the blood clot. If it went backward, it would enter my heart and cause a heart attack, possibly a fatal one. If it went forward, it would enter my lung and cause sudden death.

While a lot of people in a situation like that would have been anxious and fearful, for some reason, I wasn't. During those many days in the hospital I felt a profound sense of calm because I knew I was being watched over both by the hospital staff and from the beyond. I knew it wasn't my time.

Six days later, I was discharged from the hospital and given an appointment to see a lung specialist, a doctor I knew from my job at the hospital. We looked at a poster on the wall showing the body's vascular system and all its capillaries, veins, and arteries. He pointed to where the embolism started and how it traveled through my body and into the artery, lodging at the cusp of my lung. I told him about the thirteen-hour road trip and asked him if the embolism went through my heart to get to the artery, why didn't I die on the road trip? I've never forgotten what he said.

"I don't know. That's a question you're going to have to ask God, and it's my job to make sure you don't get to ask it anytime soon."

It's now been nearly ten years since that blood clot almost took my life. Even though I suffered multiple clots in early 2020 and know that I have a high risk of developing more, I don't walk around wondering if today is my last day on earth, if that little tightness in my chest is another embolism or just garden-variety heartburn. A person can't live like that or rather, I can't.

One thing I do know is that I experienced a miracle both in 2011 and 2020. Not everyone gets a second or third chance. I was given those miracles for a reason. The least I can do is try to live a life worthy of the extra time I was given. Anyone who comes close to death knows it changes a person. With newfound clarity you reflect on what is important and you don't take a single day, hour or moment for granted. I'm pretty sure that's why the voices in that long-ago dream invaded my sleep. It wasn't my time and they knew it.

—Jeffree Wyn Itrich—

The Great Physician

Nothing ever goes away until it has taught us
what we need to know.
~Pema Chödrön

"Please God, just give me one more chance," I prayed from my doctor's office. "I promise I'll quit skating this time. I promise."

It was the third time I had said this prayer in the past three months. This time I was seriously injured and facing surgery without insurance. God had been telling me to stop playing roller derby but I wouldn't listen. I had been competing for four years and it had taken over my life. I was putting it before Him and everything else. The first time God relayed this message in the form of a broken finger. A skater rolled over the tip of my index finger sending blood shooting out the top. Did I stop? No. I didn't even stop skating in that game. I got up, hid my wound from the refs and scored a few more points. I played in the game after as well.

The second time, God had to hit me over the head—literally. I was knocked out and suffered a concussion. I woke up, gave the EMTs my name and the President's name, and was taken off the track. I tried to get back in the game but the referees confiscated my helmet and put me in the custody of the EMTs. "Okay God, I hear you," I said. "I'll quit." I went back two months later without clearance from my neurologist.

The third time God tried to reach me was during a roller derby convention in Las Vegas. This time I strained or tore ligaments in my ankle — I don't know which. I never sought medical attention. I just loosened my skate to make room for the swelling, took some photos of it to show off on Facebook, and finished the game. I joined the group skate down The Strip that night. I told God I'd take a break after the week-long junket.

God was quiet for a few weeks so I released myself to go back. But a few days before my health insurance ran out, He tried to get through to me one more time. This time, I flew off the top of the banked track and tore my ACL. It felt like it went up in flames. I rolled around on the ground as if I was trying to put out a fire. I dragged myself to the bench and told no one about it.

The next morning, my leg was so swollen from hip to heel that I couldn't put pants on. I had a bruise that ran half the length of my leg and a big pocket of blood under my skin. I couldn't put any pressure on my leg, but I got myself to my doctor's office the day after with crutches and by driving with my left foot.

"You tore your ACL," my doctor said. "You may need surgery but we'll have to do an MRI to know for sure."

"Surgery?" I shouted. "But my insurance runs out in two days."

"Well, there's no way you'll be ready for surgery in two days," she said. "Hopefully you won't need it and it will heal on its own."

While my doctor wrote up my radiology order, I sat in the waiting room kicking myself. Why hadn't I listened to God? He was trying to tell me. He gave me chance after chance.

Is it possible that He'd give me another chance? I asked myself. *Would it be right to even ask?* It was my only hope. I prayed one last time, asked God to forgive me for putting derby first, and then got my church on the phone. I called my friend Linda, the prayer warrior, and asked her to have the ladies pray during our weekly Bible study that night. "I will," she said. "And I'll start praying now too." She prayed with me over the phone. I wasn't alone in the waiting room but I didn't care who was listening.

I got my order and crutched my way to the radiology department. The technicians took one look at me and cringed. My right leg was so grossly disproportionate that it looked like I had two different people's legs, and the bruise had turned eggplant purple. "That may be the worst bruise I've ever seen," one of them said. "Here, let us help you." They got me onto the MRI table and then helped me to a chair where I waited for the results. I could see the technicians looking over the images with the radiologist. I couldn't make out what they were saying but their tone told me something was seriously wrong. The radiologist walked out slowly as if he was in no hurry to relay the news.

"Uh, I don't know how to tell you this and I don't know how you're going to take it," he said. "But according to the MRI, there's no injury to your leg."

"What?" I said. "But look at it."

"I know," he said. "We can see the hematoma, but we can't see the source of it. Everything is intact."

He handed me the results:

"The lateral supporting structures are intact. The extensor mechanism is intact. The anterior and posterior cruciate ligaments are intact. We checked and double checked. I assure you. This happens from time to time and there's no explanation for it."

He looked embarrassed. "I'm sorry," he said, with his head down. "I don't know what to tell you."

"It's okay," I said, smiling. "I believe you."

I popped up, thanked them, and walked back to my doctor's office holding my crutches in one hand and my results in the other. I marched into the waiting room, raised my crutches over my head and proclaimed, "I'm healed! I'm healed!"

Everyone stared at me in amazement. "Oh, my God," the receptionist said. "The hair on the back of my neck just stood up. I've got to tell the others."

A man in the waiting room dropped his jaw, covered his mouth and got tears in his eyes. "I overheard you on the phone," he said. "And I prayed too."

"Thank you," I said as I did a little happy dance. "It worked."

My doctor and the rest of the staff came out, laughed, and cheered.

"It's a miracle," my doctor said. "They do happen. I have seen it."

I hugged everyone, walked out, drove home with my right leg and told my captain to fill my spot on the team. I spent the rest of the summer walking around with that bruise on my leg and the MRI report in my pocket because no one would believe me otherwise.

— Adrienne A. Aguirre —

The Greatest Cinco De Mayo Gift

Each day offers us the gift of being a special occasion if we can simply learn that as well as giving, it is blessed to receive with grace and a grateful heart.
~Sarah Ban Breathnach

I had been feeling a little out of sorts. Food didn't seem to appeal to me anymore. My wife Rhonda would make fabulous meals that I would either throw away or feed to one of our three dogs. A few weeks passed and my lack of appetite got progressively worse until my daughter Christa said, "Dad, you seem sick. We need to have you see Dr. J."

Doctor Jelicorse, or "Doctor J" as everyone called him, is a slow talking man from Mississippi, a doppelganger of the comedian Jeff Foxworthy. He examined my abdomen, looked in my mouth, and asked some general health questions. Then he ordered some bloodwork.

Three days later my daughter Jena called me to the phone. "It's Doctor J; he wants to speak with you." I thought we were well past the days of doctors making personal phone calls but this is semi-rural Georgia so I didn't think of this as anything too unusual. He asked me if I could come in later that day after regular office hours; he wanted to discuss my labs with me and maybe bring some family. I asked, "Wow, is it THAT serious?" He said we should talk in person.

My wife and I, accompanied by Jena, nineteen, and Christa, sixteen, sat down in the doctor's office. He adjusted his reading glasses and swallowed hard. "Benjamin, you have acute kidney failure. You have approximately fourteen percent of your kidney function remaining, and we need to refer you to a nephrologist immediately. You'll need to be put on dialysis and have surgery for a fistula in your arm, but you need a port inserted in the meantime. This is end stage kidney disease."

"End?" I said. "As in THE end? I had never been sick a day in my life.

He just drawled "Yes, sir" with a hint of pain in his voice.

The nephrologist, Dr. Maria Oreg, deemed this situation so serious she worked me in and met with me and my family. She was a very cheerful lady but certainly pulled no punches. She said I could extend my life a bit if I submitted to regular dialysis. But she also admitted that many people who rely on kidney dialysis become depressed and hopeless: the five-hour treatments three days a week are often physically and emotionally draining, for the patients and their entire families.

She warned it would not be an easy transition, but we could still travel as long as a clinic was near our destination and I didn't skip any treatments. She advised me to go through the permanent disability process and make this my new "job," for lack of a better term.

I started dialysis as soon as possible. The treatments were everything she described and more: tremendous nausea, weakness and a constant feeling of lethargy. The doctor visited the clinic once a week and assured me that my body would acclimate and the side effects would lessen. I felt great on Tuesdays, Thursdays, and weekends, but my treatment days — Mondays, Wednesdays, and Fridays — were dreadful. And I watched with dismay as my clinic friends died or had medical emergencies.

After two years, Dr. Oreg said, "Ben, I've looked at your monthly labs. Your numbers have all improved significantly. Being only forty-six, I think you might be an excellent candidate for a kidney transplant at this point."

She was sending me to a hospital in Atlanta for a battery of tests to see if I would be a good candidate. I would receive a kidney from a deceased donor, or if my family members were willing and compatible, possibly a kidney from a sibling, a child, or even my wife.

"Wife," I laughed, "how does THAT work?" After all, my wife was not a blood relative.

She told me thanks to advancements in rejection medications a spouse could be tested and oftentimes made great donors. I kept this information to myself for about six months and mentioned it one day randomly because it sounded so absurd.

Rhonda said, "I can do this! We can go through the program! I know I'll match; you're going to live and stay with me… I'll call right now."

I agreed, feeling this was all nonsense. But then a year later, someone from the transplant center called and said my wife was a near perfect match, as compatible as anyone could be without being a sibling.

And that was it. Fast forward thirteen years, and I am thriving with Rhonda's left kidney, We have five grandkids and I'm living well beyond my wildest dreams. The transplant surgery was on May 5th, 2009. I never celebrated Cinco De Mayo before but now it's a very special day in our lives; we call it Kidney Day.

— Ben Partain —

Trust Your Instincts

Learn to trust your inner feeling, and it will become stronger. Avoid going against your better judgment or getting talked into things that just don't feel right.
~Doe Zantamata

Have you ever had a gut feeling that something bad was going to happen? That's how I felt one evening when I was in tenth grade. But I dismissed the feeling as anxiety over a presentation I had to make the next afternoon and went to bed.

I woke up that chilly morning still nervous from the night before. I tried to talk my mom into allowing me to stay home, but she thought I was trying to avoid the presentation and told me to take the bus. I remember stepping onto the bus, listening to music, and exiting the bus, but that is the last memory I have of the next hour and a half.

I was told that I went to my creative writing class where I proceeded to talk to some friends and work some math problems on the board that most of the class did not understand. I acted like I normally would, but something just seemed "off" about me, which intensified as class began. I completed my work and finished well before the rest of the class, but I kept sneezing, holding my head, and zoning out, so my teacher sent me to the nurse. The only recollection I have during this time was meeting the vice principal halfway down the hallway; but I did not know where I was going and he sounded "fuzzy" to me.

The next memory I have is sitting in the nurse's office with both principals, the baseball coach and the nurse surrounding me. When the nurse looked at my throat they all went pale and I heard, "Find her EpiPen and call 911." They bombarded me with questions while we waited, but the only answer I could give them was that I did not remember anything after stepping off the bus. As the nurse dialed 911, she checked my vital signs. The nurse, this being her first day, was hesitant about sticking me, but after seeing my oxygen and blood pressure, I stabbed myself with the EpiPen. Then ten minutes later, I was instructed to use the second EpiPen by the dispatcher. That new nurse looked like she was going to pass out before I did.

Finally, the ambulance arrived. The paramedics checked my vitals again, and I remember the EMT that was checking them looking shocked. My blood pressure was 81/56 when they arrived, with my oxygen only 64. I insisted on walking to the ambulance instead of going on the stretcher. Once inside the ambulance, I got an IV along with heart monitors, oxygen, and two more EpiPens. I remember seeing my grandfather pull up behind the ambulance and my principal climb in the truck with him.

After pulling out of the parking lot, I do not remember much besides the nurse trying to talk to me, but I could not hear anything. We passed the Walmart distribution center, and I remember pushing myself and calmly saying, "We have to go NOW." At that moment all the monitors started to go off. I knew that I had to sit up and stay calm so my throat wouldn't close faster. I remember telling the nurse who was holding my hand that everything would be okay. And then I remember arriving at the hospital and giving the nurse permission to do what needed to be done because they couldn't reach my mom to ask her.

I was rushed inside and surrounded by doctors and nurses. I saw two nurses who'd been there for my previous attacks. They were crying as they took me into the trauma room. I later learned that my blood pressure was only 46/23 and my oxygen was at 32 and dropping.

Everything faded into darkness at that point, and then all I saw was white for a second. It was like I was up above the room but I could see everything that was going on. And I was not alone. There was a boy, around the same age as me, but I did not know him. He told me that I would be okay, and that it was not my time yet. We watched them do

CPR, use the AED and repeat the process four times before my body started jerking uncontrollably. After that he told me it was almost time, and my grandmother appeared. I hugged her while a bright, almost blinding light appeared again. Then, I remember coming to as they were about to intubate me. There was a nurse crying again.

The nurse, the doctor and the EMTs stayed with me for a while, and I told them what I had seen. Everyone was shocked because what I saw was what happened. I had flatlined twice, with the first time being a little over four minutes and the second time being about two minutes.

They later concluded that someone had exposed me to peanuts, which I am severely allergic to. I was given a total of eight EpiPens that day.

I still have nightmares about that day, but it taught me some valuable lessons, including to trust my instincts and to live every day like it is my last. I know it's a miracle that I survived to talk about it.

— Alexis Floyd —

Blessed and Grateful

Prayer is man's greatest power.
~W. Clement Stone

"What seems to be the problem?" my doctor asked me on a cold, gray day in late December.

"I feel my heart flutter sometimes like it's missing a beat and I get so shaky," I answered. "It's often hard to get my breath when I'm going up the stairs."

"Well, let's get some definitive tests to see what's going on," she said after listening to my heart. She smiled and gave me the phone number to call and set up the test.

I had the scan a few days later. After seeing the results, that doctor said, "Judee, I see a blockage and I want you to see a cardiologist right away. I am putting in an emergency referral."

I was pretty scared when I went to see the cardiologist. "Well," he said, "my colleagues and I are confirming a major blockage."

Four doctors can't be wrong, I thought to myself. I was so frightened that I really didn't comprehend his detailed description of what needed to be done. I think the doctor could see how stunned I was and softened his approach from clinical facts to gentleness. He patted my hand and said, "It is quite serious, but we found it in time, so try not to worry. We are going to do a heart catheterization and try to remove the blockage by putting a stent in that artery to hold it open."

"Oh Lord, please help me," I prayed silently as I stared at him.

"When will you do this?" I asked him.

"I think it is important to do this right away," he answered quietly. "My nurse has set up the procedure for the day after tomorrow."

"We will go in through an artery in your wrist," he continued. "It is less invasive than going in through the groin. If we can't place the stent effectively, we will schedule open heart surgery in a week or so." He patted my hand and went on. "I want you to go home and rest. Don't have any caffeine, stress or worry and only go up the stairs once a day — when you are going to bed."

Right. Don't worry after receiving news that could change or even end my life!

He handed me two prescriptions for medications that were supposed to slow down my heart rate and keep plaque from forming in the arteries in the future.

"Remember, don't worry. We've done this procedure many, many times," he assured me.

I called my daughter, Michele, in Minnesota to let her know I was going to have the heart catheterization procedure. She got on a plane the next day and flew out to support me and take care of my disabled husband, John.

I called the rest of my family and friends at church. They spread the word and soon people were praying for me everywhere. My book club, couples' Bible study, pastors, and people I didn't even know were praying for both me and the doctors.

I felt like I had a ticking time bomb inside me! I was almost afraid to walk around the house. I spent most of the time sitting in my recliner. Michele took care of us and handled all the calls coming in.

I checked into the hospital on the appointed day and the nurses prepared me for the procedure. I was praying hard that I would come though the ordeal alive.

Michele hugged me. "Don't worry, Mom. I'm right here for you," The nurse gave me a shot to calm me as Michele held my hand and prayed with me before they took me to the operating room. "I will be right here with John waiting for you." I could see her encouraging smile as they wheeled me down the hall.

When we reached the operating room, they were trying to put

the IV in my arm to put me to sleep. My whole body was trembling so badly that a nurse had to hold my arm still. Instead of being calm from the shot and the IV, I dreamed that I was drowning in a lake. I was fighting to stay above the wild waves, but I kept sinking. Every time I got my head above the water, the shore was farther away! I kept yelling for help but there was no one around and I was getting weaker. In my panic I called out to God, "Lord, please save me!"

I heard a quiet voice say, "Fear not; for I am with you; don't be afraid; for I am your God: I will strengthen you, and yes, I will help you." I recognized the soothing words from the Bible. The waves quieted and I heard the reassuring voice again. "I am the Lord who heals you."

When I began to wake up, I was a little confused about where I was. But when I turned my head I saw Michele and John just where she promised they would be. The nurses taking care of me were working to raise my blood pressure. Apparently, the shot they had given me had slowed my heart too much during surgery and I had almost died. That must have been when the Lord stepped in during the dream I had.

"You gave the doctor quite a scare in there," the nurse told me. "Just lie quietly for a while and let the medicine get your heart rate up."

It was quite a while before the doctor came in. He looked puzzled as we waited for him to speak. Finally, he said, "Well, we've gone over the previous scans and tests and today's results several times." I was anxious to hear the result, but strangely, I wasn't frightened.

"We really can't explain it. The obstruction was plainly visible in all the tests but when we got in there, the blockage was not there. I don't have any medical explanation for it, but we didn't even have to place any stents. I do want you to stay on half doses of the medicines just to be sure and I want you to come back in three months to be checked again."

If I hadn't been hooked up to all those tubes I would have jumped up and danced! Michele, John and I hugged each other. I felt so blessed and grateful! Every day is now a celebration of life,

We eat dessert first sometimes. I donated our old towels to an animal shelter and we use the good ones every day. We volunteer and open our home and hearts to family and friends. We cherish every moment and never end the day without counting our many blessings.

— Judee Stapp —

Saving Two Lives

A mother's love for her child is like nothing else in the world. It knows no law, no pity. It dares all things and crushes down remorselessly all that stands in its path.
~Agatha Christie

I remember sitting in the exam room at my doctor's office one July morning. My fingers were trembling as I dialed my husband Lincoln's phone number. What followed was years of new and unfamiliar vocabulary—medical jargon that we were forced to understand and to utilize to make intensely difficult decisions. Positron emission tomography. Primary refractory state. Autologous stem cell transplant.

Still in shock and disbelief, we were bound to make crucial decisions about not only my health, but the health of a five-week-old fetus in my womb. My worst nightmare had come true—I was pregnant and had cancer.

On paper, I quickly became a pregnant Stage IIB classic Hodgkin's lymphoma patient. I was no longer a healthy thirty-four-year-old mother of one- and three-year-old little girls.

I began to seek opinions. Some oncologists stated the unthinkable: "Save yourself. You already have two children. Abort the baby and begin chemotherapy immediately." Others said I could "hold off from chemotherapy until the baby is born, but you will risk the cancer spreading and taking your life." Or we could follow the advice of the experts at the James Cancer Hospital in Columbus, Ohio and begin chemotherapy immediately to ensure that the aggressive cancer did not spread. This would require unwavering faith that our baby would be unharmed.

I became so furious with God. Where was He? Why was this happening to me? Why did I have to make these hard decisions? I had suffered three miscarriages before my two baby girls. I had prayed so much to be able to raise a family, and now I didn't even know if I would get to see my girls grow up.

With an army of family, friends, and prayer warriors, I reluctantly began the nauseating regime of chemotherapy while hosting a fifteen-week-old fetus inside my womb. It was an eight-hour infusion every other week. Both sets of our parents dropped everything and came down to Virginia to take care of me and the two girls. Lincoln held my hand through treatments and then went to work to finance this expensive, long treatment.

We prayed. We put my name on every prayer chain that we could think of. Our church held prayer services for us. They showered us with prayer quilts and prayer shawls. Friends delivered weekly meals. Neighbors came over to babysit. All we could do was leave it up to God to heal me.

Dominic (meaning "belonging to God") was born by C-section at thirty-six weeks, weighing in at four pounds eight ounces with loads of dark fluffy hair. Perfect and precious in every way. Our prayers were answered!

While Dominic received a perfect medical report, mine was not. The cancer hadn't budged after seven months of nauseating, debilitating chemotherapy treatments.

Again, we regrouped with my oncologists and sought help. We prayed even harder. Various church members even came over to my house and prayed for me while I was in New York seeking expert opinions.

The few options the doctors gave me were grim. I was not a candidate for much of anything, and the survival percentages were low. I was told to go home and spend as much time with my family as possible. I would likely not make it to Christmas.

Having run out of options, I desperately began searching online for a clinical trial. I prayed that I could find a trial that I would be eligible for. It's difficult to get into most trials and they usually take place at major hospitals in major cities. How could I expect my weary family and friends to continue all of this childcare?

I stumbled upon a clinical trial and brought it to my local oncologist. Miraculously, he was able to set up a clinical trial just for me at his local office and administer the treatment there.

Remarkably, after only four weeks of treatment, that miracle did happen! The tumors were shrinking and almost gone!

Now what? Would/could the cancer return?

I made an appointment in New York City with the oncologist who developed this new drug combination. He questioned me: "How did you find these drugs? Who authorized this clinical trial?"

This expert oncologist came up with a new treatment plan for me that would hopefully guarantee that this cancer would never return. The plan involved numerous painful treatments that might have long-term negative side effects. I was ready to risk it all for a complete healing.

My husband and I submitted to this plan and began the six-week treatment in New York City. It was grueling. Our families and friends unquestionably stepped in again and took care of our children.

After about six months of rehabilitating my strength and stamina, the scan showed no signs of cancer. Our prayers were answered a second time.

I am now a healthy, daily dog-walking, Sunday school teaching mom of three healthy children, and I will watch them grow up.

— Lynn Baringer —

Do You Believe in Miracles?

The most glorious moment you will ever experience in your life is when you look back and see how God was protecting you all this time.
~Shannon L. Alder

"I'm sorry Adrienne, nothing can be done. I'm afraid you're terminal." The pulmonologist closed the file in his hand, shook his head and walked out of the exam room. I was shocked beyond tears and dumbfounded by the news.

It had begun one night in February 2012. I was admitted to the emergency room's twenty-three hour holding unit, for intravenous pain medications for a migraine headache. I had been in the room about two hours and was feeling well enough to call my husband, Greg, who I had sent home when they had decided to admit me.

However, as we were talking, I began coughing, then choking on blood. I was able to push the nurse call button before passing out. My husband just heard gurgling as I dropped the phone. He ran upstairs to change and rush back to the hospital when he received a phone call from the nurse's station. He was told that I was being intubated, scoped, and transferred to the Intensive Care Unit. When he arrived back at the hospital, later that same evening, it was clear that the situation was dire. I was on life-support for five days and in the hospital on oxygen a week longer.

After much testing, they were able to diagnose pulmonary arterial venous malformations, or AVMs, and pulmonary hypertension as the reason for the bleed. These malformations occur at the connection of an artery and can burst, spewing blood when under pressure. The only treatment available at that time was embolization. The procedure requires the surgeon to go into the lung and seal the affected artery shut.

Unfortunately, they said I could not be treated, because I had too many AVMs and they were present in both lungs. A geneticist confirmed that it was a hereditary disorder that had likely been there since birth. As an adoptee, I had no knowledge of my birth family's medical history. One specialist called me a "ticking time bomb" just waiting for the next hemorrhage to occur.

My husband and I began to research the disease and that led us to Cleveland Clinic; a "center of excellence" in this disorder. That first day of appointments was filled with all different kinds of specialists and a repeat of all the same scans and tests that I had back home. The second day, we met with the pulmonologist in charge of my case. The prognosis remained the same and other than increasing the amount of oxygen I was on; he said nothing could be done. We drove the four hours home in stunned silence as the feelings of hopelessness overwhelmed us.

I was placed on our church's prayer list, and I began contacting friends and family across the United States and Canada asking for prayers. One friend called the nuns at the local convent and another friend told her rabbi. I knew that I had people of all different religions and creeds praying for me.

I was still in shock from the diagnosis and my prayers became those of anger, fear, and frustration. I was only fifty-six years old. I had already buried my only child eight years earlier and now I was told that I might not live to see sixty. I could not understand God's plan for me. It took quite a while, and some counseling, but eventually my husband and I both found a level of acceptance. We decided we had to just leave it all up to God.

On a routine follow-up with the pulmonologist at Cleveland Clinic, around the second anniversary of my original AVM bleed, all the imaging and breathing tests were repeated. However, this time, when the doctor came into the room with my file, he had a big smile on his face. He looked directly at me and said, "Do you believe in miracles"? I said we had been praying for one and he replied, "Well, you just got one. Your scans and tests are all normal, completely normal. I've never seen anything like this."

We were stunned and a bit doubtful, but he reassured us that there were no AVMs present, only scar tissue from the very first bleed. I no longer even needed supplemental oxygen. He went on to say that the only explanation was divine intervention since they had provided no treatment. I was completely cured, and he was completely baffled.

I was blessed with two miracles during that illness. The first was that I was already in a hospital when I suffered the first AVM hemorrhage. If I had been anywhere else, I would have drowned in blood before they could get me on a ventilator. The second, and bigger, miracle was that I was completely healed from an inherited disorder that would have killed me sooner rather than later.

When I turned sixty we celebrated with a large birthday party that included family, friends, doctors, and neighbors. All those people who held me close in prayer for over two years were there to witness my miracles.

I continue to see a neurologist who just shakes his head and says, "Adrienne, the angels are definitely on your side." Do I believe in miracles? I am now sixty-five and my scans still show no more AVMs.

— Adrienne Matthews —

Miraculous Connections

Last Act of Love

To him, the name of father was another name for love.
~Author Unknown

Witnessing a miracle, is in and of itself, a miracle. And you know how special and rare it is when it occurs, the once in a lifetime feeling that touches your soul in a way that changes you forever.

The miracle that I saw started at 1:30 in the morning. My brother, who lived with us at the time, came into our bedroom to tell me that I needed to wake up, that my husband Michael had gotten a call: My father-in-law was in the hospital and it was serious.

I remember waking up groggy, as I'd gone to bed early, not feeling well and running a fever.

"What? What happened?" I asked, as I rubbed my eyes open.

"You need to get up, Trish. You need to go. You need to go now. If you don't you won't forgive yourself if he passes."

My husband was still on the phone, pacing and unsure what to do. We packed our bags and made arrangements for our baby for the next few days, and then we drove two and a half hours to the hospital.

When we arrived, my husband's father was not conscious. The machines were beeping and he was covered in wiring and tubes. He was in critical condition in the ICU from an aneurysm that had ruptured.

We weren't able to get an update from the doctor that early, so we slept on the ICU floor, using our coats as mats on the cold floor. And we waited until morning.

When we were able to see the doctor and get the prognosis, we knew it wouldn't be good. My husband's father had been struggling medically for years, and also had cancer. Hospice was his best option, choosing quality of life over whatever additional time he would have gotten by going through painful, debilitating treatments.

We spent the next few weeks visiting him in an inpatient hospice facility. My father-in-law was aware and conscious, albeit the bleed was still active. We brought our son to spend time with his grandpa. We brought him his favorite foods from a Chinese restaurant and a steakhouse.

For a short while, my father-in-law seemed to be getting better, laughing and joking, playing the piano. We thought he might get more time.

But then, after four weeks, he started to decline again. It was time to say goodbye.

It was somber. And surreal. How do you process that? My husband's parents had separated when he was small. His father got visits every other weekend. He and my husband loved each other fiercely, and it seemed they were still feeling the loss of all that time during my husband's childhood. There just wasn't enough time to make up for it now.

My father-in-law entered what we were told was a "death coma." He was medicated, so he was in no pain. We talked to him and hoped he heard us, but we received no response. Not an eye flutter, not a word. As we were getting ready to leave, we said our goodbyes. I held his hand and said goodbye, no response. My husband approached him, leaning over him.

"We're leaving, Dad. I love you. I love you."

And then I saw a miracle. I was the witness to a true miracle.

My father-in-law, unable to move, speak or respond, immediately moved. Death coma is a very deep state of unconsciousness right before death in which a person cannot be roused, cannot be woken, cannot move, cannot speak.

But move he did. My father-in-law put out his arms and pulled my husband close. He didn't open his eyes, he didn't say a word, but he held on with all his might. And I cried silent tears as I watched one of the most beautiful things I'd seen.

He passed away that night. The love between father and son had been enough to break through the death coma for one last hug. All we had hoped was that he could hear us. But he held onto his son one last time.

In that moment, at my father-in-law's bedside, as he left our world to move onto the next and he reached for my husband, I SAW love. Love is a miracle in and of itself. Being able to witness the intangible emotion of love in a way that makes it tangible, a father on his death bed holding his son when he shouldn't have been able to, shouldn't have been able to move; being there to witness that and see such beauty in such a moment of grief and disparity, is a miracle. I saw love.

— Patricia Ruhaak —

Kismet

Love recognizes no barriers. It jumps hurdles,
leaps fences, penetrates walls to arrive
at its destination full of hope.
~Maya Angelou

The way we met could have been a Hollywood movie. I called it kismet. But it was literally an accident.

There was a hotel in Santa Monica, The Huntley, on the corner of 2nd and California. Way back when, they had an amazing happy hour on the top floor. Margaritas were only two dollars and there was a free all-you-can-eat buffet of tasty appetizers. I wasn't much of a drinker, but I did appreciate the food.

It was late afternoon on a Friday in August of 1990 and I was going to meet a friend. I had just gotten off work at Robert Redford's Wildwood Company where I read scripts for potential films and stamped his signature on photographs to fans. (I love adding that detail.) I was coming up California Street looking for a parking space. As I crossed 2nd, I heard the squealing of brakes and was stunned as I felt the impact of a car broadsiding me.

Thankfully, the car hit the passenger side and as I scanned my body there didn't seem to be any noticeable pain, only the shock. I sat there for a few minutes, gripping the steering wheel, as I tried to figure out what had just happened.

A few minutes later, a man came around to see if I was okay, apologizing profusely. I got out and looked at the damage with him, surprised at how bad it looked, even more grateful that I wasn't hurt. Turns out, he'd gone through a stop sign and then hit me. He was most apologetic, more than willing to accept the blame.

As we pulled out licenses and insurance, he told me his name was Mike and he'd just moved out to California from Ohio six weeks earlier. As the shock wore off, I was able to look at him more closely. He was a nice-looking man, obviously coming from work. He asked if I'd be open to letting him pay for the damage rather than go through insurance companies. He didn't want his rates to go up.

In a world of scams and cynics, I briefly considered insisting on insurance companies, but he seemed genuine enough, so I agreed. Since we both lived in Venice and worked in Santa Monica, he offered to drive me back and forth. True, it was cheaper than him getting me a rental car, but he was charming!

As we were parting, he told me he'd been heading to the hotel to meet a colleague for a drink.

"Really?"

"Really."

"So was I." He offered to buy me a drink when we met up there.

Somehow, I found parking and made my way to the bar, still shaking from the event. It was packed that evening, but I finally spotted my friend in the middle of the room. He was already on his second drink. I quickly grabbed my own and started to share the story. A few minutes later, Mike found me and came over to say hello, offering to buy the next round.

Then he sat down… right behind me. The only chair available in that crowded room was back-to-back with mine. I watched as Mike pulled off his jacket, noting the sweat stains on the back of his white shirt. We made brief introductions to our companions and then went back to our own friends.

Over the course of the following week, he was true to his word. He'd pick me up on time, then take me back home again. We got to chatting about our lives and experiences. He was easy to talk to. On the last day, when he took me to the shop to pick up my car, I offered to buy him lunch to thank him for being so gracious. He said yes, lunch would be wonderful, but what if we made it dinner.

And the rest, as they say, is history.

Every time we shared that story, each of us with our own version, I couldn't help thinking it was kismet. There is no other way we would have met; we lived such different lives. He was an economist working with the City of Santa Monica. I worked in the entertainment industry by day and performed on stage at night.

My first impression of him was accurate. Throughout our courtship and twenty-five years of marriage, he was always honorable, steadfast, and loving. He wanted nothing but for his family to be happy and taken care of.

About eighteen months after he died, I was stopped at a red light, lost in thoughts of him, when suddenly, I felt a car bump into the back of mine. Startled, I looked up to see a young woman spring out of her car, deeply apologetic. I stepped out, feeling a bit shaken, but unharmed. We looked at the back of my car; there was no damage. It was just a bump.

As I got back into my car after she'd left, I started to smile. I couldn't help wondering if that was my Mike, who had reached across the veil to give his love a nudge, a sweet reminder of how we had met.

— Marianne Simon —

The Woman in a Babushka

A grandmother is like an angel, who takes you under her wing. She prays and watches over you, and she'll gift you anything.
~Author Unknown

I didn't know my father growing up. My parents divorced when I was very young. Mother eventually emigrated to the U.S. with my brother and me. Father remained in Slovakia.

As a young adult, I reconnected with him a couple of times. But when I got married it had been fifteen years since I'd seen him. I had a desire—a need—to have the two most important men in my life meet. Larry and I decided to fly to Vienna for a second honeymoon, followed by a romantic day-long Danube cruise to Bratislava, my father's hometown.

Dozing off on the overnight flight to Vienna, I was awakened by a tap on my shoulder. I turned and gazed into the penetrating eyes of a stranger. She was wearing a babushka—a headscarf often worn by older Slovak women.

"Go see your father. Go soon," she encouraged me.

I smiled and answered, "That's exactly what I'm doing."

How did she know where I was going? Had I been talking in my sleep?

The next time I felt a tap on my shoulder it was Larry, waking me for breakfast.

"Where is she?" I asked.

"Who?" Larry asked.

"The woman in the middle seat."

He smiled, saying, "Wow! You must have slept soundly. There's no middle seat — just yours and mine."

I could have sworn there had been a seat between us.

"How much wine did you have with dinner last night?" he teased.

When we landed in Vienna, I learned that my luggage — not his — was lost. The airline assured us that it would be found and sent to our hotel shortly.

We checked into the hotel and took a much-needed nap. Once again, the vision of the woman with the babushka appeared. She repeated, with more urgency:

"Go see your father. Don't wait!"

Seeing her again started making me nervous.

Vienna is a glorious city. After our nap, we wandered around visiting sites about which we had only heard. I was still wearing the clothes I had worn on the plane, waiting for my lost luggage. When it had not arrived by Friday afternoon, I decided to go shopping. I didn't want my father to see me in clothes I had worn for two days.

The following morning, we found a lovely shopping center in Vienna. I thought, "Perfect! I'll treat myself to some stylish European fashions."

Imagine my disappointment when we learned that the shops were closed for the weekend. They wouldn't open until Monday, after our planned departure on the Danube cruise.

Frustrated, I found myself rummaging through Larry's wardrobe.

Larry is taller and larger than I am. But what choice did I have? He wasn't thrilled sharing his brand-new slacks but what is marriage for, right? I borrowed his belt, pulling it tightly around my waist.

"So, the trousers are hanging down to the ground. The better to hide my tennis shoes," I reasoned with the mirror.

I wondered where my stylish high heels were flying in the European sky.

When my father had last seen me, I was younger and more focused on presenting a picture-perfect appearance.

"A father loves his daughter, no matter what," my husband assured me. "Just don't stretch my clothes," he added.

Glancing down at my chest, I replied, "I'm not THAT big."

"I meant the pants," said my Mr. Wise Guy, pointing at my belly.

We often joked that way.

Saturday night I tried to sleep but the face of that mysterious woman in the babuska returned. This time she demanded more intently: "Go see your father. Don't wait!"

We had originally planned to stay a few days in Vienna, but I was becoming increasingly uneasy. I insisted we go to my father's city right away.

Sensing my urgency, Larry arranged for a private car to take us to Bratislava. It was faster than the Danube cruise, taking only an hour.

What a delight it was introducing my otecko (Father in Slovak) to Larry. Otecko didn't speak English and Larry, a Canadian, didn't speak Slovak. No problem. Soon I had Larry saying "Na zdravie," ("Cheers") in Slovak and my otecko had learned to use the Canadian "Eh?" in every sentence.

The two men in my life, although worlds apart, were so much alike – both caring, and both with a delightfully weird sense of humor.

When Larry asked Otecko if I had changed in fifteen years—which I had to translate—he looked me up and down and replied, "Well, she's not the fashionista I remember but she is beautiful in my eyes."

Larry wanted his clothes back, so I tried shopping in town. But it was hopeless. The Communist regime had only recently disappeared from Slovakia. Walmart had recently opened, but the shelves were bare!

Besides, what good are high heels on cobblestone streets anyway?

The three of us spent every waking moment together. We visited parks, castles, and the popular beer pubs where entertainers sang American songs. I don't remember a moment without smiles or laughter and even an occasional tear.

When it was time to leave, Otecko came to see us off. He presented me with a small, rusty metal box which, he explained, included photos from his childhood and of his parents. I'd never met my grandparents, who had died in an automobile accident before I was born. I stashed the box into my bag, eager to delve into it later.

I can't tell you how touching it was to see Otecko and Larry hugging warmly as we said our goodbyes. Then father and daughter embraced one more time. Holding him tightly, I never wanted to let go.

Over his shoulder I thought I saw the face of the woman in the babushka, who had visited me in my dreams, urging me to go see my father quickly.

That delightful reunion will live in my heart forever because soon after we returned home, the call came. My precious Otecko had passed away two days after we had said our last farewell. He'd known he was ill but didn't want to reveal it. I can only guess he had wanted to make our last meeting joyful instead of one filled with sadness and grief.

Had we not shortened our Vienna holiday who knows if we would have been able to spend any time with him at all?

When I opened the rusty little box my father had given me, I found faded but treasured photos of him as a little boy, in the arms of my grandmother. Although I had never met her, gazing at her face in the photos, I knew I had seen her before. She looked familiar. Larry explained it as "family resemblance," but I knew that wasn't it. The face of my grandmother is the mysterious face that I kept seeing — the one who kept pressing me to visit my father right away. As heartbroken as I was, I was ever so grateful that I listened to her before it was too late.

— Eva Carter —

Phone Home

Intuition is your soul's perception.
~Compton Mackenzie

Barb peeked around the office door she held open, thinking I was right behind her. "Forget something?" my co-worker asked, as I stood there looking perplexed.

I'd stopped in my tracks, momentarily startled by an urgent thought: *Call Ken now; he needs you*. Really? I had a lot of errands to run.

"What's wrong?" my now concerned friend asked, approaching me.

"I have to call home. Ken needs me," I replied, making the decision while turning back into the office. She followed, quizzing me as we walked around the counter heading for the nearest desk phone. "What just happened here?" she asked, looking at me oddly. "Didn't you have a list of errands to do? I didn't hear the phone ring. How do you know he needs you?"

"I just know it's urgent," I interrupted, and requested she wait as I dialed our number.

Ken's voice was weak when he answered.

"Honey, what's wrong?" I asked.

"I don't know," he mumbled. "Sick. Headache. Can't remember if I took aspirin."

My strong hero who never seemed to get ill sounded so far away! "Do you want me to come straight home?" I foolishly asked, for I was already mentally canceling my errands while trying to calm a mounting fear.

"Yes. I need you."

Barb's eyes widened as I told her something was wrong with Ken. I raced out to the parking lot.

My daughter lives next door to us and she happened to be on the porch when I screeched into the driveway. I yelled for her to get her husband Frank, not knowing if I would need help.

I found Ken on our bed, curled into a fetal position, mumbling about meatloaf and aspirin. I dialed our medical clinic and thanked God when I was connected with a nurse-friend who calmly instructed me to get Ken to the emergency room. Frank helped me get Ken into the car.

By the time we arrived, I knew something was really wrong, as he could not tell the nurse where he was. A medical team soon surrounded him. They took him for tests while I went back to admitting to complete the paperwork and answer questions. I explained his condition when I found him and that he was fine when I left the house in the morning. I also told them how I was just leaving the office to do errands that would have taken an hour or two when I "heard" or "felt" the urgent message: *Call Ken; he needs you.*

Finally, the doctor in charge called me from behind an emergency room curtain. He explained that Ken appeared to have had a stroke and that he had been brought in just in time to receive medication to stop the attack. He questioned me thoroughly as to Ken's health and activities in the past several days. Two other doctors joined him, both insisting that Ken must have been ill and called me for help, or that he was ill that morning and I called to check on him before leaving work, or that we always called each other at that time of day. I felt like I was being grilled on some police show and finally I realized that the admitting nurse must have repeated my story and how incredible it must have sounded.

Each time a doctor made a new suggestion of what "really" happened, I repeated the story. One doctor summarized his feelings by skeptically raising his eyebrows and questioning if what I was basically saying was that God told me to phone home. I said that was exactly what happened. He walked away shaking his head in disbelief, only to return with a neurosurgeon who also wanted to examine Ken and hear the story.

Ken had returned to normal by that time and was amazed to hear about what stirred me to call him. We were shaken as the doctor explained that if I had done my errands before I returned home, it would have been too late for the medication to help Ken. Sobered by the narrow escape, Ken quietly acquiesced to follow the doctor's recommendation of an overnight stay for observation. Word apparently spread, as the following day was filled with a parade of nurses, doctors and lab technicians checking on him, shaking their heads in wonder, and asking, "Are you the one?"

For several months after, repeated testing showed absolutely no damage from the stroke. I was asked to join Ken for his exit appointment. The goal, the nurse explained, was to see if the patient had omitted sharing any changes or side effects of the trauma—if he indeed had returned to normal. The doctor chuckled when I assured him my husband was as "normal" as I'd ever seen him. He laughed outright at Ken's teasing thankfulness that for once his somewhat rebellious wife had listened to a still small voice of authority.

We all joked a bit, but the lowered tone of the doctor's voice as he left stopped our teasing. Like the conversation bubble in a cartoon, the words seemed to hang in the air—the only explanation for Ken's continued health was the perfect timing of a "message" to phone home.

Temporarily silenced, we waved back as the doctor turned the corner, and repeated his whispered farewell... "Amazing."

—Delores Christian Liesner—

A Moment of Clarity

When we are touched by something, it's as if we're being brushed by an angel's wings.
~Rita Dove

It is a cold, sunny winter day.
Snow mountains line the curbs.
Some are taller than my eight-year-old self.

I am bundled up,
only eyes peeping out above my scarf
as my booted feet crunch across the snow.
I'm on my way home.

The school day is over and done.
There is a stillness all around me.
The air is sharp and tingles with frost.

I breathe out,
white puffy clouds lift to the sky.
I look up at the blue heavens,
where the sun is slowly lowering
and suddenly, I feel it!

A sense of belonging!
It wraps itself around me,

Loving and warm like a heartfelt embrace.

Without a shadow of a doubt,
I know I am part of everything.
I've been here forever,
just like the sun and the sky.

I'm enveloped in an unshakeable certainty,
I have always belonged.
I seem to see the neighbourhood
All around, all at once.

How can that be?
Am I suspended?
I look down and see I'm still walking
yet I am now on the next street.

I stop in amazement,
to ponder, what just happened?
There is no fear, only peace.

When I reach home, I am happy,
filled with a natural serenity.
I go on with life.

It takes me years to remember,
that one splendid moment of clarity,
that innate sense of connection,
of unity, of absolute truth.

The beauty of it, the message.
I hold it gently in mind.
My treasure.

—S.K. Naus—

The Phone Call

There is hope, even when your brain
tells you there isn't.
~John Green

Many nights I cried myself to sleep. Sometimes, I even cried during the day, when my children were in school and my husband was at work. It was my secret. I was good at keeping secrets. I'd had years of practice pretending I was okay.

When my marriage ended, depression still lingered like an unwelcome guest. One night, I was all alone in my apartment. My sons had moved away, and my foster daughter was visiting her mother. I had managed, for her sake, to keep my emotions from unraveling. But now that she was gone, a dam had opened, and I was drowning.

Everything I had clung to for twenty-two years had crumbled around me. All I had left were fragments of my former life. My husband and I had been leaders in our church so when our marriage fell apart, so did our church involvement and everything that had given my life meaning. I looked in the mirror at my vacant eyes and thought, *You're a failure. Everyone would be better off without you.*

I sat down in my living room, hands folded on my lap, staring into the darkness. I prayed for death, knowing it was a futile request. There are some things you just have to do yourself.

I bent forward to grab the bottle of pills, clenching it so tightly it formed ridges in my skin. Were there enough to do the job? Trembling, I began to raise the bottle to my mouth.

Suddenly, the phone rang, piercing the stillness. I flinched and almost dumped the pills.

Rarely did anyone call, and never so late at night. Reluctantly, I lifted the receiver and heard a familiar voice. It was my son. Before I had a chance to speak, he asked, "What's wrong Mom?"

How could he possibly know? I hadn't told anyone. I'd kept my secret.

I steadied my breathing. "Thanks for calling, son. I'm okay. Really. I'm fine."

It wasn't my son's job to fix his mother. This wasn't his burden to carry.

Hanging up the phone, I reached for the bottle. Not even a call from my son could pull me out of the black pit I'd fallen into.

The phone rang again.

"Mom, hang on. An ambulance is on its way. I want you to go to the hospital. Please do this. For me."

Confused, I heard myself agreeing as if in a trance.

I managed to grab some pajamas, my housecoat and a few necessities before I heard the buzzer. A man in uniform stood at my door. He had kind eyes. Suddenly, I was in the back of an ambulance. The kind-eyed man said something about God being with me and knowing what I was going through. I wondered if he was allowed to say that. Still, it gave me comfort.

I was wheeled into the emergency ward and left alone inside a curtain-shrouded room. I sat there clutching my purse to my chest. I waited for more than an hour and my thoughts began taunting me again: *You're all alone — no one's coming — no one cares.*

Then, the curtain flew open as a nurse bustled in with a clipboard, asking me for information. "Someone will be with you as soon as possible. Sorry, it's been a busy night."

Fighting to keep my eyes open, I decided to lie down.

"Mom?"

I looked up to see my son's face peering around the curtain and began to weep. He lay beside me on the narrow gurney as he hugged me and told me he loved me. He had driven for two hours to be by my side, feeling sick to his stomach, sensing his mom was in trouble.

My son saved my life that night.

After several hours, I was finally admitted to the psychiatric ward where I lay in bed, sobbing uncontrollably. I remember asking myself why I couldn't stop crying. Something had broken inside me.

A few days passed, and a nurse asked me if I felt ready for a visitor. I cringed at the thought of anyone seeing me, but I told her to let the person in. It was my foster daughter's sister.

"Micki, I'm here because God has a message for you."

Her words caught me by surprise. Skeptical, but desperate to end the pain, I decided to hear her out.

"You need to forgive yourself and everyone who has hurt you."

It seemed too simple — naïve — foolish, even. But what did I have to lose? I didn't have the strength to pray, let alone believe, so I asked God to help me to do both. It was then that I felt something change.

Another visitor showed up — the minister from my church. She wanted to apologize for some hurtful things she'd said to me. I told her I forgave her and, as I spoke, a strange warmth replaced the emptiness that had plagued me for so long. Later, that afternoon, I finally felt ready to leave the safe confines of the hospital.

The next day, I arrived home and, just as I was settling in, I received a call for a job interview. I was offered the position the very next day. It was clear to me there was something happening beyond my control and, instinctively, I knew I was going to be okay.

The psychiatrist on duty during my hospital stay had suggested I start attending some mental health management classes. I followed her advice and not only learned better coping skills, but I also discovered that I wasn't alone in my struggles. I won't pretend everything was better, but it was the next, real step on my healing journey.

Some days were harder than others — Christmas, especially. So, I decided to pack up my keyboard and sing carols to the patients who were stuck in the hospital over the holidays. I wanted them to know they weren't forgotten. And, as I looked at the faces smiling back at me, I was able to forget about my own loneliness, if only for a while.

As life went on, I still battled depression, mostly due to toxic relationships and childhood traumas still playing out in my mind. But I was learning how to silence them.

These days, I'm grateful that I'm no longer depressed, although sadness does creep in occasionally. Now I recognize the signs and can stop myself from spiraling downward to that dark place. I'm also more open with my feelings and no longer ashamed to reach out for help. Looking back, and seeing how far I've come, it hardly seems possible that I was once that lost, broken soul who thought that ending her life would be the answer to her problems.

Often, we have no idea what people are struggling with. Many hide their pain, as I did. Words of kindness and compassion can sometimes make all the difference.

And, like an unexpected phone call in the middle of the night, maybe even save a life.

— Micki Findlay —

Friendship, Round Four

Wherever we are, it is friends who make our world.
~Henry Drummund

In 1995, I moved from Washington State to Haugesund, Norway with my husband Gordy and our children, five-year-old Aimee and nine-year-old Tyler. I loved Norway and took Norwegian lessons, as in our neighborhood, few families spoke English. My Norsk-Engelsk dictionary was in constant use.

To get our English fix, every few months we made the day-long journey to Stavanger, to the North Sea Baptist Church. The service was conducted in English by an American pastor. We met expats from nineteen different countries, including Canada, the Netherlands, South Africa, and other interesting places.

Getting to and from Stavanger was sometimes a challenge, especially after adding baby Elisa to our family. During the ferry ride home after Elisa's dedication at church, waves crashed over the bow as her infant carrier slid on the floor! But it was always worth the trip.

During one visit, I mentioned to some ladies that I'd worked in occupational therapy. One got excited. "Occupational therapy? Oh! Have you met Kristen yet? She's worked in OT! You two would get along so well, too!"

When I met Kristen, charming mother of three children — ages three, five, and eight — we chatted a bit. Then she suddenly stopped and stared at me, saying: "Wait… we already know each other!"

I stared back at her, confused, trying to drum up some memory of how and when.

She continued, excited. "Remember? We did OT training at the same time at University Hospital in Seattle."

I fought through foggy memories. There was only a six-month window during which we could have met at that hospital, and sixteen years had passed since then.

Kristen persisted. "You had me over for lunch at your mobile home in Redmond. You'd only been married a little while. But I remember your wedding ring, a marquise shape." She pointed at my ring finger. "Yes, that's it! And you had a picture on your wall your mother-in-law had stitched, with your names and wedding date."

That gave me goosebumps. We still have that framed cross-stitched picture made by Gordy's mother, and it was weird she remembered the shape of my ring. Kristen's memories were so precise. How could I not remember her? It was embarrassing and mystifying. But her face looked vaguely familiar.

I asked, "How in the world do you remember those wedding details?"

She said, "I'd just broken up with someone I cared deeply for but was unable to share my new faith with. You and Gordy were a newly married Christian couple starting your life together. It was a beautiful thing, and I wondered if the Lord would ever bless me that way. It gave me hope for the future."

When Kristen and I had met back then in Seattle, she'd come from New York. After our lunch at my home, we lost touch as she moved to three different states. She then married the love of her life and lived in four more states before Norway. It would have been like playing chess to keep up with her!

Then both our husbands were transferred to Norway for their jobs, with two different companies.

While in Norway, Kristen and I only had an eighteen-month window of time in which to reconnect, since we didn't go to Stavanger often and she had moved to Norway only six months before me. It was interesting that the woman who introduced us knew what occupational therapy was (a bit rare). Of course, she had no idea it was Round Two for Kristen and me.

After Norway, I lost track of Kristen again. She and her family returned to Texas, and I moved to Washington, Iowa, then North Carolina. I imagine God shaking his head, saying, "Wasn't connecting you twice, enough? What's it going to take to get you two to stay in touch?"

Then twenty-four years after I'd seen Kristen in Norway, forty years after we first met, came Round Three. In North Carolina. while cleaning out boxes, I found my old 1970s address book. There in my own handwriting was Kristen's maiden name, helping me find her on Facebook.

We reconnected immediately and admired photos of each other's grandkids online. We Skyped and discovered that my younger daughter Elisa and Kristen's eldest daughter had both moved to Charlotte.

After we confirmed the facts about the crazy ways we'd connected three times, I wrote a story about it. I ended that with: "I can only imagine God's expression if He has to re-introduce us a fourth time! We'd better stay in touch. Perhaps writing Kristen's name in my address book forty years ago was a hint of a promise she and I will always be connected, no matter where in the world we end up."

But our story wasn't over. Last October came Round Four, when my connection with Kristen went from crazy to miraculous.

My middle child Aimee, now a young mother living in Washington State, texted me:

Aimee: "I went hiking with a new friend today who moved here from Texas. Her family lived in Stavanger, same time frame as our family." (She added a head-exploding emoji.)

Me: "What's her name & maiden name?!"

Aimee: "Her name's Laura. She has a sister the same age as Tyler who lives in Charlotte now, near Elisa. So random. And she said in Norway they went to an international church…."

She texted me Laura's maiden name. Kristen's married name. My jaw dropped.

Me: "Oh my gosh, her mom and I are friends, with way more to the story! Will call you. I am in shock."

It turned out that Aimee and Laura met at church. But first, Aimee had met Laura's little boy Aiden in the childcare ministry. He got along so well with Aimee's daughter Lucie that Aimee suggested a playdate for the two families, including their younger boys.

Ponder this: two preschoolers — Kristen's grandchildren and mine — reconnected our families for Round Four.

It is bizarre to think that only months earlier Kristen and I simply enjoyed looking at each other's grandkids on Facebook. Now we're looking at pictures of our grandkids *with each other* on Facebook.

I recently found a printed photo of our families together in Norway, back when Aimee was five and Laura was three. Only God knew they'd grow up separated, then have their children reconnect them.

Today, while I was typing this story, Aimee randomly Skyped me. I told her I was writing about her and Laura.

"Funny," Aimee said. "They'll be at our house in a few hours."

Picture a double mind-blowing emoji.

I'm so glad Kristen and I had our first "playdate" more than forty years ago. Will preschool pals Aiden and Lucie still be friends forty years from now?

— Laurie Winslow Sargent —

A Flicker of Hope

Love is something eternal; the aspect may change,
but not the essence.
~Vincent van Gogh

I have lived with depression for most of my adult life. The years have taught me to manage it with medication and talk therapy, but I still have days that feel like I'm swimming through wet concrete in the dark. When I feel swaddled in a dull gray darkness that smothers my usually hopeful outlook on life, I call on the miracle that occurred between my grandparents and remember that sometimes hope looks like just hanging on.

My grandparents Antonia and Giovanni were a young married couple living in southern Italy when World War II wrenched them apart. My grandfather was drafted into the Italian army and sent to the Balkans. My grandmother, born an American citizen, returned to the States pregnant with my mother to wait for his return.

They would not see each other again for eight years.

Some may recall that Italy was allied with Germany until September of 1943, when Italy signed an armistice with the allies. Germany's reaction was swift and brutal—Italian soldiers were considered enemies and were taken prisoner by German troops. Over 700,000 Italian soldiers were transported to Germany to serve as forced laborers. Hitler branded the Italians as traitors to the Third Reich and classified them as Military Internees who were denied the rights of prisoners of war, one of which was receiving and sending mail.

My grandmother Antonia heard nothing from my grandfather Giovanni for years while he was a forced laborer in Kassel, Germany. She did not know that he faced each day with the possibility of being arbitrarily killed by the German guards. She could not know that each day was a misery of starvation and disease. She would not know until the war ended that the memory of her kept him alive and gave him the strength each day to just hang on.

She heard nothing from him for years. It could have been that he was alive. It could have been that he was dead. She faced her own sense of uncertainty and despair, made worse by friends who encouraged her to move on — after all, she was a beautiful woman who had attracted the attention of many would-be suitors. Her hope that he was alive was beginning to wane, but something in her told her to not give up. Something told her to just hang on.

My grandmother's determination was rewarded one spring day in 1945 when she took my mother, now seven years old, to the movies. It was a time of pre-feature newsreels and as mother and daughter watched the reel play, my grandfather's face flashed on the screen for a few moments as the film showed the liberation of Italians from German camps. He was alive.

My grandmother rushed from the theater with my mother in tow and pleaded with the manager to see the newsreel again. The manager was a kind man — he listened carefully to her story, took her to the projection booth after the movie concluded and played the newsreel on a viewer. It was him — he was emaciated, tired-looking but still handsome. My grandmother Antonia wept tears of gratitude, pointed to the flickering images and told my mother that this was her father. They would see him soon.

It was a year before my grandfather Giovanni was able to emigrate to the States. My mother recalled their emotional reunion and said her parents wept and held each other for the longest time. Then her father, a man she had never met, knelt, kissed her forehead and told her how very nice it was to finally see her.

It is a story that has inspired me for years and sustains me during my darkest times, when I feel as though I have lost my way. Their story reminds me that even a momentary flicker of light in the darkness can give me the strength to hang on until things get better.

—John Kevin Allen—

Dolphin Love

Miracles come in moments. Be ready and willing.
~Wayne Dyer

It happened during my parents' older years. They had so many needs. My dad was a perfectionist and his expectations of me were high. I was working two jobs to support my single household. My jobs were stressful; my health was suffering.

I needed a miracle.

Some friends from another state offered me a trip to Hilton Head Island. We walked along the beach. We shopped; we ate out. It was a lovely trip. I kept trying to ignore the feeling that the trip was not complete. I had an urge to hire a boat and go out in the bay looking for a dolphin. Like a siren song, the urge grew stronger. Finally, I reserved a boat and captain for two hours.

We headed out into the bay. We could see groups of dolphins swimming together in the distance, but none were near us. I asked the captain to stop the boat. He stopped and turned off the motor. I held my hands out over the side of the boat toward the water sending out my intention to meet a dolphin. Within a few moments, a dolphin swam up and placed her head in my outstretched hands. She smelled salty and her skin felt wet and rubbery. The captain said she was an adolescent.

When the captain saw that we were making physical contact he began to bluster. "Do not touch the dolphin. No touching is allowed."

I responded, "I am not touching her. She is touching me." The dolphin and I stayed like this for about ninety minutes.

What was it like to hold a dolphin's head in my hands? It was a loving, joyous step outside of time. Her energy felt exuberant and playful. I felt her gently probing to get to know me. She was full of curiosity. Her mind was not full of human chatter and so, for that period, neither was mine. There was a strong, ancient communication occurring. I felt like I was teaching human knowledge to her, and she was healing and filling me with love. I felt I was receiving a glimpse into dolphin life.

At the end of the ninety minutes, the captain said we had to go back. The dolphin still had her head on my hands. The captain started the boat and began to drive back toward shore. I began to cry, to sob. I am crying years later as I write these words.

I did not want to leave the dolphin and she did not want to leave me. She followed the boat. At first, she was able to keep up with us but as the captain accelerated to fifty miles an hour, she fell behind and disappeared. On the way back to shore the captain told me that in his seven years as a captain he had never seen anything like my dolphin interaction. I had few words to explain it to him.

All I knew was that a miracle had occurred; cross-species communication had happened on a deep level. Since that time, I have always carried the dolphin love within me. It has seen me through some bleak times in life. It helps me understand that I am not alone in the world.

Meeting a dolphin was a true gift, a miracle from the universe. The love of a dolphin changed me and makes me feel more grateful to life, to know I walk in grace.

— Linda Healy —

Messages from Heaven

One Missing

Death ends a life, not a relationship.
~Jack Lemmon

The canisters were set up side by side. The fuse was lit. There was a long hiss and then BOOM! As the smoke cleared, we watched the red and blue paper parachutes drift toward us. Five children scrambled to catch the chutes before they hit the ground, even running among the trees to find them. They knew they would each get two. But in the end, only nine parachutes were located. A red one was missing.

It was July 4, 2006, ten months after the death of our youngest son, Brian. In many ways, this holiday was much worse than Thanksgiving, Christmas or Easter. On those days, surrounded by a large extended family, there were distractions that eased the pain of his absence. The Fourth of July was different, though. It had always been a very special holiday for Brian, who had been the one who selected the fireworks for our immediate family's display.

I was amazed that he remembered the names of the colorful cones and rockets we "oohed" and "aahed" over each year. He worked so hard to make each year's display, searching far and wide to find the best possible fireworks.

In a strange way, the drifting parachutes mirrored my own fall through grief. They hung in the air and floated to unknown destinations, carried by the breeze. I was drifting, too, searching for answers in my cloud of grief.

As nighttime approached, we said our goodbyes to family members and proceeded home. During the forty-five-minute trip, we decided to spend a few minutes at the gravesite. Brian's absence during the day had been overwhelming. Tonight we needed to feel his presence.

It was already dark and the community fireworks had already begun when we got to the cemetery. My husband positioned the car at an angle, using the headlights to illuminate Brian's headstone. Before I could garner enough energy to get out of the car, I saw my husband walk to the far side of the grave. He bent down and picked something up from behind the headstone. Since he was beyond the lights of the car, I did not immediately see what it was. When he held it up, I gasped. In his hand was a red parachute, just like the one we failed to find earlier.

Goosebumps ran down my spine as I burst into tears.

Brian's spirit was with us after all on that July 4th. And his choice for the year's fireworks finale was spectacular.

—Janet M. Todd—

Visits from Dad

A father is neither an anchor to hold us back
nor a sail to take us there, but a guiding light
whose love shows us the way.
~Author Unknown

Five days before Christmas 2008, Dad collapsed in the hallway while I was in the bathroom getting ready for work. I saw him go down, and I was there immediately. I slapped his face while simultaneously calling 911, only to get a recording telling me all the operators were busy.

The heck with that; I needed both hands to work on Dad. I hung up and kept slapping his face, desperately calling, "Dad! Dad!" His eyes were open, but he wasn't there. 911 called back and asked if I'd called and hung up. I was still working on Dad; I told them, yes, and I explained the situation. Finally, I tried a couple of chest compressions and he gasped and the light was back in his eyes.

I helped him to his feet and walked him to the rocking chair in his bedroom.

The paramedics got there shortly after that, but he refused to go to the hospital, insisting, "I just needed to go to the bathroom."

"Dad, going to the bathroom and collapsing in the hall aren't connected. Something else happened, and we need to find out what it was."

Children of the Great Depression and World War II veterans have the attitude "I'm walking, talking, breathing, and not bleeding. I used to change your diapers. I'm fine. Leave me alone, I have things to do." Even when our LDS bishop, who had been driving past as the paramedics arrived, tried convincing him to go to the hospital, he refused.

I needed to get to work. The last Saturday before Christmas in retail is always mega-crazy, and I couldn't leave our small store shorthanded. My older brother and brother-in-law traded off watching Dad.

Monday morning, he was fine, driving all over the valley to finish his Christmas errands. It appeared we'd dodged that bullet.

But then on Christmas morning Mom found him on the kitchen floor. She banged on the floor with her cane for me to come up, calling, "Dad's on the floor." I rushed up the stairs, wearing only my sweatpants. I dialed 911 again, once more calling his name and slapping his face. They coached me on how to resuscitate him, but he was already gone.

Nothing could have prepared me for losing him. The impact was worse than I could have ever imagined. He was gone. Even after almost eighty-nine years, it was still too soon. He'd always been there like a rock, a refuge in the storms when I needed one.

Everything had changed. Mom and my sister wouldn't get their annual Christmas rose. We'd never read the letters he wrote and put in our stockings on Christmas morning. I'd never see him smile when he opened the scripture tote he'd asked for that I'd hunted all over the city to find.

As original settlers in the neighborhood, we were well known, and soon friends and neighbors gathered to help. One niece packed up her family's Christmas lunch and sent it with my nephew for Grandma. When he arrived, he brought the food in, grabbed the snow shovel, and went back out to clear the walks and driveway.

Guilt welled up in me because our last conversation hadn't been the best—not an argument, but we had snapped at each other. It wasn't what a final conversation should have been. The pain from everything hammered away at me all day and followed me to bed and kept me tossing and turning all night.

His funeral was on New Year's Eve, a clear, cold day. As a World War II U.S. Navy veteran, he received full military honors: a bugler playing taps, a twenty-one-gun salute, and the flag which covered his coffin folded three-cornered and handed to Mom by a Navy lieutenant on bended knee.

Adjusting was hard. His passing didn't just leave a hole, it left a crater. I couldn't wrap my head around it. I would have given anything even to argue with him again.

Two weeks after the funeral the big toe of my left foot was pinched while I slept. Strangely, I didn't panic or feel any fear. When my younger sister and I were teens and dating, Dad said he didn't want to wait up for us to get home from our dates and asked us to come in and pinch his big toe when we came home.

Dad was home.

His second visit was about two weeks later. I dreamed I walked in through the back door, and he was standing on the other side of the dining room table. He was with my best friend from junior high and high school. And he was wearing a bright blue — neon almost — cardigan sweater. He'd never owned one of those. He looked at me and said, "I didn't have a heart attack and die on Christmas Day." I answered, "No, Dad, you had a stroke and died on Christmas Day." Then he said again, "I didn't have a heart attack and die on Christmas Day, and to prove it, I'm going into my living room to watch TV."

Well, I'd wanted to argue with him again, and here I was arguing with him again!

A few days later, I came home from work, and Mom was sitting at the kitchen counter eating the dinner a neighbor had brought her. She looked at me with a smile and said, "I saw Dad today."

"Really?" I asked. "Where did you see him?"

"I was sitting here at the counter, I looked up at the patio door there, and I saw him standing there, on the other side of the sliding door."

"What was he doing?"

"Just looking in, and then it looked like he'd dropped something because he looked down and was gone. He was wearing a bright blue cardigan sweater."

I hadn't told her what he'd been wearing in my dream.

His last visit came on a Friday in the first days of March.

It was a relatively warm winter day, and I was taking down the Christmas lights. As I rolled up the string of lights I'd just taken down, I looked up, and there, flying over the roof, against the gray pre-spring sky of early March, was a beautiful butterfly with neon blue wings and a long gold tail. It was the kind of butterfly you'd see in a Brazilian rainforest, but certainly not in a desert state like Utah on a cool morning at the beginning of March.

Years later I learned that in many cultures butterflies are viewed as messages or messengers from Heaven.

I never had any more visits from Dad, and Mom never told me if she saw him again. Thirteen years later I still feel his absence deeply. Questions still pop into my mind, and I think, "I need to go ask Dad about that," but he isn't here to ask. Those four visits were enough, though. They gave us the peace and assurance that he was still nearby.

— Rich Rogers —

The Song

Music gives a soul to the universe, wings to the mind, flight to the imagination and life to everything.
~Plato

The phone buzzed on the nightstand, jolting me awake. When I looked at the clock, and saw it was 10:00 P.M., I knew. This was "that" call—the one I had wished would never come.

"I'm sorry, but your mother has passed away," said a sympathetic nurse. "I checked on her shortly after you left, then again at nine-thirty, and she was still breathing softly. When I checked back a few minutes ago she was gone. I'm so sorry for your loss."

I had expected this but I was still unprepared. I stumbled around the room in shock, feeling lost, no longer sure how to dress myself. I couldn't focus.

I was only eight years old when my mother first faced death. A radical hysterectomy due to an ovarian cancer diagnosis had resulted in internal bleeding, which posed a greater threat to her life than the cancer. Somehow, she beat the odds and survived both.

Blessed with an additional eighteen years, my mother lived on to raise me and cherish her life with family and friends. Then death challenged her once more. This time, it was colon cancer that forced her onto the operating table.

We talked privately before her surgery, sharing our thoughts, fears, and hopes with one another. My mother's deep green eyes sparkled with a love that reflected our unbreakable mother-daughter bond, and she patted my hand tenderly as she spoke.

"Don't worry, dear. I've survived worse. And, if my time has come, I know I'll walk with God." She smiled warmly. "I'm not afraid, even though I have so many unanswered questions, so many things I'd like to know before I go."

I nodded reassuringly, wishing I could say something to soothe her worried mind.

"I've often wondered," she said, her eyes wandering off in thought, "once we are on the other side, whether our heavenly spirits can communicate with our living loved ones." She looked at me, her eyes glistening. "I hope so."

I smiled in understanding but fought back the lump in my throat and a wave of tears.

"You mean the world to me, sweetie," she continued, "and if anything happens to me, I'll want you to know I'm at peace and everything is okay."

I squeezed her hand. Candid discussions were not uncommon with my mother, but what followed caught me off guard.

"When I die, whenever that day comes," she said. "I promise to find some way to send a message to you and put your mind at rest. What do you think?"

I looked at her for a moment in silence, then finally said, "I would like that." I hugged her, hoping such a thing was possible but praying that "that" day would be far, far into the future.

The surgery was successful, and chemotherapy would not be required. We celebrated, and she never took a solitary moment for granted. Eleven more years passed before the extraordinary woman I called my mother faced death once more.

Pancreatic cancer inflicted another grueling surgery upon her, and then a post-operative collapsed lung threatened her life. As strong as she was gentle, she pulled through. Granted two more years, my mother gained another precious gift of time with family and friends. Like before, she counted her blessings and never squandered a second. Then the day came when I received an urgent call from my father.

"Your mom collapsed. I rushed her to the hospital and an MRI revealed a huge mass. She just came out of emergency surgery. There's nothing they can do."

"I'm on my way," I said.

For three months, my father and I took turns sitting at her side in the palliative ward, all day and most nights. I slept on a cot next to her until she slipped into a coma.

It was the evening after Mother's Day when "that" call finally came. I managed to get myself to the hospital to see her while she was still in her room. A few minutes after I got there, my father came into the room with their pastor. I hugged both men. Like lost souls, we stared at a woman who had filled our lives with so much love and hope, unable to absorb the reality that she would no longer grace our lives.

After a long silence, I asked my father. "Did the nurse call you, too?"

He shook his head. "She called Pastor Sam, and he showed up at my door a few minutes ago. I guess I gave him a bit of a shock."

I tilted my head. "What do you mean?"

"I answered the door dressed and ready to go."

A strange feeling crept over me. "So, how did you know?"

My father smiled as tears stained his rosy cheeks. "You know the hymn I wrote for your mother?"

I nodded and fought the urge to weep again. I knew the song. She had begged him to finish it before she was gone, but time had run out.

"I haven't had a chance to work on it or think about it for months," he said. "But tonight, the song woke me up. I swear, I heard your mother softly humming it to me, like when she was at home. After that, I couldn't sleep. So, I got dressed and sat down at the piano to finish her song. By the time Pastor Sam knocked on the door..." My father choked up. "I already knew she was gone."

We sobbed into each other's shoulders, then looked back at my mother. She looked so peaceful.

On the car ride home, I remember my mother's promise so many years earlier. That's when I realized the significance of what my father had said. A feeling of calm washed over me as tears streamed down my face.

"Mom, you found a way!"

Through a song written in her honor, a hymn that symbolized her faith and precious bond with family, my mother had found a remarkable way to keep her promise and say farewell.

— Cate Bronson —

My Miracles and Me

Through the eyes of gratitude, everything is a miracle.
~Mary Davis

It was the weekend after Thanksgiving, with three weeks left in the first semester. Like many high school seniors, I looked forward to skating through the second semester, filled with fun times with my friends and family.

As any kid from a small town will tell you, hanging out in parking lots, driving around back roads, and munching on fast food are peak activities for students with plenty of time on their hands and little money in their pockets. On this particular night, my friends and I climbed into my 1997 Oldsmobile Cutlass Supreme and headed for the Valdosta mall to grab some pizza. After eating we headed to a small playground outside of our school's football field. We talked, laughed, and joked together until it was time to head home.

On our way home, the car ran slightly off the road and before I could correct the steering, the right tire hit a pothole that ripped the front end from under the car. The Cutlass began to spin out of control and we hit the concrete railing of a bridge. The air bag deployed, knocking me unconscious and permanently blinding me.

I was not wearing a seatbelt and was thrown from the car after it flipped. I landed among trees, bushes, and vines. The vines actually softened the impact, preventing further damage to my body.

Then a miracle happened.

My grandfather, whom I called Papa, had died several years earlier.

But there was Papa right in front of me. He told me with genuine love in his face, "Bubba, now it ain't your time to be here, so you just get back down there. You'll be all right son, now don't you worry, God ain't finished with you yet."

Leaving Papa and returning to my broken and bloody body I heard bushes shaking and someone calling my name. I managed a grunt and the searchers eventually found me. Before I passed out again, I said clearly, "Tell my mama that I'm going to be all right." I was confident in that statement because Papa never lied to me and he'd just told me God wasn't done with me yet.

My parents got the phone call no parent ever wants to receive. My mama quickly threw my little sister into my grandma's arms and rushed to the hospital where I was being airlifted. She was told there was no way that I would be alive when I arrived but she told the doctor, "Well you ain't God and He is the one that decides life and death."

When my mama saw me for the first time in the hospital, she leaned over me and said, "I'm not leaving your side until I carry you home with me. We are stuck together like super glue." Over the next couple of months, we faced many trials and tribulations. I had setback after setback, but we kept holding on.

I spent seven days in Phoebe Putney hospital in Albany, Georgia. Due to the damage from the air bag, I was unable to take breaths as normal, so a breathing tube was placed in my airway. At one point, it slipped and no one was aware for several minutes. I was told later I went for almost ten minutes without oxygen and yet I did not suffer any brain damage.

It was another miracle.

Later, a common antibiotic used to treat infections caused me to run a fever so high that I had to be put in an ice bath. It turned out I was allergic to that medication.

After a few weeks, I was taken to Children's Scottish Rite Hospital in Atlanta. Since my trauma was so severe, the doctors decided that it was best to keep me in a medically induced coma to prevent more damage, manage the pain, and keep me calm. Then the surgeries began.

To rebuild my facial structure, a titanium metal plate was installed, the bridge of my nose was repaired, and several eye surgeries occurred. My jaw was tightly wired shut and I was put on a liquid diet, causing me to lose a significant amount of weight. After a particularly hard night, a kind nurse named Kim came to change my bedclothes. As she turned me in my bed, my trach slipped again and I began to suffocate. Once again I saw Papa. Shaking his head, he simply pointed behind me and said, "I done told you that it ain't your time. Now get back 'cause you worrying that nurse something bad." Following Papa's instructions, I came back to my body and shook nurse Kim's arm to alert her to the problem.

It was yet another miracle that I did not suffer any brain damage despite the lack of oxygen.

By the spring, I managed to attend my senior prom with the girl who was also in the accident.

I am eternally grateful for the paramedic who found me in those woods, the doctors and nurses who cared for me at Phoebe Putney and Scottish Rite Hospitals, the Life Flight crews, and my family who stayed by my side throughout this journey. I thank God no one else was injured that night. And I thank my Papa for sending me home, twice.

— Richard Bennett —

Spirit in the Doves

Faith is the bird that feels the light
when the dawn is still dark.
~Henry Ward Beecher

My grandmother loved birds. She loved to watch them sitting in the trees. She loved to walk down to the park and sit on a bench, feeding all the birds that happened to stop by. She loved to look up at the sky as they dipped and swooped at sunset.

She and Grandpa had bird feeders in the front of their house and a birdbath in the back yard. Grandma often told me that birds were the gentlest and most peaceful of all God's creatures. And although she loved many different kinds of birds, her favorite was always the gray dove.

I remember going to the pet store with her when I was a little girl. She would usher me past all the cute puppies and kittens. She would hurry me along by the tropical fish and furry hamsters. She would guide me away from the funny-looking turtles and fuzzy rabbits. On every visit, she would make a beeline straight to the back of the store; straight to where the birds were housed.

There were always lots of people milling around in "Paradise Cove," which is what they called the bird area. The cockatiels would be strutting back and forth. The brightly colored macaws would be talking, squawking and eating their crackers and sunflower seeds. However, while most of the crowd was busy looking at the gregarious and colorful birds, Grandma would stop me right in front of the doves' smaller cage.

"Doves are magical creatures," she would say quietly. "Watch how they move. Watch closely when they look at each other and coo." Then she would lean over and wink at me. "It's like they have a secret that they only share with each other."

Many years went by and my grandmother became very ill. I was living in Fort Worth at the time, completely self-absorbed as only a twenty-something can be. The rest of my family lived in and around the Austin area. My mother was at her mother's side in the hospital, day in and day out. Other family members would stop by here and there, but my mother was there every single day.

One morning back in Fort Worth, I woke up and opened my eyes to see a little gray dove sitting on my windowsill. It was comforting to see the dove, so peaceful and serene, but it was strange too, because I lived in a very busy part of town. I had never seen any birds around my noisy apartment building.

I lay in bed and continued to stare at the dove. It stared back at me for a few minutes, preened its feathers a bit, cooed softly, and then stared some more. It seemed to wink at me and then it flew away. I ran to the window, searching for a sign of the dove, but it was gone.

I immediately picked up the phone and called my mother.

"Grandma passed away this morning, didn't she?" I said, already knowing the answer.

My mother started crying softly. "How did you know?"

"I just had a feeling."

Time went by. I didn't tell my mother about my dove encounter until several years later. When I told her about that unusual morning, she smiled as her eyes filled with tears. "Your grandmother always worried about you," she said.

"She did? I didn't know that."

We sat quietly for a minute and then she said, "I think that was her way of saying goodbye."

I don't live in Fort Worth anymore. In fact, I live fairly close to my family now — near where I grew up. Ever since I told my mother about that morning when Grandma passed away, I see doves all the time — always right outside my window.

There might be one or there might be ten, but they're always there. It's reassuring in a strange sort of way. In fact, it reminds me of that scene in the movie *City of Angels* when all the angels come out on the beach at sunrise. It's one of those beautiful moments when you come to understand that there's something out there a lot more powerful than you.

And to this day, whenever I'm going through a hard time, I take solace in seeing those doves. It's like Grandma is right there with me, comforting me and telling me everything is going to be okay. And it always is.

— Susan Taylor —

The Blue Spiral Notebook

A happy marriage is a long conversation
that always seems too short.
~André Maurois

When my mother died six months ago, I felt an overwhelming sense of loss. It also triggered thoughts about how I coped following the death of my husband twenty years earlier.

Sadly, I couldn't recall missing Larry during those first six months as much or at least not in the same way that I missed my mother. That insight spawned regrets.

In an attempt to ease my guilt, I checked with the kids, none of whom could recall to what extent I functioned during the months following their father's death. However, they tried to assure me that there was no way I wouldn't have missed him tremendously. But that wasn't good enough.

So I went directly to the source. Every night before going to sleep I asked Larry to enlighten me as to how I handled his death. Even though I knew in my heart there was no way I could have grieved his loss any less than Mom's, I'd convinced myself I had to hear it from him.

Although Larry often appeared in my dreams, he was a no-show for an entire month beginning the day I started asking him for a sign.

I eventually elected to let things lie while I prepared to move back home after caring for my mother at her house for several years. My house was in need of numerous updates, so it was important to go over renovating ideas with my son who had offered to help.

On my first day back at the house, I ran upstairs to my bedroom for a quick peek while Chris busied himself measuring the downstairs windows. It had been ages since I'd been in my bedroom, but it appeared that everything was as I'd left it.

I sat down at my desk and, out of curiosity, opened the center drawer. There amid the pens, pencils and other office supplies an unfamiliar blue spiral notebook caught my eye. Flipping through it quickly, I recognized my handwriting but didn't remember writing the words. The first page was dated a few days following Larry's death. After reading a couple of lines, the worries about my lack of grieving were promptly replaced with joyful tears. Here's what I had written:

"Honey, I love you and miss you so much! Although we knew it was coming, it's so hard to believe you are gone! Oh how I wish I could be kissing you goodnight, but all I have left is your picture on the nightstand."

I glanced at a few of the other pages, but it was a lot to take in. I gently slid it back into the drawer where it would be safe until the next day.

After scurrying downstairs, eager to share my news, I found Chris much too busy to participate in my enthusiasm. He nodded as though he was listening, but he added very little to the conversation.

Later that afternoon I called my daughter. She appreciated my relief as I shared a few of the heartfelt words I'd written for her father so many years ago.

Having made it my mission to finish reading the journal, I got out of bed soon after sunrise the following morning. I needed this closure more than anything I could ever remember.

I drove the two miles from my mother's house to mine in record time. I rushed up the stairs to my bedroom, slid into the chair, hurriedly opened the desk drawer — and froze!

It wasn't there!

I couldn't believe my eyes!

I searched frantically through every drawer without success, vowing to continue looking until the journal was once again safe in my hands.

For two days I looked in every nook and cranny, upstairs and downstairs. There wasn't a cupboard, drawer, or closet that I didn't ransack thoroughly. I searched under the chairs, couches, and all the beds. I even checked the garage.

Upon returning to my mother's house in the evenings, I searched there as well just in case I absentmindedly took the notebook with me the day I first laid eyes on it.

After a couple of days, Chris helped me comb the entire house one more time. When we were finished, he sprung his thoughts on me.

"Mom, you're not going to like hearing this, but I'm pretty sure you must have had a dream about finding a journal."

"How can you say that, Chris?" I retorted. "You were here when I found it, and you agreed that it was amazing!"

"You didn't tell me anything about a journal until the other day when you were looking for it."

It took me a minute to recall that he had been too busy measuring windows to pay much attention to what I had told him.

My only witness didn't remember. Now what?

Conflicting thoughts ran through my head: Could it have possibly been a dream? No, it was way too real. But I did ask Larry to come to me in a dream. And, if the journal was so important, why didn't I take it back to Mom's house that night? But, I remembered holding the journal, and I recognized my writing, and I'd nearly memorized the first several sentences. It had to be real!

It was difficult to sleep that night. But the next morning I awoke remembering that I'd told my daughter about the journal on the day I came upon it. She would remember!

"Hi, Sis. Think carefully before you answer this question. Did I call you the other day and tell you anything about a journal I found at the house?"

"Yes, you did! You said that you'd started writing in it soon after Dad died."

"Are you certain?"

"Of course! You were ecstatic! You said it was a blue spiral notebook in which you told Dad that you were worried about me because I was having a difficult time dealing with his death. You also told him that you kissed his picture every night before going to sleep."

She was right! I DID see the journal!

I felt a remarkable peace knowing that I had received the affirmation from my husband that I so desperately needed. It didn't come in a dream as I had expected, but as a message from heaven that I was able to hug close for one miraculous moment — and that was exactly what I needed!

— Connie Kaseweter Pullen —

The Fire

Those we love never truly leave us. There are things that death cannot touch.
~Jack Thorne

It had been a tough year for us. My mother had passed away, and my husband fought to keep his job during the recession. Dark clouds of stress and grief hung over us, but I was determined to enjoy one evening of relaxation with a backyard bonfire to unwind.

It was November 1st, and in west-central Florida, that is a good thing. It means hurricane season is all but over, and the weather is cool enough to enjoy a comfortable evening outside. We stoked up the fire and settled into our lawn chairs. The approaching nightfall was heralded by croaking frogs and a steady thrum of crickets, but otherwise it was quiet. The occasional fruit bat greeted us, dipping low at dusk to feast on mosquitos.

As the night grew darker and cooler, we kept the fire roaring and drew up closer. The hypnotic glow and the sound of the flames licking at the logs relaxed us into a trance, melting away a year's worth of worry and heartache in seconds.

I sipped a new seasonal craft beer, a red harvest stout. It had grabbed my attention, not because I like stout (which I do), but because the story on the back of the can intrigued me. The limited release beer honored an old Celtic festival celebrating summer's end. The festival ran from All Hallows' Eve into the following night and centered around a bonfire to mark the end of the fall harvest and the beginning of winter. It marked the beginning of a new year.

I thought that tradition was fitting as I felt a need to wipe the slate clean and start fresh. But the fire festival does something else. It welcomes the dearly departed home for one night to share in the love and celebration. I had not given that aspect much thought, but maybe I should have.

We reclined in our chairs, watching the flickering fire cast its dancing shadows along our six-foot-tall wooden fence. We listened to the snapping, sputtering logs that soon offered the only noise besides our hushed conversation. Our yard was secluded and private, and we felt secure, but as the evening wore on, I had the strange sense we were being watched. As Steve stoked the fire, I looked around, then gasped.

Two big eyes beamed down at me.

"Steve, look!"

He turned, and we stared up at a tiny owl perched on the fence behind me, its round white face and big yellow eyes clear in the radiant light. The owl continued to watch us with an intent, warm gaze. It was not at all spooked by us. An inner calm washed through me as I watched the bird.

"Don't owls represent messengers of the dead?"

My husband shrugged. "Maybe."

Tears welled, and for no apparent reason, I blurted out, "Hi, Mom."

I've never believed in ghosts, animal spirits, or messengers from beyond, but at that moment, I questioned my conviction. Our little winged visitor, a burrowing owl, seemed to be connected to my mother in some strange way. Maybe because my mother loved owls—they were her favorite bird. Or perhaps because the animal was so out of place. Owls stay as far from cities and people as possible. Sure, we lived in a quiet neighborhood, but it was one of many in a bustling metropolis only five minutes from busy streets and the I-275 Highway, not an owl-friendly place.

Or maybe, I simply wanted to believe the bird's presence meant something special because we needed a sign that everything would be okay. Whatever the reason behind its mysterious appearance, the owl shocked us.

When we weren't paying attention, the little owl disappeared, but the odd sensation of seeing it lingered.

The next day I researched the myth behind owls, discovering they are one of the most symbolic animal spirits. Owls hold significance in most cultures, ranging from totems of wisdom to harbingers of death. The owl I'd seen was no bad omen, but as I read on, my impression from the night before grew stronger. Owls supposedly represent spiritual icons of "death" or the animal spirits of loved ones themselves. As messengers, they symbolize new beginnings and enhanced perspectives. Goosebumps rose all over my body, and I began to cry. I wanted so much to believe the owl represented my mother returning to say hello.

I never mentioned the incident to my father, unsure how he would take it, and soon forgot about the owl.

Years passed, and so did my father. On a chilly evening in late February shortly after his death, we sat around another bonfire and made a toast to celebrate his life. I had visited my father a few months earlier but could not be at his side the night he died. As I reclined in my chair and watched the flames dance before me, I thought about how much I missed my parents.

We stoked up the fire to a dull roar and huddled closer to keep warm. As the night grew later and the sky darker, we could see our breath. No crickets or frogs serenaded us this time; not even the bats joined in. The night was silent and black, except for the smoking oak logs and the bright crackling fire.

The evening grew colder, and I went inside for a jacket. When I returned, I stopped dead. On the fence, directly behind my chair, perched not one but two burrowing owls. They stared at me, and I stared back, my eyes as wide and round as theirs. I'm not sure if owls have facial expressions, but I swear they were smiling at me. A lump rose in my throat, and tears welled again. Steve turned to see what I was looking at and sat transfixed. We watched the owls as they held us in their fixed gaze. There was nothing remotely eerie about them, only a sense of serenity and calm, so I spoke to them.

"Hi, Mom. Hi Dad. I love you!"

The birds never moved but continued to watch us with warm interest. So, I seated myself. Now and then, we stared up at them, and they beamed down at us. At some point, after the fire dwindled, they departed, and we returned indoors. My sorrow did not fade entirely, but the owls delivered a sense of ease and comfort to my troubled soul. I could let go.

Since then, we've had numerous bonfires and have watched for the owls, but they've never returned. Maybe they were angel messengers, or my parents as animal spirits, or maybe they were simply burrowing owls, but the memory of them makes me smile. If nothing else, they gave us a sense of peace at a time when we needed it most.

— Cate Bronson —

I'm So Happy!

The love of a mother is the veil of a softer light between the heart and the heavenly Father.
~Samuel Taylor Coleridge

Throughout my thirty-eight years, my mom was always there. We saw each other nearly every day and spoke several times a day. Sometimes she drove me crazy, but when she left this earth, she took a part of me with her.

When my family and I moved from the Chicago suburbs to San Diego, it made sense for my mom to move too, especially since my brother and his family were already living there. When she got sick, she moved in with my brother. The kidney failure she suffered due to chemotherapy took her from being completely self-sufficient to needing twenty-four-hour care in a matter of months. She was unable to sit or stand on her own, and she suffered from hallucinations and delusions.

Mom had to undergo dialysis three times a week for three hours. It was extremely taxing for her. My brother and I agreed to continue helping her through it until she expressed the desire to stop. If that happened, we'd respect her wishes.

One morning it was my turn to take Mom to dialysis. After the first half hour, she started asking to go home. I told her she had two hours left and tried to distract her. She continued to insist she wanted to be done.

"You want to be done for today, or you want to be done overall?" I asked carefully.

"I want to be done overall." She sounded sure.

I swallowed hard, knowing it was important she understood the implications of what she was saying. "Do you know what that means?"

"Yes, it means I won't survive."

"The doctor advised us that after stopping dialysis you'd only have one to two weeks with us." It was painful to say, but she needed to know.

"I know, and I'm sad about it, but this isn't living."

"Are you sure, because when the doctor spoke with you, Scott, and me in the hospital you said it was your choice to continue dialysis so long as it would prolong your life."

"I know, but that's not my decision anymore. This isn't living and it's my choice to be done."

This was the most lucid conversation I'd had with my mom in months.

At that moment the nurse came in.

"Miss," Mom said, "can I go now?"

The nurse looked at me. My mom, a strong, independent woman who'd been a successful real estate agent for forty years and lived on her own for fifteen years, no longer had a voice. I was her voice now.

My mom looked into my eyes, her own eyes filled with pleading and child-like trust. She knew I was the only one who had the power to free her.

"Tell her. Tell her what my decision is. Tell her what I told you. Tell her I can go."

I looked at my mother—the woman who'd spent the last almost thirty-nine years caring for me, talking to me, being there, and sticking up for me. I looked at the nurse, who was still watching me.

"She wants to go. I'm taking her home."

"Okay," the nurse said. "We'll get her unhooked then. I'm going to need you to sign an AMA form."

"I understand."

She left to get the paper and another nurse helped get my mom disconnected from the dialysis machine for the last time.

I put my hand on my mom's shoulder. "They're coming to unhook you, okay? I'm taking you home."

The agitation drained from her body. She rested her head in her hands. "Okay."

From the car, we called my brother. We both told Mom we loved and supported her. "You're my mom. I love you and want you to be here, but I don't want to see you suffer anymore and I respect your decision. I'm proud of how resilient you've been," I told her.

My mom stayed at my brother's home with the support of hospice. A priest came to give her last rites. Three days later, she passed peacefully, surrounded by my brother, my niece, and me, her favorite hymns playing. The last thing we ever said to each other was "love you."

The night we returned home after Mom's burial, my emotions were tender and raw. In the unbearable silence of that night, when there were no more phone calls to make, treatments to schedule, or a funeral to plan, I asked my mom for what I needed. When she was alive, my mom always went out of her way to cheer me up when I was feeling down. That night I needed comfort more than ever.

"Mom," I said as I lay in bed waiting for sleep, "if you're able to, can you please come visit me in a dream tonight?" I believed she would do this for me if she could.

True to form, my mom did what I asked. That night I dreamt we were at my brother's house, where my mom had died. My mom and I sat at the kitchen table. She was so vibrant and radiant. Always a lover of bright colors, she was wearing her sky-blue shorts and her white and blue shirt adorned with yellow daisies. Her hair, lost at the end of her life to unforgiving chemotherapy, was long, full, and blond. Her face was familiar but looked younger, smoother somehow. Most vivid was her beaming smile.

"Mom," I asked, "what's Heaven like?"

Her smile widened and her face lit up. "Oh, Kathleen, where I am, it's magical. It's absolutely magical, and I'm so, so happy."

My mom had suffered so much. Even prior to her illness, I'd never seen her this happy. The joy was radiating from her. Her demeanor held no trace of the chronic anxiety and worry that had plagued her during her earthly life.

"But what's Heaven like?" I persisted.

"It's not for you to know now. You're here." She tapped the table with her finger. "You'll be there one day, and besides, I couldn't even describe it to you except to say it's just magical."

"Well, can you at least tell me if Dad's there?"

The smile never left her face. "Yes, and he's so happy!"

She kept smiling and repeating how happy she was. I woke up with a smile on my face. Before my mom passed, my sister-in-law had asked her to let us know she was okay once she reached Heaven. She promised that she would.

I'll always miss my mom. I still expect the phone to ring. I still hear her voice in my head telling me to drive carefully and giving me advice. When I think about her, I don't picture her as the sick, frail woman she was at the end of her life. I think of her radiant smile when she visited me in my dream. I think of how happy she is now, and how happy we'll both be when we see each other again.

— Kat Clark —

Peace that Passes All Understanding

Those we love don't go away; they walk beside us every day.
Unseen, unheard, but always near; still loved,
still missed and very dear.
~Author Unknown

The words hit me like a fist to the gut. "She's already coded three times. We are doing all we can to save her."

My sister-in-law Peggy had survived brain surgery for an aneurism just a year earlier and had been doing fine. But this morning she had been rushed to the hospital with breathing problems.

The family was crowded into a small room when the doctor returned a short time later. "I'm sorry. We just can't keep her heart going."

Shocked silence settled on the room. I looked over at Peg's daughter. She was shaking. Peg's son was crying, as was her husband. Then one by one, we all began crying softly as the realization set in that she was truly gone.

We all left the hospital feeling numb. Peg had been the spark in the family. How could we ever fill the cavernous hole left in our lives with her passing?

That night I cried and wrote to her in my journal for hours, telling her how much I was going to miss her. Then I turned out the light, ready for a sleepless night. I lay awake staring up at the dark ceiling, praying.

"Lord, I don't understand. But I trust You. All I ask is that You give me some sign that she is with You so I can live with this."

My body must have been exhausted from the stress of losing Peg because I fell into a deep sleep almost as soon as I stopped praying. And I began to dream...

I was in the hospital room where the doctors had been trying to revive Peg. But there were no doctors there now, only Peg lying on the bed.

As I gazed at her lying there, she sat up and got off the bed. She was smiling. I was amazed and filled with joy, even though I somehow knew she wouldn't be staying.

"I can't stay," she told me, still smiling serenely. "I have to go back."

"I know," I said, wiping tears from my eyes. "But I need to know one thing. Have you met Jesus?"

"Oh, yes," she told me enthusiastically. "I have." Her eyes were shining. "I love you."

"I love you too, Peg. I'll see you again one day."

"Yes, you will. Know that I'm happy and at peace."

She embraced me and then she was gone. I woke up immediately. I sat up in bed and blinked in the darkness. What had just happened?

But I knew. God had answered my prayer in a wonderful and miraculous way. He let Peg tell me herself that she was okay, and that we would one day see each other again.

Oh, what peace filled my heart!

We don't always have all the answers we would like here on earth. But sometimes we are allowed a glimpse of the happiness to come.

And sometimes we are permitted to hear from our loved one's own mouth...

"Know that I'm happy and at peace."

— Denise A. Dewald —

The Miracle Message

Miracles are not contrary to nature but only contrary to what we know about nature.
~Saint Augustine

The cafeteria workers at Doctors' Hospital in Montclair, California knew us well. It was February 2002, and the family gathered there, playing cards, eating ice cream, singing songs, and waiting for a time to visit my eighty-four-year-old father, who was in the intensive care unit. He had suffered a heart attack and was not expected to make it. My son Rob and I had flown in from Massachusetts to join my four siblings, the grandchildren, in-laws, and friends.

Every morning we arrived at the hospital, ordered breakfast, and waited. Two people at a time were allowed in the room. There were long waits between visits.

Rob brought his guitar to California and, unbeknownst to us, composed a song for his grandfather during those waits in the cafeteria. One night while at Grandpa's house he typed the song into Grandpa's computer and labeled it "Rob's Song." At the end of the week, he took his guitar into Grandpa's hospital room and sang it to him.

Despite the initial prognosis, my father continued to improve and after a week we all flew home. He was moved from the hospital to the health care center at his retirement community. We hoped he would continue to improve and we would have a few more years with him. But it was not to be. A week after I returned to Massachusetts

I received a call from my sister in California. She said Dad had only two to three days left.

I returned to California immediately. After visiting Dad, I settled into his small house at Pilgrim Place Retirement Community and checked his e-mails for any messages I could print out for him. I noticed a file on the desktop titled, "Rob's Song." I opened the file and printed out a copy of the song. When I noticed all the spelling errors, I corrected them and printed it out again.

Forty-eight hours after I arrived in California, Dad died. Family again flew in from Massachusetts, Minnesota, and New York City. Neighbors at the retirement community offered beds for family members while I stayed at Dad's where we gathered to plan his memorial service and close down his house. The grandchildren picked out items that reminded them of their grandparents. The rest were packed in boxes and donated.

On the day before his memorial service, early in the morning, I sat at Dad's computer to type out what I wanted to say. As I started to open a Word document to type something, I noticed a file on the computer I hadn't seen before. It was titled "thank you rob." The file "Rob's Song" was no longer there.

I opened the file. There was the song Rob wrote. I saw it had been spell-checked again. Then I noticed something typed at the bottom, in bold, in a different font. It said, Thank you Rob… finish school, and take care of your mother. Rex, Dad, Grandpa." That was the way Dad always signed his letters.

How was that possible? I didn't know and never will but I do know I wasn't alone in the house anymore. I felt my dad all around me and I wept, tears of grief, tears of comfort. Rob, at the age of eighteen, and only three months away from his high school graduation, was falling into a deep-dark hole, making poor choices, heading in a dangerous direction. He needed to hear from his grandfather. He needed a miracle.

The rest of the family arrived at the house in the late morning. I asked if anyone had worked on the computer, if anyone had changed the song. No one had. I showed them the message. We felt surrounded again by Dad's presence.

My brother-in-law suggested I place that file in a folder and see when Rob's Song was last modified. I did. The date and time popped up. "Date Modified. February 20, 9:36 P.M." It was minutes after my father died, at a time when no one was in his house.

That message from my dad was one that Rob desperately needed. It hangs in a frame by his bedroom so that every day he can see the message from his grandfather. The miracle message. A message sent from beyond that helped my son know that Grandpa was still there watching over him, rooting for him, loving him. That message let us all know that my father wasn't gone. He would always be there when we needed him.

— Trudy Knowles —

Meet Our Contributors

Kristi Adams is a *USA Today* bestselling author and travel writer, with fourteen stories featured in the *Chicken Soup for the Soul* series. When she's not writing, you'll find her crocheting, reading, or laughing at the family cat Tiki and his latest antics, with her husband of sixteen years. Learn more at www.kristiadamsmedia.com.

Adrienne A. Aguirre is an ordained minister with an M.A. in Theology. She works as a chaplain and death doula providing spiritual and end-of-life care through her nonprofit Mobile Ministers. Adrienne is also a prison minister in San Diego, CA and humanitarian aid worker in Uganda. Follow her @ChickChaplain or ChickChaplain.com.

Sharon E. Albritton studied journalism at Fullerton College in California. She and her husband are currently enjoying retired life in the Lakelands of South Carolina. Sharon is an active member of her church choir and loves singing praises to the Lord!

Emily Allen is lead writer for an international labor union, a certified life coach and a freelance writer based in the Midwest. She's written for dozens of organizations, including the Discovery Channel, *Kansas City Star* and *Weekly Reader*. Learn more at www.emilyrallen.com.

John Kevin Allen is a minister and chaplain ordained in the United Church of Christ. He is at work on his first novel, a historical fiction account of his Italian grandparents' separation and miraculous reunion during World War II. E-mail him at johnkevinallenwriting@gmail.com.

Monica A. Andermann can be found on most sunny days sitting on her porch, writing, with her cat Sammie at her feet. Her work has been included in such publications as *Woman's World*, *Guideposts* and

Sasee as well as many titles in the *Chicken Soup for the Soul* series.

Donna Anderson is a wife, mom, and grandmother who lives in Texas with her husband and two dogs: a Border Collie who wants to rule the world and a tennis ball–obsessed Golden Retriever. Her hobbies include genealogy, photography, antiquing, and writing. She can often be found volunteering at the local museum.

Mary Ellen Angelscribe is a pet columnist and author of *Expect Miracles* and *A Christmas Filled with Miracles* and has nine stories in the *Chicken Soup for the Soul* series. Her swimming cats were featured on *Animal Planet*. Read heartwarming, inspirational and miracle stories on her two Facebook pages: Angel Scribe and Pet Tips and Tales. E-mail her at angelscribe@msn.com.

J. Ross Archer is a retired U.S. Army Colonel. Besides bravely and proudly serving, he earned a master's degree in psychology. After military retirement, he was vice president of a college and proprietor of a strategic planning firm. He is a Gideon and Rotarian. John Ross has had twenty-plus short stories and three books published.

Dave Bachmann is a retired teacher who taught reading and writing skills to special-needs students in Arizona for thirty-nine years. He now lives and writes poems and stories for children and grown-ups in California with his wife Jay, a retired kindergarten teacher, along with their fifteen-year-old Lab, Scout.

Paul Baribault's newest work of nonfiction, following his first in 2019, *Our Brilliant Eternity*, will be titled *Comedy & Grace* and feature "Midnight Rider" as one of its short stories. As a produced playwright Paul has written plays and screenplays, a volume of sonnets, and four children's books available on Amazon.

Lynn Baringer received her Bachelor of Science, magna cum laude, in 2000 from Kent State University, where she met her loving husband, Lincoln. She lives in the beautiful state of Virginia with their three amazing children: Layla, Bryn, and Dominic. Lynn enjoys camping, teaching Sunday school and long walks with her dog.

Susan Bartlett, a seasoned registered nurse, started writing when her daughter went off to college. What was meant to be a distraction in the uncomfortably quiet house became a joyful way to share her work and life experiences. Art museums and offbeat literature provide inspiration for trying her hand at poetry.

Richard Bennett received both a networking and a programming degree from Wiregrass Technical College in 2009. He lives in South Georgia and enjoys cruising, reading, cooking, devotionals and listening to sports.

Tom Bentley is the author of three novels, a book of short stories, and a how-to book on finding your writer's voice. He has run a writing and editing business out of his home in California for many years. Learn more at www.tombentley.com.

W. Bond received her Bachelor of Arts and her Master's in Education from Lewis & Clark College. Wendy retired from education and became a full-time volunteer for the Alzheimer's Association. She enjoys traveling and taking classes to learn new skills. She loves to spend time with family and friends.

With a lifetime passion for the written word, **Angela J. Bonomo** loves sharing her nonfiction stories. As a writer, she has spent many years training and perfecting her craft. A mother and grandmother, sharing time with her large family is one of her favorite things to do. Angela resides in Saint Charles, MO.

Cate Bronson is an accountant turned author whose nonfiction work reflects her devotion to family and animal welfare. Cate lives in Florida with her husband and rescued racing dogs. She enjoys reading and writing in the sunshine while giant hounds lounge by her side.

Cheri Bunch is an educator, working with children of all ages with reading challenges and disabilities. She is the mother of five children, grandmother of nine. She is passionate about traveling, reading, and gardening. Her all-time favorite pastime is spending time with her family.

In addition to his writing, **Jack Byron's** experiences in life include various endeavors, with careers as a freelance illustrator, gallery artist, and even a tattoo artist, as well as a decade spent working with patients dealing with Alzheimer's disease. He lives in Southern California.

Kim Carney is a freelance writer, music supporter/promoter, dog rescuer and entrepreneur. Kim has her own online music magazine, as well as her own licensed Internet radio station. Kim makes her home in western Colorado with her rescue dog, Penny. You can find links to all her ventures at https://linktr.ee/tenaciousk.

Eva Carter is a freelance writer with a background in finance and telecommunications. She lives in Dallas, TX with her husband Larry and their two cats.

Tammy Childers resides in California and enjoys a variety of artistic pursuits. Having a creative outlet to express her feelings has been therapeutic in coping with her grief since her son's passing. She's currently designing a coloring book to help grieving parents and grandparents who have suffered a similar loss.

Pastor Wanda Christy-Shaner is a licensed minister, missionary, and writer. She currently resides with six furry kids and is involved with animal rescue and rehab. E-mail her at seekingtruth65@yahoo.com.

Kat Clark is a writer and mom to her two boys, ages nine and thirteen. She has a degree in psychology and has a passion for raising awareness for mental health. Her first novel, *The Voice of Reason*, was published June 1, 2020. Her first children's book, *Spider and Friends Café*, was published March 8, 2022.

William Clark is a native of Muncie, IN. He and his wife live in Jefferson City, TN. Clark is a graduate of Ball State University. His fifth inspirational book, *Smoky Mountain Rising: The Day That Changed Everything*, was released in April 2022. Clark has two sons and is an author and inspirational speaker.

Christine Clarke-Johnsen is a retired English as a Second Language teacher. She is a performing storyteller from Nanaimo, BC, Canada. Christine enjoys telling stories that touch people's hearts or make them laugh. She also enjoys singing in a choir, playing badminton, strumming her guitar, and gardening.

Elizabeth Delisi is an award-winning author of romance, mystery, suspense and paranormal. She wrote her first story in first grade. When she's not writing, Elizabeth loves to read. Elizabeth also enjoys working with tarot cards, knitting, and watching old movies. She lives in New Hampshire with her husband Dan and dog Gypsy.

Denise A. Dewald writes inspirational fiction and nonfiction, as well as Christian verse. She has two grown sons and resides in

Michigan. She has many publishing credits to her name, including two print books and one e-book.

Kim Garback Diaz has her master's and SAS in education, and a bachelor's in marketing. She is the owner of Educational Solutions, a consulting business for parents, families, students, schools, and departments of social services. She lives in the Adirondacks in upstate New York with her husband Ray. They have a beautiful daughter, Jessica.

Pamela Dunaj has written a corporate parody newsletter and has been published in a university-affiliated literary journal. In addition, she was awarded second place in the "Unknown Writers" contest hosted by the Denver Women's Press Club. Currently, she is working on new writing projects, including one with a companion multimedia facet to it.

Erin Eddy resides in Illinois. A 2002 graduate of Macomb Jr/Sr High School, her days are spent immersed in books, homeschooling her boys, and writing. She aspires to become a full-time author, penning stories of encouragement and everyday life. She has been featured on the popular website "Her View from Home."

Micki Findlay's stories and poetry have been published in several books and magazines. Besides making readers laugh, she writes her life stories to help others see their own self-worth, find hope in difficult circumstances, and realize they are not alone in their struggles. She lives on Vancouver Island, BC, Canada.

Alexis Floyd is currently a nursing student at Northeast Mississippi Community College where she plans to obtain her associate's degree in nursing, then continue on to obtain her bachelor's and master's degrees. She enjoys working, reading, and helping others. Alexis plans on becoming a pediatric nurse in the future.

Gail Gabrielle's writing career continues to broaden. Her focus is on creating family memories, always turning to her children Danielle, Zachary, and Alexandra as sources of inspiration. A book entitled *Zack Attack* is evolving, and her website "Gail Gabrielle's Gospel" is under construction.

Renny Gehman enjoys writing both fiction and nonfiction. She's been published online with *Risen Motherhood*, *Agape Review*, and in two previous titles in the *Chicken Soup for the Soul* series. Renny lives in Gunter, TX with her husband, has two married daughters and six grandchildren. She enjoys gardening, birdwatching, and cooking.

Barbara Gladue was born and raised on the dusty prairies of Canada. Barbara works in the healthcare industry as a caregiver. She enjoys her spare time with her granddaughters and her Great Pyrenees dogs. Barbara likes camping in the Alberta Rocky Mountains, gardening and reading. E-mail her at Lb6067@outlook.com.

Bobi Gentry Goodwin is a native San Franciscan. She has been writing since childhood and her mission has been working with women and children. She is married and has two daughters. She is an author, podcaster, and Bible study teacher. Bobi enjoys tea, long showers, and living out loud. She is the author of *Revelation*, a novel.

Gina Gronberg is a wife, mother and grandmother who writes about this journey of her "staggeringly beautiful life," which has included the walk toward death with both her parents in the past four years. The miraculous has certainly been a part of that experience.

Terry Hans, a retired dental hygienist, is compiling a collection of hilarious stories as told to her by patients in the exam room. A previous contributor to the *Chicken Soup for the Soul* series, Terry enjoys time with her family, writing, and cheering for her grandsons at their sporting events. She and her husband are enjoying retirement in North Carolina.

Linda Healy is a registered nurse who worked as a hospice nurse for seventeen years. She enjoys writing poetry and legacy pieces. Linda is a visual artist specializing in color pencil drawings and Zentangles. Her favorite pastime is watching her grandchildren grow.

Jessica Hinrichs lives in Florida with her husband and son. When she's not writing, she's probably at the library, beach, or Disney World. Jessica is a member of SCBWI and is actively pursuing picture book publication. She has placed in several writing contests, and she holds a degree in English from West Virginia University.

Nancy Hoag was a young mother of three when she graduated cum laude from the University of Washington in Seattle. Today she's a grandmother and an award-winning author of more than 1,200 stories and four nonfiction books including *Storms Pass, So Hang On!*

She currently lives with her cowboy husband in Bozeman, MT.

H. R. Hook writes about real life, faith, and family. Her next step is certifying her miracle dog, Bailey, as a therapy animal for her local children's hospital. Follow their progress and connect with H. R. Hook on Facebook @hrhookwriter, Twitter @hrhookwriter, Instagram @ hrhookwriter or her website at www.hrhookwriter.com.

Shannon Hurley looks for the miraculous in everyday life. She is a mother and grandmother and her goal is to love God and love others.

Jeffree Wyn Itrich has been writing most of her life, from childhood stories to attending journalism school to freelance writing to a career in medical communications. When people ask why she writes, the answer is simple. It's in her DNA. For her, writing is as essential as eating, sleeping, and breathing.

Carolyn Jaynes, M.A. is the author of true inspirational stories of her spiritual journey to becoming a spirit medium. Her books include *Sprinkles from Heaven: Stories of Serendipity*; *Twinkles from Heaven: The Mystical in the Mundane*; and *Ripples of Faith: Living Inside Out*. Carolyn lives in San Diego, CA. Learn more at CarolynJaynes.com.

Jessica Joe is a creative writer passionately exploring and deciphering the depths of this dazzling matrix we call life: a vast universe that she believes is always communicating with us in a plethora of subtle and sometimes not-so-subtle ways. She enjoys chess, writing and reading science fiction and standup comedy.

Trudy Knowles is a retired college professor. She is the mother of five and the grandmother of four. When she retired, she had a five-point plan: sing more, dance more, play more with her grandkids, write more, and do more social justice work. So far, she has been successful in her retirement.

Brenda M. Lane received her Engineering Tech degree (Drafting/Design) from Pacific Union College. Simultaneously, she began a secondary passion as a composer/author/producer. Three grown children and five grandkids are her enormous blessings. She is actively involved in writing her fifth book. Learn more at www.laneprojects.com

Geno Lawrenzi, Jr. is a beloved world traveling gadabout journalist who has settled into creative short story writing. He has written over

2,000 articles in his lifetime. Among his passions are poker, the Wild West, famous people, the Caribbean, and justice. He evokes a unique visual mastery, truth, humor, and wisdom.

Laura Lewis received her Bachelor of Science from Central Missouri University at Warrensburg, MO in 1987. She has self-published a historical novel, *Where Roses Grow*, and is published in three anthologies, *KaleidoscopeWOJO*, *The Willows*, an anthology of adoptees, and *Chicken Soup for the Soul: Grieving, Loss and Healing*.

Storyteller **Delores Christian Liesner** writes and speaks about activating faith, inspiring others to be the miracle for others. Her writings include *Fill My Cup, Lord* (Facebook page), CBN, *Crossway*, a 21st Century Grandma column, the *Chicken Soup for the Soul* series, and a compilation of thirty-one stories and challenges in her devotional, *Be the Miracle*.

Represented by five talent agencies, **Vicki Liston** is a multi-award-winning voice actor, producer, and writer with several national companies among her many credits. She's most proud of her award-winning YouTube how-to series, "On The Fly… DIY," which raises money for no-kill animal shelters and rescue organizations.

Don Locke worked as a fine artist in Laguna Beach in the 1970s. He was in charge of graphics for *The Tonight Show* with Johnny Carson and Jay Leno for thirty-three years. He enjoys writing movies and has had two novels published. He spends his time writing songs and oil painting, but what he enjoys most is making his grandson laugh.

Singer, songwriter and worship leader **Allison Lynn** is drawn to the power of story to grow hearts and communities. Allison and her husband Gerald Flemming form the award-winning duo, Infinitely More. Their ninth album of original music will be released in 2022. Learn more at www.InfinitelyMore.ca.

Katherine Mabb received her Master of Science degree in elementary education, graduating summa cum laude, while single parenting her daughter. She is a freelance writer and a previous contributor to the *Chicken Soup for the Soul* series. She is forever grateful for the loving foundation her parents gave her.

Irene Maran is a freelance writer living at the Jersey shore with her cats and turtles. She currently writes two bi-weekly newspaper columns, runs a prompt writing group and is a professional storyteller. This grandmother of five enjoys sharing her humorous stories with adults and children.

Emily Avery Martin lives in Santa Cruz, CA with her husband, three children, dog and bunny. She loves travel, boats and all things related to the sea including sharks! She teaches literature and writing to fifth and sixth grade homeschoolers and writes middle-grade fiction.

Adrienne Matthews received her Bachelor of Science, with honors, from Bowling Green State University and Master of Social Work from Indiana University. She is retired alongside husband Greg and is proud mom to Eric. Adrienne enjoys traveling, entertaining and sharing her stories of God's miracles and the blessings in her life.

Lisa McCaskill received her Bachelor of Arts from the University of North Carolina at Greensboro in 1987. She is a teacher, writer, and mother of four grown men. Lisa enjoys writing, playing piano, making pottery, and any kind of crafting.

Joan D. McGlone enjoys writing, reading, and spending time with her three children and seven grandkids. Retired from the Franciscan University of Steubenville, she lives in Ohio with her husband Mark. Her novel, *The House on Seventh Street*, follows an immigrant woman's life and struggles. She's working on her next book.

Christina Metcalf is a full-time writer/ghostwriter and part-time curmudgeon. She's the author of *Getting Jinxed* and *West of You*. When she's not chauffeuring her kids, she's complaining to her husband about the number of exclamation marks people use these days. Her book *Someday. Never. Always.* will be out in late 2022.

Amy Mewborn has been published three times in the *Chicken Soup for the Soul* series. She is a 1992 graduate of East Carolina University and teaches high school English in eastern North Carolina. Writing is her favorite pastime — especially when she is blogging or posting at thepecanseeker.com. Besides writing, she reads, gardens, and enjoys family and friends.

Lava Mueller writes and teaches creative writing in Central Vermont. Her novel, *Don't Tell*, is currently being optioned for a movie. Lava is an ordained minister and the founder of a non-traditional worshiping community called Love Church. Lava sends love and blessings to all of you! Yay for love!

S.K. Naus has enjoyed writing since grade school and likes to enter contests on a lark. Words are important and arranging them in the right order can create wonderful stories and that's her favourite part of writing.

Linda O'Connell, a former teacher and accomplished writer from St. Louis, MO, is a positive thinker who writes from the heart and finds humor and inspiration in everyday situations. Linda enjoys a hearty laugh, dark chocolate, and long walks on a beach.

Ben Partain is the co-founder of Inspiravate Enterprises LLC with his wife of thirty-seven years, Rhonda. The company represents Rhonda's public speaking endeavors worldwide both physically and remotely. Together they share a blog entitled "Love Really is Blind."

Julie M. Phend is a retired middle school teacher. The author of *D-Day and Beyond: A True Story of Escape and POW Survival*, she currently writes fiction for children and blogs about kidlit topics. Julie also enjoys cooking, walking, water sports, travel, and spending time with her family. E-mail her at julie.phend@gmail.com.

Connie K. Pombo is a freelance writer, international speaker, and published author of three books. She has two grown sons and four precious grandchildren who visit her often on the West Coast of Florida. She loves dark chocolate, coffee, and seashells—not necessarily in that order. Learn more at www.conniepombo.com.

Connie Kaseweter Pullen lives in rural Sandy, OR near her five children and several grandchildren. She earned a B.A. degree, with honors, at the University of Portland in 2006, with a double major in psychology and sociology. Connie enjoys writing, photography and exploring nature. E-mail her at MyGrandmaPullen@aol.com.

Kathleen Cox Richardson is the author of two books: *Canal Zone Brats Forever*, a memoir of growing up in the Panama Canal Zone, and *Taking Life Back*.

Kate Rietema is a registered nurse, camp manager's wife, and children's author. She and her husband have five forever-children through birth and adoption and have cared for many more in their ten years as foster parents. Kate has been deeply impacted by the kindness of God, and she loves to share her stories with others.

Rose Robertson and her husband have three sons, two daughters-in-law, and four grandchildren. Rose enjoys gardening, reading, writing, and needlework and works as a grief companion with children, and parents who have suffered the death of a child.

Robert B. Robeson, LTC, USA (Ret) has had his articles, short stories and poems published 930 times in 330 publications in 130 countries. His work has also been featured in seventy anthologies. He flew 987 medevac missions for over 2,500 patients during the Vietnam War. He retired from the U.S. Army after twenty-seven-plus years flying on three continents.

Rich Rogers received his Bachelor of Arts degree from Brigham Young University in 1989 with a double major in English and Italian. He has been a freelance writer since 1995, specializing in arts and entertainment. His wife, Giovanna, is from Florence, Italy. They have one son.

Patricia Ruhaak was born and raised in Colorado. She has a degree specializing in psychology. She has a son, daughter, and husband Michael. Her family continues to reside in Colorado and Patricia currently works in healthcare administration. Patricia enjoys traveling, reading, writing, and spending time with family.

Judy Salcewicz is thrilled to be a frequent contributor to the *Chicken Soup for the Soul* series. She lives, writes, and gardens in New Jersey. Judy is a cancer survivor who believes in miracles.

Laurie Winslow Sargent loves sharing amazing God stories but the events in "Round Four" stun even her! Laurie's own books include *Delight in Your Child's Design* (2nd Edition, Kindle). She's contributed to thirteen other books, twenty-two magazines and now writes historical fiction. Visit her blog and say hello at LaurieSargent.com.

Lu Scannell has been writing short stories and poetry most of her adult life. One of her stories was published in *Reflections from McNally's Mirror* (Compilation), XLibris, 2013. In addition, she has stories on Medium.com. Lu also enjoys journaling and writing stories about and for her dog, Frosty.

Michael Jordan Segal, MSW who defied all odds after being shot in the head, is a husband, father, social worker, author (including a CD/Download of twelve stories entitled *Possible*), and inspirational speaker. He's had many stories published in the *Chicken Soup for the Soul* series. Learn more at www.InspirationByMike.com.

Mandy Shunnarah (they/them) is a writer in Columbus, OH. When they're not writing, they enjoy walks by the river, roller skating at the local skatepark, collecting books from the late 1800s, chasing butterflies, and snuggling with their five rescue cats. Read their essays, poetry, and short stories at mandyshunnarah.com.

Lauren Signorelli is a New Orleans girl who loves coffee and all the vintage things. She has two children and a husband who make her life the best adventure. She enjoys reading and writing and aspires to have her own book out in the world someday.

Marianne Simon was born to a family of artists and has spent her life exploring creativity in its many facets. She has worked as an actress and director for more than twenty-five years and has been writing for longer than that. She also discovered a passion for nature that inspires many of her writings. E-mail her at Marianne@Poeticplantings.com.

Heather Spiva is a freelance writer from Northern California. She is a married mom and has two sons of the teenager and young adult variety. She loves selling (and wearing) vintage clothing, thrifting, drinking coffee, and of course, reading and writing. E-mail her at hjspiva@gmail.com.

Judee Stapp is a speaker and author who loves to share her life experiences in an engaging and inspiring way. She has had nine stories published in the *Chicken Soup for the Soul* series and several in other publications. Judee is a wife, mother, grandmother and will soon be a great-grandmother! E-mail her at stappjudee@gmail.com.

Jennifer Starr is a speech language pathologist who graduated from Ball State University with her master's degree in 2009. She lives with her husband and four children and enjoys meditation, cooking, spending time in nature and writing.

Aubrey Summers enjoys running, exploring trails, cycling, and spending time with loved ones. She is currently writing a book about becoming the mother of a daughter with Down syndrome. She hopes to have her book as well as more short stories published.

Ronda Ross Taylor has been writing since she was her high school's newspaper editor. She's been a correspondent for the *Times-News* newspaper and has had other stories published in the *Chicken Soup for the Soul* series. She's lived in California, Idaho, Oklahoma, Hawaii, and currently resides in Redmond, WA.

Susan Taylor, formerly known as Susan Lynn Perry, is an accomplished writer and author of numerous books, short stories, blog posts and articles in both fiction and nonfiction. She lives in Texas with her amazing husband, incredible son, and a very feisty Bengal cat who excels at keeping them all entertained.

Kathy Thompson was born and raised in Kansas. She is a 1983 graduate of Wichita State University, studying communications. Kathy and her husband, Donald, have one son, Trenton. She loves to travel, read and write, especially humorous stories about family, life, and all its ups and downs. E-mail her at dthompsonjr@cox.net.

Janet M. Todd is a freelance writer from Fremont, NE where she lives with her husband, Tim. After the death of their youngest son in 2005, her writing gravitated toward helping others through grief. The goal is to help them understand and cope, while offering hope by sharing her personal stories and experiences with them.

Alice G. Waldert is a poet, creative nonfiction writer, and visual artist. Her work has appeared in *Arc Poetry Magazine*, *Misfit Magazine*, *Prometheus Dreaming*, *Survivor Lit*, *The Bangalore Review*, and the anthology *Tales from the Dream Zone*. She holds an M.A. and an MFA in poetry and creative nonfiction from Manhattanville College, 2021.

A former teacher and businesswoman, **June Weiner** has a B.A. in English from the University of California at Los Angeles. She has written a book titled *The Journey*. Besides writing, June enjoys reading, ballet lessons and playing the piano. She resides with her husband Richard in Central Florida. E-mail her at juneweiner@gmail.com.

Richard B. Whitaker is a retired Detective III for the Los Angeles Police Department. He received a Bachelor of Independent Studies from Brigham Young University and a Master of Public Administration from the University of Southern California. He is the father of seven, grandfather of twenty-one, and great-grandfather of eight.

In the past, **Susan P. Zwirn** entertained at children's events and delivered singing telegrams. She is currently working as a balloon artist at events in New York City. She has submitted about eight stories to the *Chicken Soup for the Soul* series as well as other places. Learn more at www.balloontwisternyc.com.

Chicken Soup for the Soul

Meet Amy Newmark

Amy Newmark is the bestselling author, editor-in-chief, and publisher of the *Chicken Soup for the Soul* book series. Since 2008, she has published 184 new books, most of them national bestsellers in the U.S. and Canada, more than doubling the number of Chicken Soup for the Soul titles in print today. She is also the author of *Simply Happy*, a crash course in Chicken Soup for the Soul advice and wisdom that is filled with easy-to-implement, practical tips for enjoying a better life.

Amy is credited with revitalizing the Chicken Soup for the Soul brand, which has been a publishing industry phenomenon since the first book came out in 1993. By compiling inspirational and aspirational true stories curated from ordinary people who have had extraordinary experiences, Amy has kept the twenty-nine-year-old Chicken Soup for the Soul brand fresh and relevant.

Amy graduated *magna cum laude* from Harvard University where she majored in Portuguese and minored in French. She then embarked on a three-decade career as a Wall Street analyst, a hedge fund manager, and a corporate executive in the technology field. She is a Chartered Financial Analyst.

Her return to literary pursuits was inevitable, as her honors thesis in college involved traveling throughout Brazil's impoverished northeast region, collecting stories from regular people. She is delighted to have come full circle in her writing career — from collecting stories "from the people" in Brazil as a twenty-year-old to, three decades later, collecting stories "from the people" for Chicken Soup for the Soul.

When Amy and her husband Bill, the CEO of Chicken Soup for the Soul, are not working, they are visiting their four grown children and their spouses, and their five grandchildren.

Follow Amy on Twitter @amynewmark. Listen to her free podcast — Chicken Soup for the Soul with Amy Newmark — on Apple, Google, or by using your favorite podcast app on your phone.

Thank You

We owe huge thanks to all our contributors and fans. We received thousands of submissions for this popular topic, and we spent months reading all of them. Laura Dean, Crescent LoMonaco, Jamie Cahill and Susan Heim read all of them and narrowed down the selection for Associate Publisher D'ette Corona and Publisher and Editor-in-Chief Amy Newmark. Then D'ette chose the perfect quotations to put at the beginning of each story, and Amy edited the stories and shaped the final manuscript.

As we finished our work, D'ette continued to be Amy's right-hand woman in working with all our wonderful writers. Barbara LoMonaco, Kristiana Pastir and Elaine Kimbler jumped in to proof, proof, proof. And yes, there will always be typos anyway, so please feel free to let us know about them at webmaster@chickensoupforthesoul.com, and we will correct them in future printings.

The whole publishing team deserves a hand, including our Vice President of Marketing Maureen Peltier, our Vice President of Production Victor Cataldo, Executive Assistant Mary Fisher, and our graphic designer Daniel Zaccari, who turned our manuscript into this beautiful, inspirational book.

Sharing Happiness, Inspiration, and Hope

Real people sharing real stories, every day, all over the world. In 2007, *USA Today* named *Chicken Soup for the Soul* one of the five most memorable books in the last quarter-century. With over 110 million books sold to date in the U.S. and Canada alone, more than 300 titles in print, and translations into nearly fifty languages, "chicken soup for the soul®" is one of the world's best-known phrases.

Today, twenty-nine years after we first began sharing happiness, inspiration and hope through our books, we continue to delight our readers with new titles, but have also evolved beyond the bookshelves with super premium pet food, television shows, a podcast, video journalism from aplus.com, licensed products, and free movies and TV shows on our Popcornflix and Crackle apps. We are busy "changing your world one story at a time®." Thanks for reading!

Share with Us

We all have had Chicken Soup for the Soul moments in our lives. If you would like to share your story or poem with millions of people around the world, go to chickensoup.com and click on Submit Your Story. You may be able to help another reader and become a published author at the same time. Some of our past contributors have launched writing and speaking careers from the publication of their stories in our books!

We only accept story submissions via our website. They are no longer accepted via mail or fax. Visit our website, www.chickensoup.com, and click on Submit Your Story for our writing guidelines and a list of topics we are working on.

To contact us regarding other matters, please send us an e-mail through webmaster@chickensoupforthesoul.com, or fax or write us at:

Chicken Soup for the Soul
P.O. Box 700
Cos Cob, CT 06807-0700
Fax: 203-861-7194

One more note from your friends at Chicken Soup for the Soul: Occasionally, we receive an unsolicited book manuscript from one of our readers, and we would like to respectfully inform you that we do not accept unsolicited manuscripts, and we must discard the ones that appear.

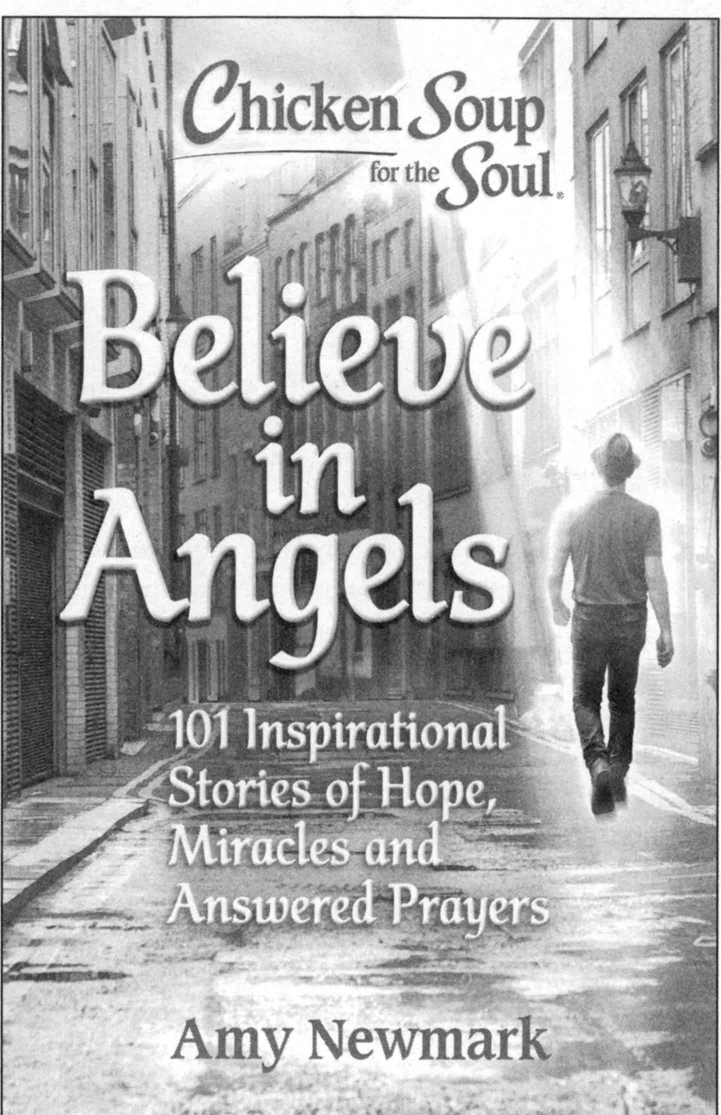

Paperback: 978-1-61159-086-9
eBook: 978-1-61159-324-2

Chicken Soup for the Soul

Miracles & Divine Intervention

101 Stories of Faith and Hope

Paperback: 978-1-61159-073-9
eBook: 978-1-61159-313-6

and deepen your faith

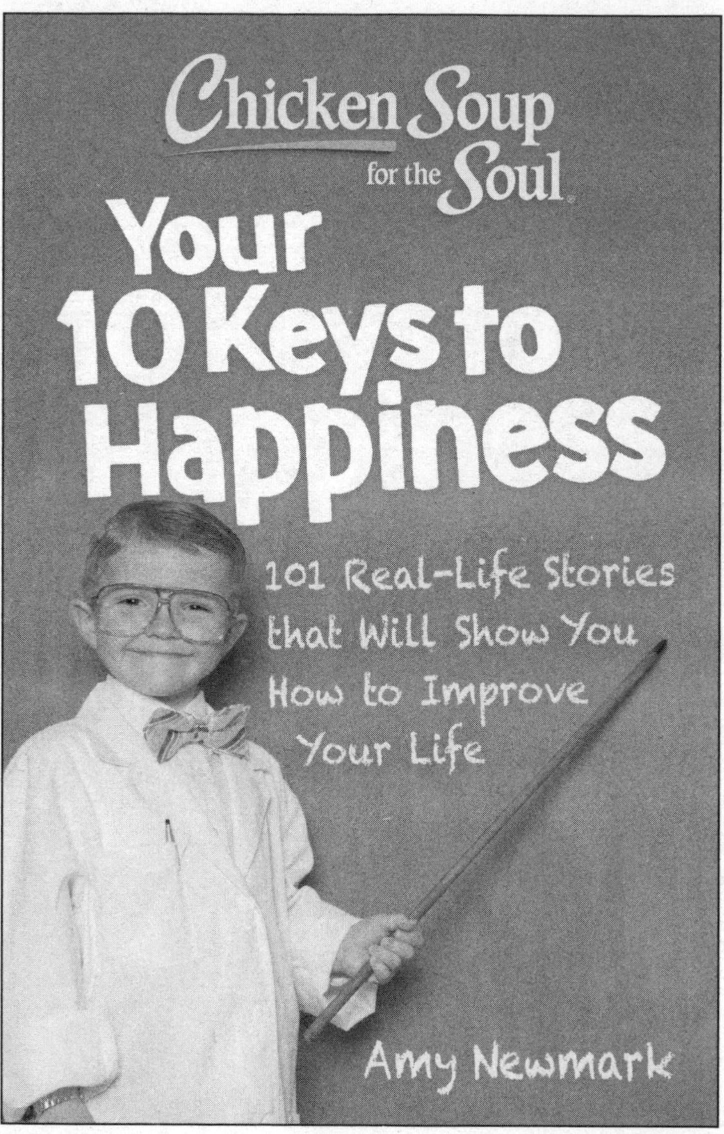

Paperback: 978-1-61159-091-3

eBook: 978-1-61159-330-3

Help yourself to a happier life

Paperback: 978-1-61159-093-7
eBook: 978-1-61159-331-0

full of blessings

Chicken Soup
for the Soul